The Other Chekhov

A Biography of Michael Chekhov,
the Legendary Actor, Director & Theorist

Also by Charles Marowitz

Books

Roar of the Canon: Kott & Marowitz on Shakespeare
Essays Om Teater (Denmark)
Stage Dust
The Other Way: An Alternative Approach to Acting & Directing
Alarums & Excursions
Recycling Shakespeare
Directing the Action
Burnt Bridges
Prospero's Staff
Potboilers
Sex Wars
The Act of Being
The Marowitz Shakespeare
Confessions of a Counterfeit Critic
The Method as Means

The Other Chekhov

A Biography of Michael Chekhov,
the Legendary Actor, Director & Theorist

Charles Marowitz

APPLAUSE THEATRE & CINEMA BOOKS • NEW YORK

The Other Chekhov: A Biography of Michael Chekhov
by Charles Marowitz

Library of Congress Cataloging-in-Publication Data:
Marowitz, Charles.
The other Chekhov : a biography of Michael Chekhov, the legendary actor, director & theorist / Charles Marowitz.
  p. cm.
Includes bibliographical references and index.
ISBN 1-55783-640-X
1. Chekhov, Michael, 1891–1955. 2. Actors—Soviet Union—Biography. 3. Theatrical producers and directors—Soviet Union—Biography. I. Title.
PN2728.C45M37 2004
792.02'8'092—dc22
      2004012377

British Library Cataloging-in-Publication Data
A catalog record of this book is available from the British Library

Applause Theatre & Cinema Books
151 West 46th Street, 8th Floor
New York, NY 10036
Phone: (212) 575-9265
Fax: (646) 562-5852
Email: info@applausepub.com
Internet: www.applausepub.com
Applause books are available through your local bookstore, or you may order at www.applausepub.com or call Music Dispatch at 800-637-2852

SALES & DISTRIBUTION
North America:
Hal Leonard Corp.
7777 West Bluemound Road
P. O. Box 13819
Milwaukee, WI 53213
Phone: (414) 774-3630
Fax: (414) 774-3259
Email: halinfo@halleonard.com
Internet: www.halleonard.com

Europe:
Roundhouse Publishing Ltd.
Millstone, Limers Lane
Northam, North Devon EX39 2RG
Phone: (0) 1237-474-474
Fax: (0) 1237-474-774
Email: roundhouse.group@ukgateway.net

For Konstantin Edward Marowitz (Kostya), whose technical expertise often saved my bacon and for which I am forever grateful (even though I eat no bacon).

Contents

From Broadway to Blighty

Hooray for Hollywood

Preface

IN THE LATE FORTIES, when I was barely a teenager, I managed to persuade my reluctant parents to enroll me in acting classes at the Henry Street Playhouse, a theater in the most abysmal reaches of New York's lower east side. My instructor was a blonde, good-looking young man with a cultivated, brisk and authoritative manner named Blair Cutting; his students, like myself, youngsters whose diction was rooted in the slovenly habits of unpolished New York argot. Our absence of vocal technique was surpassed only by our ignorance of theatrical aesthetics, but Cutting was a patient teacher and, little by little, we learned something of the etiquette and the goals that professional actors were obliged to strive for.

My memory of those classes are hazy but I do remember sessions in which we expended a lot of energy "radiating" to one another and trying to conjure up atmosphere. What I remember most vividly is a class in which Cutting explained that, on stage, even if one were playing a vicious and ugly character, there had to be some intrinsic beauty about the way it was being done. He demonstrated this first by rolling his body into a constricted little ball, his voice strident, rasping and demonic, the blood vessels in his forehead strained almost to the point of bursting, his eyes compressed into two narrow slits, eyeballs swiveling maniacally. I no longer remember the speech that accompanied this grotesque incarnation but I, and

everyone else, was relieved when the demonstration finally
came to an end. The demon now banished, Cutting then
repeated the speech with ardor and controlled malice, making
it clear as a bell and conveying the facade of the character that
concealed the monster we had just seen take possession of him.

At another session, he magically demonstrated how an
actor of only average height could, by pumping himself up
with a kind of self-generated helium, become a towering figure
far taller than his actual height. This too was a demonstration
that remains etched in the mind like an astonishing magic
trick which, neither now nor then, one could ever explain.

During all those classes, the name of Michael Chekhov
was never mentioned and I had no idea that Blair Cutting was
one of Chekhov's most talented disciples, a leading member of
his companies both at Dartington Hall and Ridgefield,
Connecticut, and a charismatic teacher of the Chekhov technique. It wasn't until many years later in England, when I had
become an avid champion of Stanislavsky (by then considerably watered down by the Method) that I became aware of the
personal connection between Chekhov and Stanislavsky; the
divergence of their views and the ideological nuances that colored and differentiated their respective acting theories.

As I matured, I came to realize that I had unwittingly
caught glimpses of Chekhov en route to my conversion to
Stanislavsky—as the ebulliently camp agent with the out-
landish Russian accent in Ben Hecht's film *Specter of the Rose*,
which I had seen as a teenager at the Irving Street Playhouse
off 14th Street in Manhattan, and later as the avuncular,
Freudian analyst in the Alfred Hitchcock film *Spellbound*. My
discovery of Chekhov in maturity was a gradual realization
that, as a green and awkward pupil in Blair Cutting's class, I
was actually being exposed to the mind and philosophy of an
actor theorist who would gradually displace Stanislavsky's position in my personal Parthenon and lead me into intriguing
new areas of aesthetic discovery never dreamed of in my
staunch Method days.

In the intervening years, I was too busy hatching my own theories and developing my own techniques to concern myself with the prescribed ideas of any conventional aesthetician. Directing was a pragmatic pursuit in which discoveries made in the rehearsal room and in workshops automatically influenced the interactions I was having with actors of very different stamps and in various theaters throughout Europe. But the niggling, tantalizing, and challenging ideas of Michael Chekhov slumbered beneath my work in the theater, occasionally throwing up inferences, provocations, and wrenching doubts. The more one became disenchanted with Naturalism in all its mundane varieties, the more the specter of Chekhov returned. I was like a man who, having renounced religion in all its sundry forms, suddenly becomes aware of a burgeoning spirituality that could no longer be ignored.

It would be false to suggest that I gradually became a convert to all the aspects contained in what we loosely refer to as the Chekhov Technique, but what is undeniable is that over the years I have become more and more drawn to the persona of the man himself and the provocative implications of the ideas to which he devoted himself throughout his relatively short life. For me, Chekhov represents that ineluctable quality in the theater that transcends all methodology no matter how persuasive or impressive it may sometimes be. When one examines how art happens, particularly performance art, one is constantly confronted with an impregnable mystery. Sometimes effects are achieved not because of theories but in spite of them; not as a demonstration of a logical proposition but as a dynamic refutation of all propositions and all intellectual theorems.

Sometimes, the closest we can come to getting a handle on the inexplicable combustions that produce great art is to examine, probingly and in detail, the nature of the man or woman in whom that art has manifest itself. We study the lives of great artists not to be able to duplicate their achievements but to try to understand how their life, milieu, social pressures and psychological network produced that particular result in that particular person. We call it biography but it is really a kind of theoretical exploration of cause and effect.

Because Chekhov's territory and my own turf are virtually the same, i.e., the chemistry of acting and the science of how theater produces its effects, the reader will find digressions and critiques on these subjects sprinkled through the pages of this book. I do not apologize for their inclusion and I don't believe they are tangential to the body of this work. Part of Chekhov's legacy is provocative speculation about the art form he practiced and wrote about, and to avoid the issues thrown up by his ideas would be shamefully anti-Chekhovian. Misha, whose appetite for dialectic was insatiable, would be the first to welcome challenges and controversy about the theories he espoused. A healthy disrespect for orthodoxy was the hallmark of his personality, and a biography that simply assembled the facts of his life and ignored the ideas that made that life so rich would be guilty of intellectual neglect.

—Charles Marowitz

Acknowledgements

PORTIONS OF THIS BOOK were grafted out of a manuscript copy of Chekhov's own autobiography which he had tentatively titled *Life and Remembrances*. His autobiographies will be published in the English language for the first time by Routledge under the title *The Path of The Actor* in 2005. I am grateful to Mala Powers, the Executrix of the Chekhov Estate, for allowing me access to her recollections, aid and support. Without her fifty-year advocacy of Chekhov, his reputation would not have achieved the definition it now has. I was also assisted by the recollections of Ford Rainey, Daphne Moore Field, and Mary Haynsworth, who were part of the Dartington Hall Chekhov Studio, and Jack Colvin and Jack Larson, who worked closely with Chekhov during the last five years of Chekhov's life in Hollywood. Frederick Keeve, whose film *From Moscow to Hollywood*, an invaluable record of the work of both Chekhov and his associate George Shdanoff, was extremely generous in opening up hidden areas of Shdanoff's life and thirty-five-year partnership with Chekhov. Vincent Sherman was eye-opening recalling his film work with Chekhov and others in the forties. Nikolai Guzov, one of the foremost exponents of Chekhov Technique in Los Angeles, provided invaluable assistance in filling in the Russian environment from which Chekhov sprung, and Ginny and Phil Brown generously provided rare information about Chekhov's period at the Actor's Lab in Hollywood, California.

A special gesture of gratitude needs to be made to William K. Elmhirst and the Dorothy Whitney Elmhirst Trust, which made it possible for me to travel to Dartington Hall to examine the Chekhov Archives, and Deirdre Hurst du Prey and her son Pierre du Prey, who allowed me to nose around in uncatalogued material at High Cross House in Devon, without which my knowledge of that period would have been dim indeed. William Elmhirst, son of Lord Elmhirst, was a staunch supporter of my work on Michael Chekhov from the very beginning and no amount of acknowledgement can convey the depth of my gratitude to him for his unwavering support. His presence was a dynamic correlative to his parents and sister Beatrice Straight out of which the whole Dartington Hall experiment issued.

Finally, a heartfelt note of thanks to Aighleann McKiernan, a bright and conscientious intern whose discretion, sharp eyes, and indefatigable research helped muster some of the material that has been integrated into this biography. Her acute knowledge of Russian literature and Soviet theater was a steady, enlightening and enlivening influence throughout.

—C.M.

RUSSIAN
EVOLUTION

Chapter One

IN 1928, THE RUSSIAN REVOLUTION was eleven years old. It had shed its first skin and, under Joseph Stalin, was already revealing the signs of despotism that would soon turn it into the most oppressive nation in Europe.

Lenin had died four years before and, in 1927, Zinoviev and Kamenev, two of Lenin's closest allies, were publicly rebuked for subverting the Leninist spirit of the Bolshevik Revolution. Three years later, Bukharin and Trotsky would be exiled and, in 1941, one of Stalin's henchmen in Mexico would fatally plunge an ice pick into Trotsky's skull. At the 15th Party Congress in 1927, Trotsky and Zinoviev were officially expelled from the Party and Stalin's control became absolute.

In the same year, Michael Chekhov, one of the most distinguished actors in the Soviet Union and the most brilliant disciple of Konstantin Stanislavsky, was entering his sixth year as a prominent member of the First Studio, an offshoot of the Second Moscow Art Theatre. He had already been lauded throughout Russia for his portrayal of Khlestakov in Gogol's *The Inspector General* staged by Stanislavsky, and had created one of the most memorable Hamlets in modern times. Serafima Birman, one of Chekhov's colleagues at the First Studio, had written in her memoirs, "His talent is almost inexplicable, he is a phenomenon nobody has succeeded in deciphering." For Chekhov, each performance was like a runway

on the original play from which he immediately became airborne. Even when the plays were known and the characters
already fixed in the audience's mind, he astounded audiences
with startling new interpretations that added incredible, hith-
erto unimagined, dimensions to the role. He had, as critic
Konstantin Rudnitsky, wrote, "the apparent artlessness that
only genius can achieve."

Stanislavsky revered Michael's uncle Anton Chekhov, the
playwright who had almost single-handedly created the triumphs of the Moscow Art Theatre making that institution the
envy of theaters throughout Europe and America. Michael
was virtually Stanislavsky's adopted son, and often expressed
the hope that the short, dynamic, pixie-like young man would
become his successor.

Michael had quickly and efficiently absorbed Stanislavsky's
teachings, but with the passage of time, had developed strong
misgivings about the so-called System. Stanislavsky's emphasis
had always been on the naturalistic creation of character; "living one's part" meant to him obliterating the difference
between the character and the actor, and seamlessly fusing the
two. His credo was "truthfulness" and by that he meant being
truthful to human behavior and social appearances.

Chekhov, on the other hand, had been seduced by the
Symbolists and Eastern philosophy and, early in his life, had
become a convert to Rudolph Steiner's anthroposophy; a theory that believed God was realized in man by means of intuitions, contemplative illumination, or direct communion with
unseen but palpable forces in the universe. Chekhov's truth
transcended the "monkey see, monkey do" aspects of Naturalism. The accurate reproduction of actors' emotional states was,
for him, only one aspect of artistic truth, but one that ignored
what Chekhov later came to call "the Higher I"; that part of
man's psyche that transcended his social shell. His route to
characterization was through the imagination not versimili-
tude. Consequently, he grew progressively more dissatisfied
with the very principles that underpinned Stanislavsky's art.

Chekhov and Stanislavsky discussed these differences openly and although the leader of the Moscow Art Theatre was a formidable director, a celebrated actor, and an influential theorist, Michael remained unpersuaded. Little by little, the aesthetic differences between mentor and disciple began to surface. By 1928, the cracks were visible to both men. There were other problems as well at the Second Moscow Art Theatre.

Shortly after Chekhov's somber rendition of Hamlet, the director and actor Alexei Diky, a precociously talented member of Chekhov's troupe who, like Chekhov, had trained under Stanislavsky, produced a colorful, fairground production of *The Flea*, a flamboyant version of Nikolai Leskov's novel *The Left-Hander*. It was resoundingly successful and very much in the circus-style of Vsevolod Meyerhold, who was unquestionably the dominant theatrical influence of the post-revolutionary period. Chekhov was not impressed and felt the show's flippancy was not in keeping with the highest principles of the Studio. Artistic differences apart, there was no love lost between Diky and Chekhov. In Diky's eyes, Chekhov was in his exalted position only because he was the nephew of his charismatic uncle Anton, and the whole business had a whiff of czarist decadence about it.

At this time, Chekhov was directing a production of *Petersberg*, adapted from a novel by Andrei Bely, a much admired writer and poet, but not one whose work any theatrical artist had managed to realize on the stage. Chekhov was the first to try. Bely, like his director, was also an acolyte of Rudolph Steiner, and the two men's enthusiasm for anthroposophy forged a strong link between them in regard to the project.

According to the established formula laid down after the revolution, a whole cadre of directors worked collectively on each production. It was felt that this would provide an antidote to the kind of individualism that was associated with "the bad old days" of pre-revolutionary Russia. *Petersberg* opened to very disappointing reviews, with only Chekhov's performance being singled out for any real praise. Pavel Markov, a leading critic of the period, complained of a "lack of coordination," and observed that "by placing the production in the hands of three directors, the theater condemned it to a lack of unity." As a result, he said, "the outer form of production was ten years behind the times."

The Chekhov-led production of *Petersberg* was quickly swept from the boards, but Alexi Diky's rambunctious production of *The Flea*, with its strong populist appeal, continued to prosper—although it too would soon run afoul of the censor. Chekhov's authority within the company was badly shaken by the poor reception of *Petersberg*. This emboldened Diky, who mounted a harsh campaign of criticism against Chekhov's leadership, enlisting seventeen key members of the company to his cause. The underlying objective was Chekhov's removal from his position as leader.

The schism at the Second Moscow Art leapt into the newspapers and became racy gossip throughout Moscow. Although Chekhov's talent as an actor was never in question, letters in the press and insidious gossip began to impugn both his aesthetic credo and his political loyalty. It was pointed out that the Second Studio had never produced any contemporary revolutionary plays; that its penchant was for symbolism and comsopolitan works that were not in harmony with the tastes or inclinations of the workers who, after 1917, made up the dominant faction of all theatergoers. Chekhov's admiration for the teachings of Rudolph Steiner was also brought into question. To the masses, these anthroposophical ideas were spiritual tendencies smacking of religion which had become anathema to mainstream Communist ideologues. More worrying still, rumors were flying that letters criticizing Chekhov had been written to the KGB by members of the disenchanted contingent of actors that, spurred on by Diky, had publicly withdrawn from the Second Moscow Art Theater. Carping critics drew attention to Chekhov's abandonment of "collective direction" and his bizarre notions of idealism and inspiration.

Displaying the naive indifference to looming crises that characterized his entire life, Chekhov construed these assaults as mere "demagoguery" and believed they warranted nothing more than a dignified silence, but it was a time when ideological differences were grave matters that could bring about dire consequences. In fact, the rift was not only about aesthetic differences; it also had to do with loyalty to a cause; the shaky and not yet fortified principles of Revolutionary Art that, at the Soviet Writers Congress of 1934, would lay down the commandment that Social Realism would be the guiding principle for all the arts. And it was happening at a time when political opponents of Stalin were being expelled, interrogated, arrested, and exiled. The writing on the wall was too large and ominous to be ignored.

Stanislavsky, whose Moscow Art Theatre was associated in the public's mind with the parasitic, bourgeois classes the revolution had aggressively banished, was helpless to intercede. Anatoly Lunacharsky, the Minister of Culture who at the beginning had been a staunch supporter of Chekhov, was silent. Some of his closest collaborators, sensing which way the wind was blowing, forsook Chekhov and joined with Diky. As Chekhov himself admitted afterward, he had begun to feel like "an inner émigré."

One night Chekhov received a call from a librarian who had once been his acting student and was now working in an official capacity for the Party. She intimated that an order had been drafted at KGB headquarters for Chekhov's arrest. Although he had steeled himself for some official reprimand, he hadn't anticipated detention or imprisonment. The librarian's warning was followed by a message from Minister Lunacharsky confirming that Chekhov's life was in danger if he remained in the Soviet Union. That night he and his wife Xenia made arrangements to leave for Berlin. In the next two decades there would be several attempts to negotiate a return to his homeland, but they would all be broken off. Chekhov would journey from Berlin to Paris, from Latvia to Lithuania, from Devonshire to California, but never again step foot on Russian soil.

Ironically, his last stage performance at the Second Moscow Art Theatre in 1927 was as Murmonsky, a harried and tormented individualist cruelly taunted by a souless bureaucracy in a play entitled *The Case* by Sukhovo-Kobylin. Although his character began as a hilarious little comic figure in side whiskers and shaggy beard, by the time the play reached its final scene, the puny weakling, condemned to a bureaucratic prison cell, would summon up hidden reserves of strength and rebel against both the bureaucrats and the state that had cruelly whittled him down. "His legs bend at the knee in those high boots," wrote critic Mikhail Zagorsky, "those pathetic gray side whiskers still quaver as before—and then suddenly before us stands a man who has risen up in a last desperate effort, all his blood surging to his heart, and who with the same trembling lips, cries out against the executioners and the victims. But no, it is not a cry; simply total anguish of grief, rage and pain." Murmonsky then collapses in a heap and expires.

This startling transformation from comedy to tragedy that astonished all those who witnessed it curiously presaged what lay ahead for Michael Chekhov as he set off on what has come to be known as his wandering years.

Chapter Two

EVERY FIBER IN MICHAEL CHEKHOV'S BEING, every nuance of his mind, every flaw in his character can be traced back to his father Alexander Pavlovitch Chekhov, the elder brother of the renowned playwright, Anton Chekhov. Michael (christened Mikhail Aleksandrovitch) was born on August 16, 1891 — the year of one of Russia's greatest famines and the one that did the most to radicalize the agragrian workers who ultimately spearheaded the revolution.

Growing up in St. Petersburg in what would turn out to be the twilight of the czarist era, Misha, the nickname that stayed with him for more than sixty years, was terrified, entranced, monopolized, and dominated by a paterfamilias who was ingenious, inspired, irascible, unpredictable, alcoholic, neurotic, and entirely inescapable.

In a memoir written in the mid-forties, Chekhov described his father as being "constitutionally incapable of enduring anything ordinary, habitual or conventional." Alexander, for example, owned fifteen pocket watches but preferred to tell the time by means of a wooden clock of his own making that was elaborately decorated with twigs, cork and moss. In place of pendulums, it was fitted with two balanced bottles of water. He eschewed typewriters, believing it was ridiculous to expend the same amount of effort on a period or a comma as one did on a letter of the alphabet. He abhorred telephones because their ring invariably interrupted either his experiments or the trains of thought leading to and from them. He did, however, have a fire alarm fitted to a panel immediately above his bed that roused him day or night when a fire broke out in St. Petersburg.

A prolific writer, Alexander contributed columns, belles lettres, and articles on scientific subjects to local papers, which accepted them eagerly. One of his more prophetic works was a book entitled *Alcoholism & How to Battle It*. He was once approached by a university professor who believed alcoholism could be successfully treated by hypnosis. The hypnotist tried to get Alexander to cooperate on the cure. At first he roundly pooh-poohed the idea, then reluctantly agreed to be a guinea pig. After a protracted session of intense concentration, the hypnotist succumbed to Alexander's Svengali-like gaze and fell into a deep sleep.

Alexander's alcoholism was the bane of the family's existence. On numerous occasions during the year, he would simply disappear, terrifying his wife and child. A few days later, they would receive a telegram saying, "Am in the Crimea" or "Am in the Cacausus." During these vanishing acts, he would never take any luggage. He would return sometimes days, sometimes weeks, later, unkempt and physically debilitated. Misha believed these sudden escapes to far-away places were attempts on his father's part to spare his family from the more violent manifestations of his alcoholism, and that once away, he was overcome by the disease. The homecomings were invariably shame faced. He would say contritely to his wife, "Come, Mother, let's go out for some beer." A brew he never considered to be particularly intoxicating.

Alexander's social circle consisted of thieves and ne'er-do-wells, habitués of the lower depths to whom he doled out money even as he showered them with imaginative bits of whimsy. They warmed to his humanity even more than they did to his hand outs, mainly because he erected no social barriers between himself and the lowest dregs of society. Often,

the more notorious of them approached his wife with assur-
ances of their safety. "We wish you well," they would say.
"Don't worry, we would never harm you!"

After all-night binges with the roughest of the town's rough
trade, Alexander would stumble home wasted, tank himself up
with beer and milk, refuse all solids, and fall into a stupor and
sleep soundly for hours. The frequency of these nocturnal
blackouts became so common that his wife eventually accepted them as the norm, although for the hypersensitive Misha,
they were like recurrent nightmares.

When the madness struck, Alexander took possession of his
son and, despite his wife's protests, refused to allow him out of
his thrall. Frightening as these seances may have been to
Misha, they also had a sense of enchantment about them. He
would be sucked into a netherworld far removed from the
bustling, provincial life of St. Petersburg, dragooned by a kind
of mad wizard into a Gothic castle filled with spells and magic
elixirs. "He opened up different worlds before me," wrote
Chekhov.

The sessions usually began with a game of chess, and no
matter how much liquor Alexander had imbibed, his mind
remained intensely clear. He coaxed young Misha into
becoming his drinking partner, and in the cavernous study surrounded by books and illuminated only by the smoky light of a
kerosene lamp, drew the boy into metaphysical speculations.
From there he would segue into philosophy, describing how
consciousness graduated from nothingness into the concep-
tions of Thales and Anaxagoras, then Aristotle and Plato; how
Christianity arose from Paganism through the Dark Ages into
the Enlightenment, always spicing his tale with colorful anecdotes about Diogenes, Julius Caesar and Alexander the Great.
It was a veritable cavalcade of history chronicling the progress
of ideas from one era to the next, all of which developed in
Misha a fascination with cognitive thought and laid the foundation for the aesthetic theories he would hatch and rehatch
when he became an actor and a teacher.

The history lesson concluded, Alexander would begin drawing caricatures. With a few broad strokes he could create the likeness of his wife, their nanny, and their neighbors—not only their salient physical characteristics but the tell-tale signs that revealed their innermost character. His father's love of caricature was one of Misha's earliest legacies and one that remained with him all of his life, eventually transferring itself to the bizarre makeup and grotesque characterizations he created on the stage.

After chess, drink, history, and art, Alexander treated his son to a magic show derived from his knowledge of physics and chemistry, creating multicolored plumes of flame out of ingenious mixtures of dyes and acids. As Misha watched wide-eyed, liquids came alive in test tubes, bubbling as if stirred in a witch's cauldron; colored crystals formed in flasks; wisps of steam seeped out of jars then dissipated into thin air; mini-explosions cracked bottles, showering the floor with miniature lava.

Chemical spectaculars were followed by tales of incredible adventures populated by courageous heroes who risked death and destruction to save lives. As the night stretched into dawn, this segued into astrological phenomena, with the names of stars and galaxies being pointed out as father and son pressed their faces to the window pane. Alexander spoke excitedly of comets and meteors, and of the vast populous universe that stretched far beyond the visible night sky of St. Petersburg and into regions beyond the reach of learned astronomers. Humans became insignificant appendages to cosmic forces that thundered in solar systems beyond the paltry speculations of scientists and earthbound stargazers. "The human being always appeared in father's stories," wrote Chekhov, "as an insignificant accidental phenomenon. But who made it happen? Who controls it? My consciousness as yet unsullied by materialistic speculations, could not understand and my imagination came to its aid. 'The accident,' as I saw it, was a wise, clever, huge, all-seeing, all-powerful *someone*. But he was so alone, this someone, that I felt sorry for him and tears choked me. He cares for everyone, does everything for everybody, creates the universe and yet, all shun him."

During these lengthened, liquefied, all-night sessions in which the Prospero-like Alexander initiated his son into the mysteries of the universe, Misha's sense of deity was gradually being formulated. He not only visualized a higher power that was in some inscrutable way responsible for everything in both the visible and invisible worlds, he also identified himself with it. Later, when he became a staunch believer in the theories of Rudolph Steiner and anthroposophy, there would be a traceable link between the transcendental intuitions proselytized by the German mystic and the unforgettable nights Misha spent with his inebriated father probing the mysteries that lay beyond appearances. His Christianity, like his anthroposophy and his theories about unseen powers clustered beyond the verifiable facade of Naturalism, would all meld into a *weltanschauung* that would permanently influence his life and approach to theatrical art. It would also cause both friends and collaborators to turn against him, and at times threaten his life.

Recalling his childhood, many years later, Misha said of his father: "I trembled before him, was amazed by him—but I could never love him. To me, every aspect of him was *terrifying*."

● ● ● ● ●

There was a very strong bond between Alexander and his younger brother Anton. The playwright always acknowledged the uniqueness of Alexander. "He is far more talented than I," he said, "but he will drink himself to death."

Ironically, it was after Anton Chekhov's death in 1904 that Alexander rapidly deteriorated. The binges became more frequent and of longer duration. Anton's death also caused strange transformations in Alexander's personality. He fussed aimlessly over trifles, worked less, and lived alone—rarely inviting his wife and son to visit. He took to writing irrational

letters to high-ranking government figures, and fanciful obituaries of his own death that he sent out to local editors. He
became more and more itinerant, traveling to exotic destina-
tions and then, quickly growing bored, returning to his family.
It was after one of these sudden returns that he was diagnosed
with throat cancer. He refused all attempts at surgery and
showed no outward signs of fearing what he and his family
realized was his imminent demise. He retreated to bed and
remained there, indiscriminately reading one book after the
other and drinking constantly. He prophesied the time of his
death, and on the appointed day died just as he had predicted,
in excruciating pain.

"Such a strong, always surprising, and terrifying man,"
wrote Misha "should not die like that. He gasped for breath as
nightmare visions tore at his soul, and in those moments when
consciousness returned, I was horrified by his wild rage and
malice and prolonged suffering. I expected during those horrible days and nights some new truths from him, previously
unspoken. As the last spasm ran across his face, and he ceased
breathing and lay with his mouth open and his eyes open but
unseeing, I was still waiting. But the chord remained unresolved."

Later, still musing on the same subject, he wrote: "It was
the first time I had seen death at close quarters. It made me
realize how falsely actors portray death upon the stage.
Rendering, as they believe, a faithful picture, they pay too
much attention to the physiological processes. The more accu-
rately the physical torments of the dying are portrayed, the farther it is removed from the picture of death as it should appear
in art. Death upon the stage should be shown as a slowing
down and the gradual disappearance of the sense of time."

As soon as Alexander had expired, Misha made a sketch of
his dead father; the servants thinking this to be in bad taste,
secretly destroyed it. The sense of incompletion at his father's
death remained with Misha for many years afterward; the
"unresolved chord" keening for the moment of resolution. It

came only after Chekhov, the mature actor, experienced three stage deaths. In *Ivan the Terrible*, the moment of death was accompanied by the shrieking of jesters and buffoons. Misha wasn't sure whether this racket marked the departure from life or the arrival of Ivan's tortured soul at the threshold of the world beyond. In *Eric XIV*, the character caught a glimpse of the next world, and to his surprise, raced to meet it. In *Hamlet*, death was accepted gratefully as the prince passed beyond the pale, freely divesting himself of his corporeal form.

For Chekhov, these three stage deaths were "not only departures from *here*, but also dissimilar entrances *there*." The "act" of dying, imaginatively projected through the termination of a character's onstage life, provided an insight that real life could not. They brought a proxy resolution to young Misha's conflicted feelings toward his father's passing. The chord, like so many things in life, could only be heard within the artificial context of a drama. Only then could Chekhov finally experience closure.

Chapter Three

BEARING THE NAME CHEKHOV gave Misha a certain cachet both in Russia and in his travels around Europe and the U.S., but in fact he had very little contact with the illustrious playwright, and most of it at a very young age.

His earliest memory dated from when he was six or seven. He was sitting on Anton's lap being asked a question he couldn't answer, and he became flustered and turned his face away in embarrassment. Misha also recalled the first time Alexander brought him to visit Anton in Yalta. No sooner had he been introduced than a package of books arrived for the playwright, including one entitled *Kashtanka*. "Have you read this?" his uncle asked, to which Misha answered in the negative. "Then take it, you should read it. And what of *Byelolobu*?" Again Misha shook his head no. "Read that as well," said Anton as he inscribed the book to him. In Misha's memory, Anton was always surrounded by books and doled them out as if they were medication: "This one will help you to think clearly; this one will remove your anxieties about God; this one will put you to sleep."

Misha's most vivid memory of his uncle was during a walk along a Yalta street. Chekhov—frail, bent over, walking cautiously and leaning on his stick—was surrounded by a group of dancing urchins who were shouting, "Antoshka, chakhotka, Antoshka, chakhotka!"—a play on words that rhymed the

diminutive form of "Anton" with the Russian word for consumption. Anton, with no trace of offense, merely glanced
back at the children with a gentle smile.

Misha also recalled Anton's perverse sense of humor.
Coming into the kitchen after a long writing stint in his study,
Anton sat down to have tea and suddenly cried out, "This
spoon smells of a dog!" His mother was quietly outraged and
assured him that everything in her kitchen was hygienically
scrubbed before being placed on the table. "How can you say
such a thing, Antosha? What dog? Where?" Misha suddenly
burst out laughing and Anton, having duped his mother, shot
Misha a sly smile.

At Yalta, Misha spent many hours sitting in Anton's study
watching him write, consumed with curiosity and scanning
the long locked cases in the corner bulging with books of every
description. He was irresistibly drawn to Anton's collection of
knickknacks on his desk and occasionally, sensing the boy's
interest, Anton would give him one. Before long, the boy had
amassed a small treasure trove of his uncle's keepsakes.

Misha remembered his uncle's consternation when old
friends—unannounced—would disturb him at work, but he
never betrayed any irritation. The same gentle, tolerant smile
he had shown to the mocking street urchins would always be
wreathed on his face.

Once, when the playwright was away from home and
Misha slept in his uncle's bed, he noticed a large oil painting
done by Anton's artist brother, Nikolai. It hung prominently
over the bedstead and depicted a poor seamstress with a weath-
er-beaten face, her hands clasped in her lap, her sewing crum-
pled by her feet, her thin chemise slipping off one shoulder. On
the table beside her burned a dim kerosene lamp. Misha recognized his mother in that mournful, almost tearful, face. He
was disturbed by the picture and it reverberated in his mind for
a long time afterward. When he was older, he was told Anton
and his mother, when very young, had been in love. He never
understood why they had never married, why Alexander and

not Anton had become his father. A good portion of Misha's natural inheritance stemmed from both his father and his uncle. From Alexander, he acquired his insatiable curiosity about ideas; from Anton, his ability to penetrate the surfaces of ordinary life to discover the smoldering mysteries underneath. A combination of curiosity and creativity that might best be described as Chekhovian.

Chapter Four

MICHAEL CHEKHOV'S FIRST AUDIENCE consisted of his mother and his nanny. These household performances, as he called them, involved a great retinue of costumes appropriated from every member of the family; his father's jacket, his nanny's skirts, his mother's dresses and sweaters, stray hats, umbrellas, galoshes—anything that Misha could incorporate into his improvisations. The character of the improvs changed according to the prop or costume employed, but whether comic or tragic, pathetic or absurd, they always elicited uproarious laughter rising to helpless tears from his devoted audience of two.

As his circle of admirers grew, Misha began concocting scenes from Dickens and classic Russian authors, never memorizing lines per se, but rather grasping the broad outlines of some situation and conveying it through improvisation. When he had become one of the most admired actors in Russia essaying the works of Gogol, Strindberg and Shakespeare, his penchant for fanciful improvisation remained irrepressible. For Chekhov, acting meant the inspired outpourings of his own ceaseless invention. Many of his most structured performances retained the airborne quality that one associates with the maniacal spontaneity of comedians like Robin Williams.

His first appearance before a real audience was in a local amateur club, where he was cast in the role of a comic old man. He glimpsed his doting mother and nanny in the crowd, but they were now surrounded by a large assemblage of strange faces. Misha was at a loss. "Too frightened to sit down or walk to the side," he recalled, "I stood there shifting my weight from one foot to the other, and as it was supposed to be a comic role, saying, 'Heh, heh, heh.'" His father, ever the critic, bellowed out some advice: "Don't rock, blockhead!" Terrifying as this first exposure to an audience may have been, Misha's fate was sealed. He discarded his other studies and concentrated all his energies into acting. His parents enrolled him in the Suvorin Theatre School, and after a period of acute confusion in which he considered becoming a surgeon, an author and even a fireman, he concluded that the stage was going to become his profession.

Theater schools, in the period before the advent of Stanislavsky and the Moscow Art transformed the art form, were mainly occupied with teaching students the prevailing clichés of the czarist stage; to stamp your foot in anger, to crumple your shoulders in despair, to raise your chin to convey determination — the so-called indications that would eventually be routed by the psychological truths inculcated by the Stanislavsky System. The Suvorin School itself didn't really teach Chekhov how to act, but exposure to its illustrious slate of professional teachers — Savina, Dalmatov, Glagolin, Arbatov, etc. — did. "I did not study *with* them," Chekhov recalled, "I studied *them*."

In the gallery of the Alexandrinsky Theatre where Chekhov was so often to be found, the tuition reached even higher levels of perfection. This was the theater in which Varlamov, Davidov, and Strelískaya — some of the leading lights of the czarist stage — could be found essaying Gogol, Griboyedov, and Turgenev. Recalling the giants of that period, Chekhov wrote:

> More than thirty years have passed since I saw these magicians on the stage, yet I have not forgotten, and cannot forget, thousands and thousands of details. Strelískaya brushes the dust off a portrait of her dead son

and the auditorium sobs with grief. To me, that is mirac-
ulous. Dalmatov, in a comic role, puffs on a cigar and
says: "Byron, Shakespeare, Goethe, Voltaire," and you
realize in an instant he's never even read Shakespeare.
Something barely perceptible, no, totally imperceptible is
happening to the cigar smoke, and from that we can tell
he simply hasn't read him. Isn't that a miracle? Varlamov,
as Pischik-Simeonov in *The Cherry Orchard*, learns that
the house has been sold. A short pause of five or six seconds. Varlamov looks at the chair next to him, at the window, at the portiere, at the empty expanse of wall, and
everything is transformed onstage, in the auditorium, in
the viewer's heart, in the atmosphere of the performance.
Clearly, life in this house has ended.

The telling moment is what riveted not only Chekhov, but
the theater audiences of that magical period in the first years of
the twentieth century when certain artists were outsized without being implausible. It was the mastery of these very czarist
artists that inspired Stanislavsky to try to formulate a methodology that would consciously create the effects they achieved by
instinct and God-given talent.

It was while at the Suvorin School that Misha had a brush
with Czar Nicholas II. A cycle of historical plays produced by
Arbatov caught the interest of the czar and the students were
invited to give a performance at the royal palace. When they
arrived at the train station, they were met by red carriages decorated with the two-headed eagle, symbol of the Royal Family,
and lackeys wearing embroidered gold livery. Once they got
into the palace, they found large round tables set for lunch.
The royal footmen serving the student actors from silver plat-
ters barely concealed the disdain they felt for the young com-
moners. After lunch, the company was permitted to smoke,
but as no receptacles had been provided in which to douse
their cigarettes, they used the massive silver napkin rings as
ashtrays. Members of the secret police in large civilian frock

coats patrolled the chamber. The atmosphere was fraught with tension. One of the actors whispered, "The lunch, my friends, was truly rotten," which slightly lightened the atmosphere.

The czar sat in the front row as they performed and then went backstage to greet the actors, but appeared to be embarrassed and at a loss for words. The students had been told in advance that under no circumstances were they to question members of the royal family and to speak only if and when they were spoken to. The czar's first question to one of the Jewish members of the company was voiced in such subdued tones that the actor could not hear it. "Did you say something?" he barked. "What did you say?" The czar turned his attention to an auburn-haired actress who was quietly trembling in her costume. Before he could pose a question to her, she sank down in a curtsy and fell backward onto an open piano keyboard, recovered immediately and then propelled herself forward, still bowing.

The czar then turned to Misha. "How do you glue on that nose?" he asked. "Like this, your Majesty," said Chekhov, removing the sticky mastic and spreading it over the palm of his hand. The czar then asked if he had ambitions to perform on the Imperial stage. Misha was too flustered to answer. The czar, sensing his embarrassment, smiled and put out his hand. Misha took it firmly, gluing the mastic in his palm to the sovereign's white glove. Somewhat consternated, and chuntering inaudibly, the czar shook his hand free and moved hurriedly out of the chamber. "Our behavior had not pleased," wrote Chekhov, "and we never saw the sovereign again."

Had the scene come from one of Uncle Anton's vaudeville sketches or Misha's own comic improvisations, it could not have been improved upon.

● ● ● ● ●

Shortly after disgracing himself before the true czar, Misha found himself assuming the role of another. His first profes-

sional role at the Maly Theatre where he went after graduating
from Suvorin's theater school, was as czar Fyodor Ioannovich,
the eponymous hero of Tolstoy's play.

After performances in the capitol, the company set off on a
provincial tour, it was Chekhov's first experience of the
Russian countryside and the peasant world that swarmed
beyond Moscow. He was astounded and uplifted by the adora-
tion showered upon actors and the people's reverence for theater. Provincial theatergoers, like eager children seeing their
first puppet show, were magically transported. Although the
kulaks' garments were what Moscovites would call tasteless,
and the women's attire rustically naive, the people themselves
unfailingly divined the inner content of the plays they were
witnessing. Misha watched them being transported by what
they saw, empathizing with betrayed lovers, rallying to the
hopes of struggling idealists, being downtrodden by cruel and
unfeeling bureaucrats. "It was then that I conceived a vague
idea of the role that theater could play in the cultural life of
mankind," he said.

Misha's ambition grew and took shape when he realized
how insignificant so much theater was in his native country. It
was the provincial tours that nurtured Chekhov's desire to turn
the theater into a moral force and he recognized that to
achieve this, it must first be purged of its impurities. The disease, he believed, was naturalism itself. "How could naturalism develop any further," he asked "when the audience has
already seen on the stage a husband deliberately driving his
wife mad; a man run over by a train; a vampire—in tails—
sucking young girls' blood and women slowly and skillfully
undressing on the stage?" Naturalism was destroying the public's sensitivity by coarsening it with an endless diet of behavior-
ist clichés masquerading as real behavior. In order to continue
to satisfy its audiences, the theater needed to provide more and
greater stimulation "that does not exist within the reserves of
naturalism." Although his own theories were in their most
formative stages, it was clear they grew out of a repugnance

with the limits of crudely mimicked natural behavior and an inchoate desire to transcend a theater mired in nineteenth century conventions of both style and content.

Around this time, Misha's father's legacy was beginning to make itself felt. Always hungry for intellectual stimulus and trying to grasp the immensities of life beyond the theater, Chekhov discovered three mentors who collectively monopolized his thoughts: Charles Darwin, Sigmund Freud, and Arthur Schopenhauer.

From Darwin, Chekhov came to believe that "life is a relentless battle for survival, and that morality and religion are mere illusions; that, in the final analysis, I am only my body plus all that I have inherited from my parents." From Freud, he discovered that beyond his consciousness, there was a swirling world of primitive and labyrinthine sexual impulses that, being inescapable, had to be confronted and dealt with. Schopenhauer taught him to "admire the aimlessness of human existence—the charms of melancholy and cynicism." Portraits of his new gods hung on the walls of his room. Their books lay open on his desk and bedside table. "My complex inner life became more difficult," Chekov admits. "Externally, I became coarser and coarser. I began to drink more, and frequently acted when drunk...My relations with women became more coarse and primitive. The worse my behavior became, the more I loved my mother and pitied my father." He conducted inner dialogues with his mentors, probing their works, relating his experience to theirs and gradually sinking deeper and deeper into an all-engulfing pessimism.

As Chekhov became more cynical and contemptuous of people day after day, his mother recognized that his son was sinking into a spiritual malaise. She also noticed that the more Misha brooded on the philosophies of his mentors, the more he took to the bottle. It was the first appearance of the manic depression that was to stalk Chekhov for the rest of his life.

Over time, with antidotes provided by writers such as Alexander Ivanovich Krupin, Anton Chekhov, and Tolstoy, the black mood passed and he was able to haul himself out of his nihilism. "How could these cynics who spoke of man's psyche as a mechanism, or man's soul as a dirty pit, be right?" he asked himself. Dosed up with Tolstoy and the writings of the Christian poet philosopher Vladimir Solovyov, he came to detest his mentors and, little by little, his skepticism was replaced by a transcendental notion of Christianity. He read the lives of the saints and resolved to resist all temptations to commit immoral acts. "As was always the case with me," he wrote, "my passionate nature hurled me from one extreme to the other." His mind reeled with the turbulent pros and cons of the ideas it was attempting to assimilate.

This was not the first brainstorm Chekhov experienced, nor would it be the last.

Chapter Five

WHEN THE MOSCOW ART THEATRE visited St. Petersburg, Olga Leonardovna Knipper, the widow of Anton Chekhov and one of the company's leading actresses, said to Misha, "Why don't you want to join our company?"

"I dare not dream of the possibility," answered Misha.

"I will mention it to Stanislavsky," she said. "Come back tomorrow."

Chekhov passed a sleepless night and the next day, wearing a collar that was too tight and a pair of trousers hitched up so high they looked as if they had been specially tailored to avoid puddles, he was introduced to a tall, gaunt man with a pince-nez and the imperious look of a czarist general.

"We are very pleased to have Anton Pavlovich's nephew with us," said Stanislavsky, pumping Misha's hand. "Read for us from *Tsar Fyodor*." Misha did as he was instructed. "And now, Marmaladov's monologue from *Crime and Punishment*." He followed haltingly with the Dostoyevsky. In Misha's opinion, one speech was worse than the other.

"Congratulations," said Stanislavsky, "you are now a member of the Art Theatre! Go and see Vladamir Ivanovich Nemirovich-Danchenko; he will explain the terms to you."

The interview was over and Michael Chekhov had been accepted into the most prestigious theater company in all of Europe.

But behind this marvelous assumption, one has to remember that Misha's uncle had become something of a saint in Russia. Anton Chekhov's plays had catapulted Stanislavsky's theater into the front ranks of all European companies. In 1898, *The Seagull* had literally saved the theater from dissolution, and the mating of Stanislavsly and Chekhov had produced one of the most celebrated collaborations in the modern theater. The nephew of such a charismatic playwright would naturally be welcomed into such a milieu, and the favoritism that enveloped him was not easily lost on all the other members of the company. Indeed, Misha soon became the darling of its director.

Stanislavsky personally took charge of the acolyte. Private tuition was arranged between the director and the actor in which the secrets of the "system" were solemnly imparted. When these sessions were taking place, Stanilsavsky's wife, Maria Petrova Lilina, was sent out of the room. "Maria, please go," he would say rather brusquely. "You don't understand anything anyway." Often, Misha was invited to breakfast at Stanislavsky's home, but, engrossed in exercises, the tuition would often prevent the young actor from swallowing any food. "Try eating as if some tragedy had just occurred," Stanislavsky would command as Misha tried to down a mouthful of eggs. "Forgive me, but I don't believe you," Stanislavsky would say snatching the plate out of his hands. "A grieving man wouldn't eat like that. Now, imagine that your child has just died. Now, eat!—eat!—There again, I don't believe you!"

"I don't believe you" had become something of a shibboleth with Stanislavsky. He used it time and time again when an actor resorted to some convenient acting cliché and, truth be told, it became something of an albatross around the necks of many members of the company. But Stanislavsky hoped the command would jolt actors out of their bad habits and compel them to reestablish contact with their innermost feelings. Apart from a certain insensitive directorial insolence, Stanislavsky, like most of the directors of his time, indulged in line readings and acting demonstrations, a practice that, in the contemporary theater, is heavily frowned upon. "It was impossible to duplicate his example immediately," said Misha. "Several days had to pass before one's soul could absorb all the subtlety and depth of humor of his demonstration."

Strenuously trying to drill the tenets of his system into his actors, many of whom were instinctively opposed to it, Stanislavsky would break off in frustration, cancel the remainder of the rehearsal, and bitterly complain. "Why do I do this?" he would sob like an infant. "I'm a merchant, a factory owner, why do I need to suffer so?" But with Misha, Stanislavsky was usually on his best behavior; stern but constructive. He believed he had found an heir to the throne and he was assiduously cultivating him for future glories.

The atmosphere at the Moscow Art was very different from that at the Maly. The work ethic was deeply embedded in the company and the discipline was strict. Jealousy and intrigue were practically nonexistent. Both Stanislavsky and his co-director Nemirovich-Danchenko instilled a pious love for the theater that transcended the personal ambitions that motivate most young actors. Love the art in yourself, not yourself in the art, Stanislavsky had preached, and what he preached he had inculcated. But the company's season consisted of relatively few plays, and so many of the actors' desire to perform was regularly frustrated. This dissatisfaction extended even to stars of the company like Ivan Moskvin, who had built up a large following even before he joined the Moscow Art. To satisfy his cravings, Moskvin would stage mock funerals for members of the company who willingly agreed to take part in the proceedings. The deceased would stretch themselves out on a table with their hands folded on their chest while Moskvin, drenched in tears, would conduct their funeral service. Once, Moskvin took a child's coffin from the property department, placed it in an open cab, and rode through the streets of Moscow making the sign of the cross and weeping while passersby, viewing the sorrowful spectacle of a father who had lost his young son, would likewise weep and cross themselves.

One day, just before a performance of Tolstoy's *Tsar Fyodor*, Moskvin was taken ill and Misha, who was his understudy, was told he might have to stand in for him. Having caught wind of the planned substitution, Moskvin dragged himself out of his sickbed and, burning with a fever whose temperature topped 103, staggered through the entire performance. Misha's big chance was missed. Shortly afterward, he was officially cast in the juicy role of Opiskin in *Selo Stepanchikovo*, a great step up for a young actor at the Moscow Art. But before rehearsals began, Moskvin demanded the role for himself, and, given his eminence in the theater, it was given to him. "I had already fallen in love with the part," Misha recalled, "and saw the character so clearly in my imagination that ridding myself of him, forgetting him, and ceasing to love him were no easy tasks." Stanislavsky, like a grieving father, consoled Misha as best he could, but for an actor, losing a plum part is like losing a limb, and the sense of loss was truly inconsolable—until, that is, Chekhov actually saw Moskvin play the role. "He was so splendid, surprising, and original, and I was so caught up by this latest Moskvin masterpiece, that I soon forgot *my* Opiskin." Chekhov, ever the celebrant of true creativity, was temperamentally unable to hold a grudge against an artist of such magnitude.

Despite Stanislavsky's favoritism toward Chekhov, there were, even at the start, certain glitches in their relationship. During a performance of Molière's *The Imaginary Invalid* in the 1912–13 season, Chekhov, who was playing the role of a minor physician in the play, was ticked off by the maestro for "having too much fun with the part"—no doubt one of the impish excesses to which young Misha was particularly prone. But surely, he told himself, in a comedy, "fun" was something the actor should try to convey to his audience. But not, it appeared, if it overstepped the bounds that Stanislavsky had set within his mise en scène. Another time, during a workshop class with Stanislavsky, Chekhov was asked to create an "affective memory" exercise based on the actor's personal experience. Chekhov re-created the experience of grief experienced at his father's funeral. Everyone in the room was deeply touched by the scene. Stanislavsky, genuinely affected, embraced the actor and commended his detailed powers of recall. Subsequently, the director discovered that Chekhov's father was in fact still alive and that the exercise was strictly an imaginative evocation of an incident as it might occur in the future. Chekhov was promptly ejected from the class for displaying "an overheated imagination."

He played a variety of roles at the Moscow Art Theater, between 1913 and 1923, some large, some marginal, but always distinctive. In a city highly attentive to its resident actors, he gradually accumulated a growing claque of admirers. Although some of his interpretations, like his over-physicalized Caleb in an adaptation of Dickens' *The Cricket on the Hearth*, might appear too grotesque and off the wall for a public brought up on the classical Moscow Art style, they were always discussed heatedly and the subject of endless dispute.

After a routine apprenticeship at the Maly, Chekhov was discovering the Moscow Art to be a theater driven by an aesthetic philosophy. Given his father's tuition, that was something he immediately warmed to, but it was coming at a time, the early 1900s, when all aesthetic theories were in ferment. After a short period at the Moscow Art, Vsevolod Meyerhold was taking the psychological realism of his mentor Stanislavsky and turning it on its head, espousing a bold, theatricalist form of theater, underpinned with biomechanics and influenced by expressionism. He advocated and exemplified a dynamic, highly physicalized theater that openly proclaimed its artifice. Fyodor Kommissarzhevsky, a quiet, meditative director with a love of books, precious antiques, and beautiful surroundings, was powerfully motivated by the mystical lure of symbolism. Although he, like Meyerhold, rejected the theater of the fourth wall, he was opposed to the "inhuman formalism" that had come to be associated with Meyerhold's puppetlike mise en scène. The aristocratic Nikolai Evreinov was also an enemy to naturalism; the audience, he claimed, did not need an object but merely its image. He was opposed to the Stanislavskyian idea of an audience losing itself in the pretended reality of stage events. The stage's theatricality, he insisted, must be intensified for the spectator; it is art, he contended that influences life, and not the other way around. Alexander Tairov shunned both naturalism and symbolism; he believed theater should not be based either on text, or subtext; that the director was empowered to create a purely theatrical language employing those tools that were germane to his art form.

This welter of ideas swirled through Michael Chekhov's head at the same time as he was being inculcated into a system that was predicated on painstakingly created natural behavior and finely crafted moments of emotional truth. And it all coincided with Misha's entrance into the First Studio of the Moscow Art Theatre, and the arrival of two exceptional theater artists whose practices would condition the next thirty years of his life.

Chapter Six

LEOPOLD ANTONOIVICH SULHERZHITSKY was a short man with a small goatee, a powerful physique; a lively, extravert manner; and a natural enthusiast in almost everything he tackled. In the early 1900s, he became a close associate of Konstantin Stanislavsky at the Moscow Art Theatre.

Suler, as he was affectionately known, had a checkered past. He had been a fisherman in the Crimea and a sailor who had made several voyages around the world. At different points in his wildly itinerant life, he had also been a farmhand, a revolutionary party functionary, a hobo, and a staunch advocate of Leo Tolstoy, who considered him a trusted friend and permitted him to copy his manuscripts. When he was conscripted for military service, Suler refused to serve on the grounds of conscience. He was tried and sentenced to solitary confinement, and placed in a lunatic asylum in a remote castle in the north of Russia.

Tolstoy made efforts to free him, and when he finally returned from exile, the writer-philosopher put him in charge of a contingent of Doukhobors (members of a Christian sect that, rejecting all church and civil authority, obeyed only their "inner light") as they emigrated from the Caucasus to Canada. For two years, Suler lived among the Doukhobors on the new continent, helping them to assimilate to the new culture while piously preserving their own. In addition to being a friend and

mentor to the tribe, Suler also became their attorney, negotiating their permits with the Canadian authorities. A grueling
winter in a threadbare tent seriously undermined his constitu-
tion, and when it was over he remained in precarious health for
the rest of his life. Eventually, he returned to Moscow entirely
indigent. Because he had previously been banned from entering the capitol, he lived in a railway watchman's shed beside
the tracks and often slept huddled in doorways or parks.

He came to the Moscow Art as a kind of handyman helping
with props, costumes, prompting and other odd jobs. It
seemed that whenever anything needed to be done,
Sulherzhitsky was on hand to provide useful services.
Gradually, he made himself indispensable at the theater. In
the early 1900s, he surprised all of his comrades by marrying,
his itinerant days abruptly coming to an end. He became
Stanislavsky's assistant on the director's production of
Andreyev's *The Drama of Life* and found his true métier:
teacher, director and inspirer of youth at the Moscow Art.

It is not generally realized that Stanislavsky came gradually
and painfully to what was later dubbed the "Stanislavsky
System"; a theory of acting predicated on truthful behavior
intended to coax inspiration when that precious quality was in
short supply. He had arrived at his system as a result of intense
dissatisfaction with his own work and, by inference, the work of
his fellow actors. Like Freud, who emerged from a period of
self-analysis with a batch of new theories that ultimately developed into psychoanalysis, Stanislavsky had foraged into his
artistic being to come up with an inner technique that would
banish fakery from the Russian stage. But his actors, unlike
their director, were set in their ways and rebelled against the
maestro's "monkey business," which is how they characterized
the theories that in twenty short years were to revolutionize acting throughout the western world.

When Stanislavsky found it difficult to persuade the more
established actors of the company to experiment with his newly
hatched ideas, he realized the new technique must be inculcat-

ed among the young, the neophyte actors and actresses who hith-
erto had served only as crowd members or supers in the company's productions. Only among young artists still susceptible to
new ideas could his unorthodox theories take root. Together
with Sulherzitsky, he set about creating what in 1911 became the
First Studio of the Moscow Art Theatre. Suler was the ideal partner in this experiment as he was open, intellectually adventurous,
and not grounded in any of the ossified practices that, in
Stanislavsky's view, kept the Russian theater chained to the past.

"Sulherzhitsky," wrote Stanislavsky, "dreamed of creating
with me a sort of spiritual order of actors. Its members were to
be men and women of lofty views and ideas, of wide horizons,
who understood the human soul and strove for noble artistic
ideas, who were willing to sacrifice themselves for art." At the
turn of the century, the notion of sacrificing oneself for art was
not the mawkish cliché it later became. There were abundant
examples of artists, like Gaugin, who devoutly did just that.

Anticipating the ensemble spadework which was later to
help create the Group Theatre, Theatre Libre, Le Theatre du
Vieux Colombier and Chekhov's own company at Dartington
Hall, Stanislavsky envisaged a retreat far from the teeming
streets of Moscow, where actors would live communally, work
diligently, and cut themselves off from the routine demands of
play production. In such an atmosphere, they would assiduously hone the instruments of their craft. In their free time,
they would cultivate the soil and live off the land. By means of
this structured togetherness, they would develop the intercon-
necting vertebrae that every group of actors needed to establish
an effective acting ensemble.

Of course, the dream was never realized. But Stanislavsky
did manage to take over a plot of land in the Crimea near the
Black Sea, a few miles from Eupatoria, and turn it into the
environment from which a fresh new theater could grow. And
it is here in 1911 that Michael Chekhov went along with
Evgeny Vakhtangov and a choice group of young actors to create the First Studio of the Moscow Art.

Although Rudolph Steiner and anthroposophy are often cited as powerful determinants in Michael Chekhov's work, his exposure to Leopold Sulherzhitsky, who managed the First Studio, would seem to be the more formative influence.

Sulherzhitsky's own *weltanshauung* was fashioned by his exposure to Tolstoy and the Doukhobors with whom he lived and worshipped for two years. It is with them that notions of transcendentalism and spirituality became a way of life. They believed that the highest truth resided in the deepest recesses of one's own soul, untainted by tangible or worldly concerns. The inner light that the Doukhobors revered as the source of truth and goodness bears a striking resemblance to the spiritual content of Chekhov's subsequent acting theories. Both belief systems are predicated on discerning and trusting to intuition in order to realize what was richest and most deeply rooted in their personal psyches. When Doukhobors looked within, they found God there; the theater artist, the wellsprings of inspiration.

Chapter Seven

THE SANGUINE SPIRIT of Sulherzhitsky pervaded the First Studio's production in 1911: Herman Heijerman's play *The Good Hope*, retitled *The Death of Hope* and directed by Richard Boleslavsky. Cast in the minor part of Kobe, a backward fisherman, Chekhov chose to play him as a seeker of truth. In a grotesque invention of his own, he gave the character a cone-shaped head and sunken skull and transformed a low-comedy character into a pathetic simpleton oozing lyricism. When it was pointed out to him that this ran contrary to the playwright's intention, Chekhov's response was that he went "beyond the playwright and the play" to unearth Kobe's true character.

The youth, simplicity, and collective thrust of the company enchanted the Moscow public. The company, which had perfectly assimilated Stanislavsky's teachings, created a sense of togetherness that was refreshingly new. Its second production, an adaptation of Charles Dickens' *The Cricket on the Hearth*, was even more successful and particularly delighted Stanislavsky. The more senior members of the Moscow Art who had looked skeptically on Stanislavsky's "peculiar ideas" about acting were obliged to reevaluate their views. If the system diligently applied could be put to such marvelous ends, it would have to be taken more seriously.

The opening of the First Studio coincided with Chekhov's

initial season with the Moscow Art; the same year in which
Stanislavsky took him under his wing and initiated him into
the tenets of his system; the same year in which Misha was
assigned to Evgeny Vakhtangov to be orientated into the company's aesthetic.

"I will not teach this Maly actor!" proclaimed Vakhtangov,
almost crushing the sensitive new recruit. But the assignment
had been made and would not be reversed. The two were
thrown together in the studio work with Suler merrily cement-
ing relationships on all sides, and gradually the ice was broken.
In a matter of months, Chekhov and Vakhtangov became
inseparable.

There were three outstanding disciples of Stanislavsky who
went on to forge their own unmistakable identities in the
Russian, then Soviet, Theatre: Vsevolod Meyerhold, Evgeny
Vakhtangov and Michael Chekhov. Vakhtangov had studied
with the charismatic leader during those uncharacteristic years
when, clearly influenced by the post-revolutionary generation
of directors, Stanislavsky had begun to experiment with non-
naturalistic modes of acting and staging, mounting works by
modern playwrights such as Maeterlinck, Hamsun, Hauptmann and Andreyev. It was a shortlived period that ended with
a disastrous production of Byron's *Cain*. From then on, Stanislavsky returned to the basic tenets of his system and renewed
his commitment to psychological realism, whether influenced
by his own inadequacy with symbolism and poetic drama or
the Soviet emphasis on proletarian plays and social realist principles, it is hard to say.

During Stanislavsky's brief romance with a bolder kind of
theatricality, Vakhtangov was smitten with what was then the
"new drama," a mixture of overt theatricality and a search for a
deeper, inner core. He had already become active in a students' group called the Mansurov Studio. Although their production of Boris Zaitsev's *The Lanin's Estate* was something of
a damp squib, there was a strong solidarity in the acting collective and its members remained together for some three years

under Vakhtangov's leadership, strengthening their ensemble. "A performance," Vakhtangov had preached, "is the expression of the will of a creative collective." It was 1917, the spirit of the revolution was rife and the notion of artistic togetherness, spawned in large measure by the success of the Moscow Art, remained a cherished goal among the young. After a few months, the student group became Vakhtangov's Moscow Dramatic Studio and was soon incorporated into the Moscow Art as a workshop. Vakhtangov continued to forge alliances with other workshops throughout the city—the Gunst, the Armenian Operatic Workshop, the Local Proletarian, the Cooperative, etc. He also took over the helm of Habimah, a local Jewish group that produced short plays in Yiddish and Hebrew by Sholem Asch and Y.L. Peretz (although Vakhtangov could speak neither language).

Vakhtangov never wavered from Stanislavsky's belief in humanistic truth on stage, nor did he ever abandon his obsession with bold theatricality. Although forged in the crucible of Meyerhold and openly acknowledging that director's breathtaking brilliance, he recoiled from the rigid mechanization that often made Meyerhold actors look like automata on stage. Nor was he part of the post-revolutionary movement that favored constructivism and the incorporation of technical gadgetry, slides, and film clips. His work pleased neither the doctrinaire Communists nor the champions of the avant-garde. But in dazzling productions such as Maeterlinck's *The Miracle of Saint Anthony*, Ansky's *The Dybbuk*, Gozzi's *Princess Turandot*, and Strindberg's *Eric XIV*, he established himself as one of the most groundbreaking directors in the country, and the main contender for Meyerhold's crown.

Vakhtangov believed that each play determined its own style, and the director's job was to probe its innards using the shared intelligence of the acting ensemble until that style was collectively realized; hence, his productions—unlike Meyerhold's, which always bore a Meyerholdian stamp—were consistently unique, one bearing virtually no resemblance to another. A compliment similar to that which was soon to be paid to Max Reinhardt in Germany.

Vakhtangov had a bristling and insatiable intellect, as did Chekhov, which created an immediate bond between them. They regularly played a kind of mental tennis together. It was a relationship underpinned by amiable competitiveness but rooted in a joint devotion to a developing aesthetic and one which, more and more, caused them to veer away from Stanislavskyian priorities.

The two friends shared a room during the provincial tour of *The Cricket and the Hearth*. They played mandolin duets together and their philosophical debates often stretched well into the early hours of the morning. Chekhov had become fascinated by Eastern philosophy and was constantly performing yoga exercises on the carpet of their small furnished room. Vakhtangov often found Chekhov in the lotus position as he shuffled across the room for his morning tea. Chekhov then rescued a large, shaggy dog he had found wandering through the streets of town and the dog became the third boarder. Vakhtangov was not partial to stray dogs. A tension began to develop between the two friends and they spoke of it openly. Chekhov, trying to find a way of relieving it, came up with a game called "trained ape."

"The ape," Chekhov explained, "had to wake up before the 'master' and make coffee, move and grimace like an ape, and meekly endure all of the master's whims. But the following day, the roles were reversed and yesterday's ape could exact vengeance for all his suffered wrongs. One day, the trained ape rebelled and a fierce battle broke out. Vakhtangov and I had a real fight. We fought, but we did not quarrel. After the battle, we carefully nursed each other, tending to the wounds we had inflicted on one another, and our friendship was sealed forever. Vakhtangov even became interested in yoga; he even forgave me for the dog."

In addition to mock battles, there were also verbal skirmishes. At one point Vakhtangov threw out the charge that if

Misha's uncle had not been the great Anton Chekhov, Misha would never have made a career for himself in the theater. He knew this was a criticism that Chekhov found extremely irritating and so enjoyed sprinkling salt into that particular wound. He was delighted when after a performance of *The Cherry Orchard*, in which Misha played Epikhodov, a member of the audience, pointing to Chekhov, stood up and cried out, "There he is! Just think, he not only wrote it, but he acts in it as well."

Practical jokes between them were par for the course. On one occasion during one of their southern tours, Chekhov found a taxi passing just as he alighted from the train station. He gave the driver the address where several of the actors from the company were already staying. "You wouldn't happen to be Anton Pavlovich Chekhov's nephew?" asked the reverent driver. Chekhov was flattered by the recognition and replied that, he was in fact Chekhov's nephew. When they arrived at the hotel, the driver refused to accept any payment, jumped out of the cab and smartly threw open the door so that his celebrated passenger might alight. As Misha approached the entrance, the hotel doorman hurried over to him and asked: "Are you Anton Pavlovich Chekhov's nephew?" Chekhov, surprised at being so widely recognized in this small, provincial town, replied in the affirmative. "Step this way, sir," he said as he relieved Misha of his satchel and flung open the doors of the hotel. Inside, a startled porter seeing the actor approach asked the same question and being told the answer, obsequiously showed him to the finest room in the hotel. As the porter swung open the door, there sat Vakhtangov, doubled up with laughter with both the doorman and the porter joyously joining in. Vakhtangov's little joke, beautifully staged as befit the great director, had worked like a charm.

Vakhtangov, like Chekhov, improvised brilliantly and effortlessly. He was able to appropriate the simplest prop—a pencil, a comb, a flower—and develop an extended scene that contained elements of both comedy and pathos. Sometimes, these improvisations had the comic inventiveness frequently found in Chaplinesque two-reelers: a drunkard trying to pull on his galoshes, attempting to insert a match into a narrow-necked bottle, vainly trying to light a cigarette or haul on an overcoat whose sleeves eluded its wearer. But he was also an indefatigable director spending his days in the Moscow Art Studio, and his evenings at his own workshops.

When he was rehearsing his production of *The Dybbuk* with the Habimah actors, which was destined to become a legend among Jews throughout Europe, he invited Misha to one of the final dress rehearsals. When the performance was over, the company, still in costume and makeup, was summoned before the director and Chekhov. Vakhtangov asked his colleague what, if anything, he had not understood. Misha explained that he knew no Hebrew, but that apart from a few things that were unclear, he had understood most of the performance. Vakhtangov, refusing to let him off the hook, demanded that Chekhov describe in exact detail precisely which moments had been unclear and Misha proceeded to list them. "What Chekhov didn't understand," said Vakhtangov to the cast "was not because of language, but because you acted badly. Good acting must be understood by everybody, regardless of language. We will rehearse again the scenes that Chekhov has mentioned."

Despite the lateness of the hour and the exhaustion of the company, Vakhtangov proceeded to drill his cast to clarify the obscurities that had been enumerated. The rehearsal slogged long into the night, but according to Chekhov, "with stunning results." At the end, Chekhov was astonished at the ways in which personal acting discoveries on the part of the company illuminated the literal content of the playwright's text, uprooting subtextual meanings despite the barrier of language.

In 1919, the revolutionary instability gradually began to subside and Chekhov opened his own studio in the Arbat theater district of Moscow. As a result of his ideological differences with Stanislavsky, he had begun to coalesce his own notions about acting. Instead of stressing units, objectives, and emotional memories, he concentrated on the powers of the actor's imagination; not who the actor was but what he could become as a result of extending himself into areas beyond his circumscribed personality. Hundreds of young students auditioned for the studio, but only thirty were chosen. By the end of each session, many of these had fallen away—either confused by Misha's theories or simply frightened off by his immersion in yoga and reincarnation. After a year, it was clear that the studio could not provide him with a livelihood, and he was obliged to return to acting. But just when he needed the bulwark of Stanislavsky and the Moscow Art most, he managed almost to alienate them forever.

To the general public in Moscow, there was something arcane about the Stanislavsky system—not unlike how the "method" was perceived by those actors in the fifties not directly involved with Lee Strasberg within the confines of the Actors' Studio. In Stanislavsky's case, this was a deliberate obfuscation. He forbade his students from discussing the tenets of the system with the outside world because he was well aware that it could easily be misinterpreted and distorted by people who had not experienced it. Then, one day, the director was astounded to read an article by Michael Chekhov in the cultural journal *Gom* (*Crucible*), which provided a detailed breakdown on the system that not only revealed all its constituents but proceeded to dispute the validity of many of them. Senior members of the Moscow Art were furious at Chekhov's arrogant subversion and brazen disloyalty. Even Vakhtangov felt compelled to reply to it in a chilly essay entitled "To Those Who Write About the Stanislavsky System", which appeared in *Vesnik Teatre*. The timing was also unfortunate. The article appeared at that point in the history of the Moscow Art when Stanislavsky himself was most vulnerable and many actors had already begun to question the efficacy of the ideas their director had been instilling among the company members. Indeed, one of the main objects of the recently created First Studio was to apply those theories to younger, more malleable actors who, in the opinion of both Stanislavsky and Sulherzhitsky, would be more amenable to them. Had Stanislavsky lacked magnanimity and Chekhov personal charm, that might have ended the relationship then and there, but as it was, once the maestro had fumed and fulminated for a few weeks, he forgave Misha's "indiscretion" and Chekhov was once again admitted back into the fold. But the dissensions between the director and the actor had been well and truly sewn.

In 1921, Chekhov created two of his most extraordinary characterizations: Eric XIV in Strindberg's play of the same name under Vakhtangov's direction at the First Studio, and Khlestakov in Gogol's *The Inspector General*, directed by Stanislavsky at the Moscow Art. What was extraordinary about these two roles is that they were the products of two almost diametrically opposed directorial approaches that Chekhov somehow managed to assimilate into his own burgeoning style.

The key for Chekhov in regard to the young, impotent Swedish king was that Eric is trapped within a circle from which he cannot escape. He tries continually to break the circumference of that circle by flaying his hands and arms, but it is impregnable. His hands dangle helpless at his sides; his body flails about, but remains constricted. It was by refining this gesture of escape within the deepest reaches of his personal psychology that Chekhov was able to structure the astonishing performance that emerged. He would, at this time, never have referred to it as a "psychological gesture", but a decade or so later, it would become the keystone of his own personally honed Chekhovian technique.

Eric XIV, according to Konstantin Rudnitsky "became the turning point in the work of the First Moscow Art studio." Nikolai Zograf wrote that in this production the director "created a new theatrical world far removed from the realistic verisimilitude of depiction, a world of the anti-everyday." And Chekhov, according to Rudnitsky, "played Eric as a man who has heard the firm, inevitable tread of fate; who knows that his demise is inescapable, and this is why he seems indifferent to everything, apathetic, as if transfixed in his cumbersome silver attire, then suddenly driven into furious activity by terror, the impotence of rage. The tragic was conveyed in the spare, graphically incisive, and outwardly cold figure. Abnormally dilating eyes, drooping intonation, and the nervous movement of his thin hands betraying suffering and anguish. At the moment when Eric threw the magnificent royal mantle from his shoulders with one short, quick movement, his boyish thinness, his frailty, immediately became apparent. Eric personified weakness itself, impotence itself."

At the same time, under Stanislavsky's direction in the larger theater, Chekhov was being steered toward the "personal truth" of the charlatan Khlestakov in Gogol's comedy of czarist bureaucracy. But by this time, Stanislavsky realized he was working with a highly imaginative artist who could not be easily bent to a director's will—not even his. In the face of Chekhov's ebullient inventions, Stanislavsky simply backed off. Like any astute director, he knew when he was on to a good thing and decided not to endanger it with directorial impositions.

This was a radically different interpretation from the Arts Theatre production in 1908, which took place in a dreary, roach-infested provincial setting with worm-eaten furniture and a Khlestakov who was relentlessly naturalistic. Chekhov's mistaken government inspector was lively, capricious, idiosyncratic, and constantly airborne. The mayor was played by Moskvin, with the two sycophants Bobchinsky and Dobchinsky scrambling around the civic dignitary, fastening the spurs to his boots and buffing up the leather. In the final scene, Stanislavsky broke through the fourth wall to have Moskvin, his foot perched on the prompter's box, confront the public directly with the line, "What are you laughing at?—You're laughing at yourselves!" With this indictment, the house lights were immediately switched on and the audience found themselves thrust from dramatic illusion into an embarrassing reality.

Chekhov's Khlestakov was the centrifugal force of the entire production. He cavorted through the evening with an improvisational flair that made it appear as if he were making up Gogol's play as he was going along. Chekhov's performance, wrote Konstantin Rudnitsky, "stunned with its unbelievable improvised ease and unrestrained imagination. Chekhov's Khlestakov now dived underneath the table three times in search of money, now skipped across the stage like a young goat, now lusting for the mayor's wife, gnawed the leg of a chair, now mocking Khlopov, moved a burning candle about right under his nose. Countless mischievous, eccentric pranks followed one after another, forming themselves into the dodging, confused line of behavior of the unprepossessing snub-nosed official from Petersburg, the silliest, emptiest man, gripped by a great flight of the imagination."

Chekhov's creation of character was so total that it seemed to observers at the time to have taken on a life of its own. It varied from night to night—sometimes radically—was sprinkled with new business, unexpected moves and changing intonations. It was Khlestakov controlling Chekhov, rather than the other way around. "Can this be the same man we see in our studio every morning?" an astonished Vakhtangov asked Stanislavsky.

The Gogol would remain with Chekhov for many years to come, being revived in France, then later in America, acquiring legendary stature, preserving for Chekhov a kinetic memory of some of the finest work he ever accomplished in Russia. It was a period in which, paradoxically, the actor was simultaneously developing his tragic proclivities as well as his most inspired comedic inventiveness.

● ● ● ● ●

The First Studio in which Chekhov and Vakhtangov did their earliest work was more a room than a theater. There was no raised stage, and hence, no footlights. The performances took place directly in the midst of spectators who sat in the very center of the action, so close they could smell the actors' perspiration and register every quiver of emotion expressed in their bodies and faces. If a fireplace or an oven were needed, it would be painted on the folds of fabric hanging from the ceiling. Walls were also painted drops. "We do everything by the most primitive means," Sulherzhitsky explained. "Our sets are canvases on hooks." Since there were barely three walls utilized in the performances, there was no pretense of there being a fourth wall. The proximity of the public encouraged the most detailed and psychologically nuanced acting that could be mustered. A twinkle in the eye, a thought passing silently over an actor's face, a twinge of fear, or a surge of aggression were immediately registered by the public.

The young company included Richard Boleslavsky who would later emigrate to America and make a name for himself as a prominent alumnus of the Moscow Art Theatre — despite the fact that much of what he learned in the twenties would be heavily revised by Stanislavsky after his departure, so that in a sense, Boleslavsky was spreading a gospel the master himself had already renounced. (It was this earlier training that was passed on by Boleslavsky to his American pupil Lee Strasberg. A decade later it would cause a deep rift among the members of the Group Theatre precipitated by Stella Adler, who, having gone to Paris to study with Stanislavskly, returned to the group to announce, "We're doing it all wrong.") Another member of the First Studio was the diminutive Maria Ouspenskaya. She fell deeply in love with Boleslavsky and followed him to America, where her film career included classy films such as Joseph von Sternberg's *The Shanghai Gesture* and William Wyler's *Dodsworth*, and low-budget horror flicks like *The Wolf Man* and *Frankenstein Meets the Wolf Man*—a far cry from her work at the Moscow Art Theatre.

Being the offspring of the Moscow Art and led by two of Stanislavsky's prize pupils, Chekhov and Vakhtangov, the First Studio started with a steadfast fidelity to the system inculcated

in the Mother Theatre. So much so that Stanislavsky told
Stella Adler in 1934 that the true system had never been fully
realized by the older actors at the Moscow Art; only in the studios, particularly the First and Third Studios, did it really take
root. The relative youth and inexperience of the actors in the
First Studio made it easier for them to assimilate Stanislavsky's
precepts, and Vakhtangov, one of Stanislavsky's most gifted
and most trusted disciples, did a good job of drilling them into
willing minds. But as time progressed and the entire Russian
theater was invaded by newer and more daring ideas, expressionist tendencies began to creep in and the younger, more
susceptible actors started questioning some of the acting principles handed down to them from above.

In productions such as Hauptmann's *The Festival of Peace*
and Henning Berger's *The Deluge*, the tendency of
Vakhtangov's work toward a more excitable and heightened
style of acting disturbed Stanislavsky who described it as "some
kind of disease, hysteria" with actors performing "neurastheni-
cally." His own preference was for Boris Sushkevitch's adaptation of Dickens' *The Cricket on the Hearth*, a touching and
tender Christmas tale, which Stanislavsky believed was for the
First Studio "what *The Seagull* had been for the Moscow Art
Theatre."

The first, and in many ways the most definitive,
Vakhtangov-Chekhov collaboration had been Strindberg's
Eric XIV in 1921. Here, Chekhov first revealed the extra dimen-
sionality of characterization that was to be the hallmark of all
of his major performances. Despite the inherent evil of the
character, Chekhov made the audience feel enormous sympathy for Eric. "For the first time," wrote Nikolai Gorchakov,
"this actor showed the enormous range of his skills. In his intonations, in his outcry suddenly erupting from a whisper, in his
hasty and impetuous motions, in his incredibly dynamic translation from shading to shading, he unveiled the character of a
person torn apart by contradictions."

Just as his father had been able to capture the essence of a character with a few bold strokes of the pen, Chekhov seemed to draw together a cluster of contradictory traits that, dispensed on stage, delineated the fascinating complexity of Strindberg's pathological monarch. "The performance," wrote Pavel Markov, "was marked by a cold and rigorous graphic quality. It seemed that this quality was expressed by every movement and gesture; the posture of his body in space; the hand that darted out and remained suspended in the air; the hopeless melancholic gaze of the morbidly wide-opened eyes upon the elongated, wondering face; the thin hands and feet slipping out from the silver garments; the sudden uplifts and plunges of the timid and bold movements. It seemed that his whole bearing could be put on paper and fixated in the form of a clear drawing."

By the time Vakhtangov and Chekhov had produced Strindberg's *Eric XIV*, a darker and more harrowing experience than had ever been produced at the Moscow Art, it was clear that a dissociation of sensibility had taken place between the mentor and his disciples. Vakhtangov's natural tendency was to escalate sharply from realism to a frightening grotesquerie, a constant shuttling between styles that produced highly ambiguous reactions upon the audience. Chekhov imperceptibly slithered from realism into caricature, using the ordinary as a trampoline on which he performed astonishing imaginative leaps. Disturbing rather than reassuring the public was a mutual, if never articulated, principle of their work.

Before long, a kind of estrangement developed between the two theaters that seeped over into personal relationships. No longer "Misha," Stanislavsky took to calling Chekhov by the more formal appellation, "Mikhail Alexandrovich." Although he praised Vakhtangov's work in public, he criticized it in private. In 1928, Stanislavsky and Chekhov had a frank conversation about their aesthetic differences. It was in fact their last meeting, although neither man realized it at the time.

One of the tenets of the system concerned "affective memory," the trick of an actor tapping a highly personal memory

drawn from his own experience that, in paralleling the emotion required from his character, could immediately evoke it on
the stage. Chekhov believed that truly creative feelings were
more effectively conjured up by the actor's imagination,
cleansed of all personal associations. Chekhov's experience
was that actors who harked back to traumatic memories from
their past were often upset on the stage and could not control
the feelings they had evoked.

The other point had to do with the way in which the actor
imagined his role. An actor playing Othello, for instance, was
encouraged by Stanislavsky to envelop himself thoroughly in
Othello's circumstances, and in this way project the character
through his own being. Chekhov believed "the actor must forget himself and conjure up Othello (not himself) in his imagination, from the sidelines, as it were. The actor will feel what
Othello feels, and his feelings will be pure, transformed and
not drawing into his own personality. The image of Othello,
seen in the imagination, will ignite those mysterious, creative
feelings in the actor that are usually called 'inspiration.'"

It is interesting that one of the artistic differences between
Vakhtangov and Stanislavsky also tends to coincide with those
between Chekhov and Stanislavsky. In *Princess Turandot*, by
commenting ironically on the characters and objectifying
their roles rather than losing themselves within the fiction,
many critics believe Vakhtangov anticipated Brecht's theory of
alienation; having actors play in such a way that an audience
could draw socially relevant inferences about their characters
rather than being swallowed up by their reality. Although
Chekhov never went that extra step toward alienation per se, he
was fond of leading audiences up the garden path, projecting
one set of characteristics and then abruptly reversing them—
segueing from comedy into pathos or virtue into villainy.
Anything that so dislocated the continuity of character on
which Stanislavsky's theories were based would obviously be
jarring to the more conservative director. But then, it was
Stanislavsky himself who had always encouraged actors to look

for contrasts in their roles; to seek out the villainous aspects of virtuous characters and vice versa. And so the principle of contradiction is embedded in both approaches. But Chekhov, influenced by Vakhtangov's expressionist tendencies, gravitated naturally to the external rather than the internal route toward character, and in so doing, violated one of the more sacred tenets of the system, in which psychological truth determined verisimilitude.

The more one tries to define the differences between artists like Stanislavsky and Chekhov, the more the debate seems to wind backward to Diderot's *Paradox*, William Archer's *Masks or Faces*, or the more recent controversy between the efficacy of British technique as opposed to Method acting. There is a tendency to believe these are merely quibbles between similar approaches to acting and, although in general terms this may be true, the Chekhovian theory is rooted in a very different terrain from that first hoed by Konstantin Stanislavsky. It may not produce the high-profile actors that have traceably developed from the Group Theatre through the Actors' Studio and into Hollywood films, but it is essentially different in kind, and nourishes a very different conception of dramatic art and gravitates toward a different body of work. There are very few actors who have been able to exemplify it as Chekhov himself did, but its lure is apparent to actors of a very different stripe working in different languages and in many parts of the world.

● ● ● ● ●

After the First Studio's tour of the provinces, the first signs of Vakhtangov's illness began to be revealed: stomach pains that he attributed to an ulcer, although he, and others, sensed that it was much more serious than that. Despite these symptoms, or perhaps because of them, he worked all the harder, believing that intensified periods of creativity could in some inexplicable way counter the cancer that was slowly consuming him.

"How I want to live," Chekhov recalls him saying toward the end. "Look at these stones, look at these plants. I feel them in a new way; in a special way. I want to be with them. I want to touch them." There was an operation to remove the cancer but it quickly grew back. "Feel that bump?" he would say to Misha. "That is the scar left by the operation." Standing before a mirror, his piercing eyes blinking at his image, he would say to his friend, "See how strong I look! My arms, what muscles! And my legs are very strong, see?" But what he did not see was that his face had become yellow and sunken, his arms and legs disturbingly thin. Still, he never let up. At the Moscow Art Studio, he was remounting *Eric XIV*, intending to alternate with Chekhov in the title role. Sapped of energy, he would often have to miss rehearsals. A co-director was brought in to lighten his burden.

Vakhtangov's final production of *Turandot* in 1922 was not only his most brilliant, but the one that finally synthesized all the stylistic trends he had been experimenting with since 1917. It began with characters in glittering evening attire crossing the stage, bantering with one another and making trivial, inaudible jokes. They then sat down at their dressing tables onstage and, becoming actors, proceeded to apply their make-up and don their respective costumes, which were also subject to transformation. A towel became a turban, an elongated shawl turned into a dress, and colored silk fabrics fluttering down from the flys created China. The musicians' instruments consisted of combs wrapped in cigarette paper, commedia-styled maskers hurled improvised insults to latecomers shuffling to their seats after the show had begun. "It was as if the festive beauty of the merry spectacle," wrote Rudnitsky, "refuted the everyday reality of Moscow life in the early twenties, still cold, dark and half starved."

Vakhtangov lay in his room on Denezhny Lane, barely five minutes from the theater, too ill to attend the opening. He had been given morphine injections to ease his pain. Couriers ran from the Arbat stage of the Third Studio theater to his home, delivering glowing reports of the production that was captivating the Moscow public and that was destined to remain in the repertory for decades, being successfully revived in 1971. Each report of the audience's reaction brightened Vakhtangov's enervated face; he tried desperately to climb out of bed but was too feeble to stand. He died three months later.

When one examines Chekhov's virtues as an actor and a theorist, one constantly stumbles across the ghost of Vakhtangov: the almost total immersion in improvisation, the quest for deeply rooted living matter beneath the psychological subtext, the belief that only subconscious energy can truly ignite the actors' imagination, the conviction that artifice can contain a greater dollop of truth than can ever be produced by strict verisimilitude. Vakhtangov died in 1922 at 39, but the seeds that he planted in his friend and collaborator were destined to sprout magnificently over the next three decades. In the fifties, when Chekhov himself had become something of a legend both in Europe and America, few would remember the name of Vakhtangov, and if they did, it would be strictly in terms of his discipleship at the Moscow Art Theatre. But Michael Chekhov never forgot him.

Chapter Eight

CHEKHOV'S COMMENTS on Stanislavsky's rehearsal procedure during the production of *The Inspector General* slightly tarnish the image of the great director. The rehearsals for the Gogol were many and, in Chekhov's words, "for the most part, excruciating." Stanislavsky often confused teaching with directing and tended to treat senior members of the company as if they were fledgling students, which stirred a palpable resentment from the stage. In one scene in which Misha, Ivan Moskvin, and Chekhov's widow Olga Knipper slightly muddled their lines, the stern, cold voice from the auditorium boomed, "Stop! You will repeat your lines thirteen times!" And with Stanislavsky tapping his finger on the desk to mark each repetition, the actors duly recited them aloud like schoolchildren.

At other times, applying different aspects of his system, which was constantly being mentally revised, the director would forget his previous instructions. "What idiot taught you to do that?" he would ask indignantly, only to be told, "Why, you did, Master—yesterday."

Demonstration, as we have seen, was very much the modus operandi at the Moscow Art, especially when the artistic director was himself such a celebrated actor. Occasionally, Stanislavsky would wander from the given plot, improvising scenes that didn't exist in the play at all. But it was done with such creative exuberance and consummate skill that none of the company ever thought of drawing attention to those tangents.

No one enjoyed the success of *The Inspector General* more than Stanislavsky himself, sitting in the audience, frequently laughing in anticipation of a joke he knew was coming or trailing laughter long after the scene had moved into other areas. When Chekhov played well, he would visit him in his dressing room and gently berate him. "Awful!" he would say. "Who needs it!? It's not worth three kopecks. We must rehearse everything again from the beginning!" But when he played badly, he would come backstage with a pasted-on smile and, avoiding the actor's eyes, coo, "Very good. Simply splendid. The role is clearly growing. Congratulations." In the former case, he would be guarding against the actor becoming too conceited, and in the latter, being too disheartened by a poor performance.

On rare occasions, he would offer advice on personal matters. Once, trying to intercede in one of Chekhov's marital problems, he uttered a few heartfelt words about God, and in return received a spray of atheistic epithets. This produced a look of great pity in Stanislavsky, mingled somewhat with contempt. When he conveyed warm regards from a medical acquaintance known to both of them who had spoken disparagingly about Schopenhauer, Chekhov replied that the doctor in question was "stupid" and that he didn't like him at all. "And who *do* you like?" asked Stanislavsky, sharply turning away. Misha might have honestly answered "You, Alexeyevitch," but he didn't.

The reactions to Chekhov's performances both in the Gogol and in Strindberg's *Eric XIV* were not entirely laudatory; some of them were cautionary. "If he goes on acting like this," Chekhov heard one playgoer say, "he will lose his mind." The offhand comment cut deeply into Chekhov's fragile self-confidence because, buried beneath his inspired comedy was the fear that his mind was not stable and at any moment might come unhinged. Once into the run, symptoms did begin to appear. He found himself stammering—sometimes so badly that he didn't feel able to perform. He went to Stanislavsky and said dolefully, "I sta-sta-stamm-er continually. And so in all proba-proba-proba-bil-bil-bil-ity, I will not be able to a-a-a-act any longer." Stanislavsky listened quietly to Chekhov's complaint, then stood up and said, "The moment I open this window, you will stop stammering." He flung it open and, according to Chekhov, the stammer instantly disappeared. He continued to act.

Whimsical anecdotes such as these are peppered throughout Chekhov's reminiscences, and although they strain credulity, one is constantly reminded that during this period Russia was very much the "old country," and folk tales and supernatural occurrences were regularly chronicled and implicitly believed. It is an open question as to whether many of the improbable events that supposedly took place in that more primitive world happened or not. Our twenty-first-century skepticism, demystified by science and technology, is not the best means of trying to fathom a time that has receded into an unrecoverable past.

While in Russia, Chekhov's attitude to Stanislavsky was ambivalent. He admired the actor and lauded the challenging new theories the director had formulated, and in fact, Chekhov himself practiced many of them throughout his life. When he left Russia and was formulating his own ideas about the actor's craft, his judgement on Stanislavsky hardened. "The tragedy of Stanislavsky," Chekhov wrote, "was that he had no understanding of what it meant to be a teacher. He was never able to find a way to give his knowledge to others. He was a great inventor, but as a teacher he was very ungifted. He could demonstrate, but he could not teach."

It may well be that Stanislavsky lacked the gift of entering into a healthy, reciprocal relationship with all his actors. He acknowledged the fact that he was not able to inculcate his system with the veteran members of the Mosow Art, and that greater success was achieved among the younger actors of the

First Studio, the studio led by Vakhtangov and subsequently,
Chekhov. But he certainly engendered the skills that made
Vakhtangov and Sulhershzitsky the outstanding teachers they
became, and through his example and his writings, influenced
several generations of instructors who, having assimilated the
basic tenets of the Stanislavsky system went on on to refine and
enhance that system. But it is possible to be the inventor of a
dynamic new theory and not be the best person to transmit it to
students on a one-to-one basis. It is possible to be the embodi-
ment of creative ideas, and an exemplar of those ideas, and not
be the locus from which they can be effectively relayed to others. Then again, Chekhov's criticism of Stanislavsky's teaching
ability may be nothing more than the typical actor's aversion of
being shown what to do rather than being coaxed into creating
those moments oneself, an irritation that almost every actor
has experienced at one time or another in the hands of a
demonstrative director who, unwilling to take the circuitious
route that gradually leads to personalized results, opts for the
expedient of imitation.

Chapter Nine

IN HIS YOUTH, Chekhov was a hopeless romantic, constantly falling in love with one girl after another, no sooner smitten than proposing marriage. It was a fervor commingled with fear of rejection and tremulous insecurity and it tended to frighten away the objects of his affection. During one of his early depressions, aggravated by too deep an immersion in Schopenhauer, he arbitrarily decided that marriage, unreasonable as it may be, was the stabilizing factor that he most needed. Olga Knipper-Chekhova, Anton's widow, lived with two young nieces, one of whom was named Olga Konstantinovna Knipper. Dispassionately, Chekhov decided to select her for his wife. "If you really do consider your life of no account," he told himself, "then to consciously commit an unreasoned act" would in some way confirm his nihilist philosophy.

Since he despaired of ever obtaining their parents' consent, Olga and Misha eloped, and in a remote country church bribed a priest to marry them without documents or other formalities. To his astonishment, Misha fell passionately in love with his young wife. But soon afterward, Olga, with unfailing intuition, sensed that the marriage had been something of a cold-blooded decision on the part of her bridegroom. She gradually became drawn down by his black moods. Olga tried to relieve them, but Misha remained mired in a kind of existential despair from which nothing could shake him free. At one point, the intensity acquired suicidal proportions and he actually contemplated taking his life with the loaded Browning automatic he kept in his desk drawer. (Ironically, not too long afterward, his cousin Volodya, with whom he used to stage impromptu performances for the family, stole the Browning from its hiding place and did commit suicide.)

The paranoia took a disturbing turn when Chekhov confessed to Olga that he could both hear and actually visualize conversations that were taking place in distant parts of the country.

Since the source of his depression seemed to be philosophic in origin, Misha approached a professor of psychology named Chelpanov to suggest a program of systematic study that might relieve the spiritual stress that weighed so heavily upon him. "I would suggest that you occupy yourself with questions of religion," the professor advised, "and put away philosophy and psychology." This provided no relief to Misha's torment, and he sank even further into torpor.

Chekhov's unshakeable depressive state, his suicidal impulses, the voices in his head interspersed with sporadic and uncontrollable fits of maniacal laughter, became so disturbing that Stanislavsky decided to intervene. He persuaded Misha to have a consultation with a group of leading Moscow psychiatrists.

"Three or four eminent men came to my home," Chekhov recalled, "and spoke to me in tender, serene voices as if I were perfectly normal. They asked me many questions. I received them politely and tried, in turn, to deal with them as with normal people. 'What books do you read?' they asked. I told them. 'Yes,' said one, 'but Schopenhauer never understood physiology properly and none of his discourses have any merit.'"

This offhand dismissal of his favorite philosopher caused Misha to pity his interlocutors. He wanted to persuade them about the validity of the ideas they seemed so quick to reject. As he did so, he found himself playing the character they took him to be, consciously portraying the symptoms of remoteness and spiritual malaise that had been attributed to him. Again, the dividing line between acting and being was subtly crossed. Once the doctors' diagnosis had been confirmed, he hoped they would finally leave him alone, but their probes persisted. One of them suggested he squeeze himself between the back of the couch and wall and huddle there in a kind of embryo position while the doctor put certain questions to him, a tactic Misha found particularly offensive. Another suggested Misha accompany him on a stroll. But to what purpose? Why suddenly go for a stroll? Feeling both paranoid and defensive, he walked outdoors with the psychiatrist. Chekhov recalled:

> He was short and thin. As we strolled, I watched him, and was prepared to attack him at any moment. I knew I could easily deal with him. I also knew that if I wished to, I could greatly increase my physical strength. My strength had grown to its utmost. I felt invincible and decided to spare him until the last possible moment. The unpleasant stroll was soon over, but the consultation went on much longer. I lost all respect for my unwanted visitors. I wanted to be left alone, as I knew they would be presenting their findings to Stanislavsky. Their conclusions, however, didn't interest me. I was tired and glad to see them go. This meeting with eminent scientists, whom I had previously respected, left me more disillusioned with people than before.

Chekhov's description of his session with the Moscow psychiatrists tends to suggest a classic paranoid personality, tinged with delusions of grandeur and smoldering with bottled-up fury against authority figures who clearly do not understand their patient or appreciate his state of mind. Depression of the kind suffered by Chekhov was often considered a forerunner to total mental imbalance, but it is clear the psychiatrists were treating a sensitive and cultivated artist as if he were simply a basket case. Chekhov's dilemma existed on a philosophical plane, trying to reconcile the writings of people like Nietzsche, Freud, and Schopenhauer to the events in his personal life while living in a society turbulent with revolution and foundering values.

Although a certain mental instability characterizes Chekhov's life almost from beginning to end, it is not the instability of a psychotic or a schizophrenic, but rather the reactions of a heightened sensitivity trying to sort out life's painful contradictions; the kind of internal confusions that young men frequently experience as they attempt to correlate a jumble of intellectual assumptions with emerging realities that contradict them. That sorting out of irreconcilable impulses happens to people at all ages, and it was happening to Chekhov in his late 20s. At that time in Russia—or indeed in the entire western world—psychiatry had not yet assimilated the work of its European pioneers. The first International Psychoanalytical Congress had taken place in Salzburg only eight years before; psychology itself was still a mixture of unscientific speculation, untested assumptions and deeply ingrained fallacies. Even when the theories of Freud and Jung were later disseminated, it was decades before they would take root in Russia. And so Chekhov's skepticism about the psychiatric specialists seems quite justified.

Four years after their marriage and shortly after the abortive diagnosis with the Moscow doctors, Olga left Chekhov for another man described by Chekhov himself without rancor as "elegant, handsome, charming and talented, with great inner strength which had an irresistible effect on people." Ferenc Jaroszi, an officer from the Austro-Hungarian army, had been a prisoner of war in Russia but despite his rough past had developed a suavity which enchanted all who met him. He regularly visited the Chekhovs, who now had a young daughter named Ada, and gradually cast a Svengali-like spell over Olga. It was a period during which battles were still being fought on the Moscow streets, artillery shells exploded in the distance and bullets whistled past people's houses, often shattering their windows. But Jaroszi, who came courting Olga, blithely walked the streets, visiting the family daily, imperturbable and consistently entertaining. He claimed that he couldn't be killed. "If you can hold your life in contempt completely," he said, "then it is out of danger."

Under Jaroszi's influence, Olga slipped rapidly away from her husband and, discovering he was a hopeless alcoholic and an impractical dreamer, decided to leave for good. After she had informed him of her decision, there was a memorable final parting. Caressing her husband of four years, she said: "How ugly you are. Well, goodbye. You'll soon forget." She gave him a short peck on the cheek as one might a casual acquaintance, and with their infant daughter in tow, abandoned their home.

The epilogue to Olga Chekhova's abandonment of her husband is riddled with both melodrama and speculation.

After arriving in Berlin, she quickly threw over her new lover. There, she began to develop those powers of self-preservation which would maintain her throughout World War II when she became a highly successful German film star and a favorite of the Nazi hierarchy with powerful protectors that included both Goebbels and Hitler. It is alleged that during the same period she was also a spy for the USSR, having been originally recruited by her brother, Lev Knipper. An inexhaustible mythomaniac, Olga fabricated professional accomplishments in Russia, claiming she had been an actress with the Moscow Arts and personally trained by Stanislavsky—just as she aggrandized her relationship with the führer during the war years when it added a gloss to her own career.

After the Nazis' defeat, her "collaborative" years were converted into heroic undercover work for the USSR. In 1936, her honors in Germany had included Schauspieleren or Actress of the State and, immediately after the war, the Order of Lenin was conferred upon her by the Central Committee of the USSR. She was celebrated for having been an invaluable spy for the Soviet Union throughout the war years, although no conclusive achievements in that capacity were ever demonstrated. During and after the war, she was rigorously protected by Joseph Stalin and the notorious Lavrenty Beria as well as key members of the People's Commissariat for Internal Affairs (NKVD) which, when she returned to her homeland, provided her with money, property, food rations, guards, and unimpeded freedom to travel between the East and West.

A congenital liar, self-dramatizer but supreme survivor, her highly successful film career in Germany had included stints with respected directors such as Frederich Murnau, Max Ophüls, René Clair and Alfred Hitchcock. She had also been something of a cover girl for both the Wehrmacht and the German army, and the appellation, "Hitler's favorite actress," which was pinned on her during the Nazi years, was never removed.

In 2004, the historian Antony Beevor wrote a detailed biography of her life entitled *The Mystery of Olga Chekhova* which, despite a multitude of facts about her family, her lovers, her turmoils, and her hairbreadth escapes in both Germany and the USSR, remains maddeningly inconclusive as to what spying she actually did for the NKVD and how she managed to swan through the highest realms of both Nazi and Soviet society. Chekhov himself sheds no light on any of these post-marital events, and the "mystery" of Olga Chekhova remains largely unsolved.

After the revolution there was famine in Moscow, and food and medicine were in short supply. Chekhov's mother fell seriously ill. Chekhov wrote:

> She lay in a cold, unheated room and moaned softly, day and night. She needed expert and special care, and I managed with difficulty to get her into a hospital. Her intellect weakened and her mind began to wander. Seeing this and being unable to help her, my spiritual equilibrium began to give way. Mother died without me. They moved her body to the morgue and I had difficulty

finding her. A typhus epidemic was raging in Moscow and they barely managed to bury the dead. I found her in the midst of a great many corpses lying on tables, on the floor, under benches, in freakish poses, either repulsing or enticing each other. The bodies were buried in large graves, tied to planks and logs, in pairs. The priest mechanically mumbled a prayer moving briskly from one grave to the next, accepting money as he went from those who wished to pay him. I became suddenly indifferent to what I saw around me and even to the fact that Mother was dead. Having buried her, I plunged into a long period of dull indifference to life.

As with the death of his father, Chekhov tried to evoke an emotion appropriate to the enormity of the loss but found it impossible to do so. It was as if the weight of his depression had detached itself from those more commonplace emotions, like grief and mourning, that were piled beneath it.

The recommendation of the Moscow psychiatrists was that Chekhov be interned in a mental hospital. Fortunately, the general wisdom of friends and colleagues prevailed and that advice was not taken. Instead, one of Misha's students, the wife of a well-known hypnotist named Kapterev, was brought in to treat the actor who, in fact, could no longer act and had been obliged to turn to teaching. Chekhov was skeptical from the outset, but after five sessions the hypnotist had purged his patient's obsessions and restored his aplomb. His body became light, it was pleasant to experience his limbs in motion, and he felt younger and even taller. After these physical improvements, he began to experience a spiritual change as well. Time seemed to pass more slowly, and with its passage evoked pleasant, restful sensations. Chekhov became aware of the fact that an intense, internal pressure had been driving him into a direction in which he didn't really want to go, turning him into a person he didn't want to be. Miraculously, Kapterev had led his patient out of the maze he had woven for himself with a phalanx of cynical philosophers who had darkened his soul. Applying the same kind of consciously formulated willpower that would soon develop in him as a teacher, Chekhov convinced himself he was well and turned his thoughts back to the theater.

After Misha had recovered from both the wounds of his disastrous marriage to Olga and his mother's death, his desire for marital stability returned. There were a number of pointless flirtations with Chekhov again hurling himself at passing women and being coldly rebuffed. But in 1918, he met and married Xenia Karlovna Zeller, a blonde girlfriend who had been a ubiquitous tennis-partner during Olga's pregnancy with Ada, and had seriously vexed the relationship with his first wife. Xenia, unlike Olga, was loving, selfless, and utterly supportive of Misha from the beginning of their marriage until her husband's death. She had no great interest in theatre and throughout her husband's career, in both Europe and America, was very much a background presence, but one that Chekhov relied on heavily for emotional support. It was Xenia, claimed Chekhov, who cured him of alcoholism, and certainly, under her influence, he became more stable and productive than he had ever been before.

Chapter Ten

AFTER WORLD WAR I, interest in Rudolph Steiner and anthroposophy was almost as great as that generated by Freud and the advent of psychoanalysis; among educators, arguably greater. Steiner, an Austrian born in 1861 who died in 1925, first gained prominence as a disciple of Goethe and worked for a time at the Goethe Archives in Weimar. He was then drawn to theosophy and the Eastern philosophies orchestrated by Helena Petrovna (Madame) Blavatsky, but Steiner's interests were directed more toward European occultism, mysticism, and Christianity.

Steiner believed that the same scientific investigation that had provided knowledge about our physical world could, through exercises and meditation, also illuminate our spiritual selves, and that man's intelligence was derived from a higher form of spiritual consciousness that, though latent, could be methodically activated.

He wrote only a few books but gave thousands of lectures touching on occultism, esotericism, education, music, agriculture, and economics. With his second wife, Marie von Sivers, he popularized a system of flowing movement called "eurythmics," which strongly influenced both actors and dancers in the early part of the twentieth century. Gradually, it was assimilated into educational institutions throughout the world.

In the course of espousing theories that drew on theosophy,

rosicrucianism, Christianity, and the writings of Plato and Goethe, many blunders were committed. For instance, Steiner took the gospels at face value and once argued that the fifth century Christian neoplatonist Proclus was in reality the first-century Dionysus, whereas the former merely plagiarized the latter. But his influence in education was formidable and even today, Rudolph Steiner Schools abound in England, America and on the Continent. His was a multifaceted philosophy that was entirely harmonic with Christianity and indeed, saw Jesus' self-sacrifice as a catalyst for the realization of every man's spiritual potential.

Chekhov's interest in yoga and his immersion in the writings of Schopenhauer, Freud, and the mystic philosopher Vladimir Sergeyevich Solovyov predisposed him toward Steiner's brand of spirituality. One day, when he was passing by a Moscow bookstore, his eye fell on Steiner's volume *Knowledge of the Higher Worlds, and Its Attainment.* Silently, he scoffed at the idea of such a book, believing that if this knowledge was achievable, it would already exist and there would be no need for a book on the subject. Still, the title intrigued him and he read it from cover to cover. When he was done, the seed had been planted, and from the mid-twenties to the end of his life, the vision of a rich inner world buried beneath endless layers of mundane reality challenged his mind and guided his actions both as actor and theorist.

Yoga led him to theosophy, and theosophy to clairvoyance. He began to mix with secret societies and encountered many people in Moscow who moved in what he called a "mystic haze." Many of these were either charlatans or dupes who frequently made him question the validity of the theories they espoused, and in which he himself had come to believe. Beneath all of his troubling, unanswered questions lay a profound uncertainty about Christianity that he felt driven to explore.

There were in Moscow at this time a father and son often spoken of by the faithful in hushed tones: Father Alexei, an elderly, ailing, and frail priest, and his son, Father Sergei. Despite the difficulty in obtaining an audience with the older priest, Chekhov managed to arrange one. When he found himself in the priest's presence, predetermined not to tire the frail churchman, he was astonished to find him energetic and commanding. Father Alexei sat his guest down and concisely asked what Chekhov wanted of him. Taken aback by both his vigor and his decisiveness, Chekhov quickly abandoned his carefully prepared apologies for imposing himself and began expressing his doubts about the faith. As he unburdened himself, Chekhov became aware that Father Alexei seemed not to be listening to him but instead, was scrutinizing his face and peering at a point immediately above his petitioner's head. Suddenly, he cut Chekhov off in midsentence and, as if reading it off a radar screen above his head, said, "Oh, my dear man, what chaos you have in your head. You had better go to Father Sergei. He will talk with you. I'll tell him about you!" And with this, Father Alexei was up and gone.

Although shaken by the old priest's verdict, Chekhov went on to meet with Father Sergei, who turned out to be a young, tall, dashing man with blazing black eyes who resembled the faces chiseled on ancient icons. Chekhov, who despised sentimentality whether on stage or in life, was pleased by the younger priest's bluntness. Father Sergei greeted him as an old friend, and they spoke long and deeply about the paradoxes of belief. Although Misha admitted he gained a great deal from his discussions with him about Christianity and the church, the priest's unwavering devotion to orthodox dogma left many doubts unresolved.

When he left Father Sergei, he immersed himself again in Steiner's philosophy and a kind of epiphany gradually occured. Wrote Chekhov:

> I read a whole series of Steiner's books, and this careful reading answered the questions that had always troubled me. There was no mystery, no mysticism, no desire to

impress in his style. The facts that were his subject were
made clear through his simple, lucid and scientific manner. What was inaccessible to sensory perception was
made accessible to the intellect. I learned, for example,
that the spiritual world and its beings evolve and change
just as the physical world and its beings do. Unfounded
speculation is alien to anthroposophy. Nothing derived
from the spiritual world should be accepted uncritically,
said Steiner. An anthroposophist must *reason*, not
believe. The spiritual world is a mystery only to those who
refuse to make the effort to enter it. The first and fundamental exercise devised by Steiner develops the aptitude
for logical, clear, active thought. Without this ability, the
beginning clairvoyant might fall prey to illusions and sink
into the realm of fantasy and self-deception. The main
thing I learned, and which was decisive, was that Christ
stands at the center of everything about which Steiner
speaks. Anthroposophy was revealed to me as the modern
form of Christianity. This encounter of mine with anthroposophy was the happiest period of my life.

Steiner's anthroposophy and Chekhov's acting theories
share a number of similar assumptions. Both are predicated on
the existence of a power beyond that which we can immediately hear or see, and both believe that power can be harnessed
and converted into useable energy. Chekhov's notion of "the
higher I," a zone that an actor must attain beyond the parame-
ters of his own personality, is almost a direct translation of
Steiner's belief in "levels of self" and "planes of existence."
Steiner described anthroposophy as "science of the spirit," a
path of knowledge that can ally the spiritual in the human
being to the spiritual in the universe. His methods, like
Chekhov's, depend on exercises in both concentration and
meditation. In Steiner, all of these evolve from, and return to,
a kind of idealized view of Christ, whereas in Chekhov, the
final application is between the soul of the actor and the

nature of the character he is portraying. But with Chekhov, as it was later to be with Artaud and Grotowsky, the theories stem from an idealized view of the actor's function. With Chekhov, it is never the routine application of technique—training of the voice and body per se—but a quest to achieve levels of being beyond the commonplace objectives of verisimilitude. One can follow Chekhov's theories on acting without reference or even knowledge of Steinerism, just as one can apply the tenets of psychological realism in complete ignorance of the Stanislavsky system, but in relating Chekhov to Steiner one immediately grasps certain fundamental connections between theory and practice that illuminate both.

Years later, when Chekhov was derided for being a mystic, he would vigorously deny the charge. For him, Steiner's brand of mysticism had gradually translated itself into a practical modus operandi that unraveled many of the secrets that continually baffle the logical positivists. Chekhov had diligently used rationality to arrive at a view of life that appeared to defy rationality, and he was entirely in earnest when he refuted the label of mystic. There was nothing mystical about spirituality. It was, for him, as tangible and indisputable as the Trinity is to the Catholic or the law of gravity is to the scientist.

Unfortunately, many of his colleagues failed to share his convictions, and in the coming years in a society where the prevailing doctrine was dialectical materialism, Chekhov would be viewed as a crank, a dreamer, a decadent, and worse.

Chapter Eleven

IN THE YEARS immediately following the revolution and the civil war that followed, the Russian theater went through a dramatic metamorphosis. At the center of these transformations stood Vsevolod Meyerhold, a director who even before the revolution was brazenly innovative and unconventional. After 1917, incarnating the spirit of change which the revolution prosletyzed, he became the most dominant figure on the theatrical landscape.

In the fall of 1920, Anatoly Lunacharsky, the commisar of education, appointed Meyerhold head of the TEO, the Theatrical Department of the People's Commisariat of Education, which gave him official jurisdiction over every theater in the country. He immediately took over the former Zon Theatre and filled it with young and zealous radicals like himself, renaming it the Russian Socialist Federal Soviet Republic Theatre No. 1 (RSFSR). Meyerhold's ascendance brought to the fore not only actors and directors who shared his radical views, but painters, poets and musicians who saw themselves as members of a triumphant avant-garde. These zealots included artists such as Dmitri Shostakovitch, Sergei Eisenstein, and Vladamir Mayakovsky.

To make no bones about the changes he wished to institute, Meyerhold declared a "Theatrical October," a sweep of dramatic art that would be as uncompromising as the Bolshevik

victory that had removed the czar and his family, and inaugu-
rated a new social order. Since the traditions that underlay theaters like the Maly, the Alexandrinsky, and the Moscow Art
had originated in czarist Russia, it went without saying that
they must be uprooted. The "old art" was as much an enemy to
the new Soviet state as the aristocrats, landowners and feudal
barons who had supported the old order, and with the same
vigor that the old was to be eradicated, the new was to be
installed. This, despite the fact that Meyerhold himself had
begun his career under Stanislavsky at the Moscow Art and
had, in fact, played Treplev in the groundbreaking production
of Chekhov's *The Seagull*.

Although his rhetoric was violently opposed to the "estab-
lishment" theaters, it was considerably tempered by
Lunacharsky himself, who, though he advocated "the revolu-
tionary-creative formation of new theater" also insisted upon
"the preservation of the best theaters of the past, which unconditionally deserve the state's concern as custodians of artistic
traditions." No doubt, while Meyerhold grumbled at the commisar's tolerance, Stanislavsky and the other "bourgeois" theater managers heaved a sigh of relief.

Since no playwrights had yet emerged to glorify the revolutionary splendor of the new regime, Meyerhold proceeded to
create works from the material at hand. Cutting texts had long
been a convention in the Russian theater, but Meyerhold foisted the notion of director as "the author of the production,"
fully entitling himself to revise, rewrite and transform the
material that he appropriated. The first post-revolutionary production under his aegis was *The Dawn*, by Belgian symbolist
writer Emile Verhaeren. In the Meyerholdian transmutation,
the play came to depict the struggles between the White and
Red armies that were still raging throughout the country. In
The Dawn, the Red Army was triumphant and the finale was a
forceful rendition of "The Internationale." Even the theater
building itself had been "revolutionized," with all the customary comforts of the former bourgeois playhouse stripped away.

"The doors to this theater knew no ticket takers," wrote Meyerhold's associate Boris Alpers. "The railings had been torn from the boxes. The seats and benches for the audience had been poorly constructed and ruined the regularity of the rows. You could crack nuts and smoke shag in the corridors... Everyone felt like a master in this theater. The revolutionary atmosphere of the streets had broken into the theater."

In fact, this became literally true during the performance on November 18, 1920, when a telegram arrived during the course of the performance reporting the defeat of General Wrangel's forces in Pereskop. Meyerhold spontaneously decided to read the telegram from the stage, replacing the *Herald*'s line announcing the victory over the imaginary foes in Verhaeren's play. "It is difficult to describe what occurred in the theater when this historic telegram was read out," said one eyewitness. "Such an explosion of shouts, exclamations, applause—such a universal delighted, I would say *frenzied*—roar has never been heard within the walls of a theater." Many in the audience were, of course, members of the Red Army to whom Meyerhold had doled out free tickets, and so the news of a military victory was bound to have an immense impact. So much so that all future telegrams from the front were routinely read out by actors from the stage. The excitement generated by the production was genuine, but not everyone was equally impressed. N.K. Krupskaya, who was a critic of Meyerhold's "experiment," thought the show brash and tasteless. "Someone" she wrote "conceived of adapting *The Dawn* to Russian conditions at the wrong moment...To cast the Russian proletariat in the role of a Shakespearean crowd, where any conceited idiot could lead wherever he pleases—this is an insult!" Ferdinandov, a fellow director, described the stage as "a concentration camp for actors." Alexander Tairov, a longstanding enemy of Meyerhold, called the production "a vulgar popular print" adding acidly, "It is high time to say propagandist theater after the revolution is like mustard after dinner."

Meyerhold was clear in regard to his priorities. "Up to

1917," he declared to his company, "we treated the literary work with a certain caution and care. Today, we are no longer fetishists. We do not kneel and call out in prayer, "Shakespeare! Verhaeren!... Now we are no longer protecting the interests of the author, but of the audience."

If *The Dawn* was the *forspeis* of Theatrical October, the revised version of Mayakovsky's *Mystery-Bouffe* was the grandiose entrée; a rambunctious political revue featuring grotesque caricatures that celebrated the proletarian heroes of the revolution and cruelly deflated its enemies. The curtain was eliminated, and a series of staircases and gangways constructed on the stage. The main action, according to actress Maria Sukhanova, "was carried out in the auditorium, for which purpose several rows of seats had been removed from the stalls. In front, in the foreground, a globe—or rather, a section of a globe—had been constructed. The wings had all been cleared away, *Paradise* was stacked on top of a construction beneath the ceiling at the very back of the stage. Those of us in *Paradise* (I was an angel) stood with our arms raised and with every movement our white wings, made of thin wire covered with gauze, quivered behind us." The action of the piece flooded through every gulley of the auditorium while, onstage, actions were taking place simultaneously on a series of raised platforms. The play, episodic and discontinuous (long before discontinuity became a fashionable avant-garde device) totally shunned any Aristotelian idea of unity. It was essentially a montage, similar to what Eisenstein, a disciple and a collaborator of Meyerhold's, was soon to develop dramatically in Russian films such as *Potemkin*. When working with Mayakovsky, Meyerhold took no liberties. "Mayakovsky knew what theater was; he had a command over the theater and was brilliant in the field of composition," said the director, who fastidiously interpreted the letter and spirit of the Russian poet's text.

Mystery-Bouffe was perhaps the most representative production of the post-Revolutionary period. A work written by the leading communist poet and directed by the leading Soviet director, it galvanized an entirely new Russian public who had, previously, felt excluded from the theater. After the revolution, the Russian theater became one of the spoils of victory. A new and enthusiastic public experienced works like Mayakovsky's as an extension of the social upheaval that had devastated old Russia and flung it into a century brimming with the promise of genuine socialist change. It was a period when actuality in both life and art was dynamically combined and Russians could feel for the first time a sense of artistic ownership. This theater belonged to *them*, reflected *their* struggles and celebrated *their* victories. This was audience identification on a par that has never been known since.

However, it was all short lived. By February 1921, barely one year later, Meyerhold, a great rhetorician but a poor organizer, was removed from his position as head of the theatrical department *Narkompros*, and shortly abandoned the TEO altogether. His journal, *Vesnik Teatre*, in which he rallied the forces of the new Russia with endless polemics against the bourgeois theater he was determined to destroy, shut down seven months later. The civil war between the Whites and the Reds was over, and the hype of Theatrical October began to weary even the communist diehards who had been its staunchest champions. But the new Soviet state was consolidating its gains and establishing its power structure and the ideology on which the revolution had been based was rapidly spreading its ethos throughout the land.

In March 1921, Lenin launched the New Economic Policy (NEP), which permitted a certain amount of capitalist enterprise to return to the country. There was to be private initiative, private trade, and to an extent, private ownership. The policy removed subsidy from many of the theaters that were now expected to show a profit. Costly mass pageants celebrating revolutionary victories, such as the storming of the Winter Palace, were now seen as an extravagance that could no longer be borne. Ticket prices increased. In three years, Lenin would be dead, Trotsky exiled, and Stalin installed as the leader of what was soon to be proclaimed the Union of Soviet Socialist Republics.

This was the social and artistic climate in which Michael Chekhov assumed the leadership of the Third Studio after the death of Vakhtangov. It soon became officially known as the Second Moscow Art Theatre and both Stanislavsky and Chekhov (and eventually even Meyerhold himself) were to feel the pinch of a sterner political reality, very different from the one that existed before and immediately after the Revolution of 1917.

Chapter Twelve

ACCORDING TO CHEKHOV HIMSELF, his leadership of the Second Moscow Art theater was essentially a coup d'etat. After Vakhtangov's death, he tried to steer the theater along the lines that had been previously established but, after encountering obstacles from the governing board, decided to take the management into his own hands. He declared himself dictator, and the act so stunned all the members of the studio that no opposition rose against him. (In theory, Boris Sushkevitch, a gifted actor and director who had started at the Moscow Arts and had been with the First Studio since its inception, was the co-director, but he was soon eclipsed by Chekhov.) A few days after Misha had "seized power," the People's Commissariat for Education sanctioned his directorship. A new board made up of four trusted members of the theater was installed, and Chekhov proceeded to purge the repertory of the antireligious bias that had begun to creep in after the revolution. To assert his position and to indicate the scope of his ambitions, he decided to mount a production of *Hamlet*, a production that was carefully prepared over the following eighteen months.

The approach was unconventional. The language in the play was transformed into pure sound shorn of literal content. "We listen to *what* someone says," explained Chekhov, "and we do not notice *how* his words *sound*." Exercises were created to try to isolate the sound components of Shakespeare's words from their meaning. Balls would be tossed between members of the cast, corresponding to the rhythm of the speeches. Whole scenes would be run through entirely in the actors' imagination—"incorporeal rehearsals" Chekhov called them—silently working through the beats of a scene before playing it with full voice. Chekhov devised a number of new exercises for the company. Occasionally elders from the Moscow Art proper would come by and get drawn into the unorthodox activities. "We should forbid our actors to go to your classes," said Nemirovich-Danchenko, half-jokingly. "You could easily ruin them." Underlying all these novel tactics was Chekhov's desire to give spiritual qualities a concrete and recognizable form. Steiner's theories, and particularly his ideas on eurhythmics, were the philosophic foundation from which they sprang. "I was absorbed in artistic labors," wrote Chekhov, "and lost interest in all events outside the theater walls." These included official communist party meetings, where Chekhov's absence was solemnly noted. His more politically savvy friends warned him that it was dangerous to offend the apparatchiks. They also advised him that his lectures on art given to factory and mill workers were perhaps too tinged with religious overtones to please hardnosed proletarians.

Although Chekhov's talent as an actor was recognized everywhere, he was the first to admit that he did not possess great talent as a director. Consequently, he instituted a group of three or four directors to work collectively on the productions of the studio. Three young directors—Valentin Smyshlyaev, Vladamir Tatarinov, and Alexander Cheban—were chosen as the directorial triad for *Hamlet*, and the pitfalls of collective direction were soon revealed in their work.

There was enormous interest leading up to Chekhov's *Hamlet*, which opened on November 20, 1924, in the company's new home on Theatrical Square in Moscow. It was Chekhov's first production as the Second Moscow Art Theatre's artistic director, and the first major Shakespearean tragedy undertaken by the new troupe. Chekhov divided the play into three acts and fourteen episodes. He made major cuts both in the scenes and the soliloquies, eliminating Fortinbras altogether. Nothing was permitted to interfere with the forward thrust of the narrative toward the play's tragic conclusion. The costumes and makeup were highly stylized. The focus was on Hamlet himself and the spiritual struggle he was waging with the new king. Critic B. Tikhonovich neatly summed up the conflict: "One of them—Hamlet—protesting, heroic, is fighting for the affirmation of what makes up the essence of his life. The other—Claudius—conservative, obstructing all that is holy and heroic, is trying to hold back everything that is striving forward."

No consistent style was imposed on the supporting players. Gertrude was played as a neurotic grotesque, Claudius as a sinister Machiavel, Ophelia as a subdued melancholic, Laertes as an inflammatory hothead, and Polonius as a satirical buffoon. The settings were opulent and ceremonial, but the overall effect was gloomy and remote. According to Stanislavsky, Chekhov had "a mighty talent, and there is no task whatsoever that he could not fulfill on stage." According to Konstantin Rudnitsky, Chekhov's Hamlet, "strong willed and mournful, quickly, without any special reflections, came to the conclusion that violence, bloodshed, and murder could be justified by high ethical motives—the necessity of cleansing the world of its terrible vices and restoring the integrity of the time that was 'out of joint.' The tragedy of his fate was that by fulfilling the recognized mission, he acted against his own nature. The strong-minded and active Hamlet agonizingly overcame his humaneness, goodness, and compassion for those he punished."

The result was a performance steeped in pessimism. Critic Mikhail Zagorsky saw this Hamlet "as a modern city dweller whose nerves could not endure the turbulence of the times.... Do we need such a Hamlet now? No, we do not!" Pavel Markov, the most influential critic of the period (he started on *Pravda* and went on to become the lead critic on *Izvestia*), felt it discarded all the old interpretations. "[It] took up a wholly negative attitude, without disclosing the positive foundation of the play. The philosophic side of the tragedy was disregarded, and it was interpreted as no more than the struggle between the heir to a throne and a usurper. The result was a rich, pretentious production that kept the audience in a state of unabated suspense and enthusiasm but did not bring it any closer to an understanding of Shakespeare's characters."*

The reaction was heatedly controversial and the public flocked to see the play. Perhaps the outward euphoria of the post-revolutionary period concealed an existential gloom that was only masked with banners, parades and pageants. Perhaps this dark *Hamlet* spoke to some long-suffering melancholy in the Russian people. Years later, it would be recalled as one of the pinnacles of early revolutionary theater — except, of course, by those in the higher echelons of the party to whom by then Chekhov had become a non-person. It is one of those theatrical events that, despite its legendary status, remains maddeningly inconclusive. It was unquestionably popular with Russian audiences and won him the title of Honored Artist of the RSFSR. Ironically, it was almost immediately after this accolade that his relations with the communist authorities began to deteriorate.

The advocacy for naturalism, which was seen to be the

---

* John Berry, the actor-director and student of Chekhov, was among those who saw Chekhov's Hamlet. "There was no ghost," recalled Berry. "The ghost was an image formed in Hamlet mind by his trance, and when the ghost appeared, it would be lit from below." The stage would go dark and he would go into a trance. The Soviets did not approve of this. They considered it occult and they moved to close the production." If Berry's recollection is correct, then Chekhov was the first to have the ghost's lines spoken by the actor playing Hamlet, as if the father had taken possession of the son's body. This device was used years later by Franco Zeferelli in his production of Hamlet, and by Jonathan Pryce when he played the role in London. It has since been employed in many American and European productions.

artistic ally of the revolutionary spirit, became more and more widespread and officially sanctioned. For the Bolsheviks, the theater was necessary only as a propaganda tool, and the notion of consolidating the power of the new regime went hand in hand with the desire to sell it to the masses as if it were a desirable consumer product. In 1927, a full-scale attack on the more traditional theaters began. Previously, the Bolsheviks had praised the Moscow Art Theatre as the classical outlet for Soviet social realism. Now it was assailed for the "naturalistic and impressionistic romanticism of the disillusioned, Russian, middle-class intellectuals." Its studios, according to Commissar Lunacharsky, "lacked not only any kind of social or philosophical ideology, but even an ideology of the theater." The Kamerny Theatre was attacked for being partisan to the decadent bourgeois habits it had always championed. The gifted director Tairov was labeled a pitiful eclectic. Even Meyerhold, who had actually fought with the Red Army in the 1917 Revolution and was previously considered the avatar of the postwar theater, was chastised for indulging in "mystical and symbolic experiments."

Chekhov, despite his high standing in the profession, did not escape censure. The work of the First Studio was called "mystical," "sick," "alien," and the most dangerous of all Red epithets, "reactionary." Chekhov was described by critic Nikolai Gorchakov as "a sick actor" who spurted a mystical infection toward the entire Soviet theater. His best role, Hamlet, "was a mystical nightmare alien to the materialistic cognition held by the toiling masses."

Extreme as this criticism was, there was more than a grain of truth in it. Chekhov was never a communist ideologue. While practical-minded artists quickly sensed which way the wind was blowing and lined up behind the Leninist/Marxist shibboleths of the new regime, Chekhov delved further and further into Steinerism and tried to formulate a new aesthetic that was in keeping with both his artistic and religious precepts. That it had become a time driven by rampant opportunism and doctrinaire Communist philosophy with little tolerance for "pure art" eluded the naive Chekhov. Perhaps he felt, as many artists of the period did, that art was not subject to the vicissitudes of politics; that what happened in the Politburo or the Kremlin could not possibly affect one's attitude to Shakespeare, Molière, Turgenev, Tolstoy or Anton Chekhov. The idea of a party appropriating art the way it had appropriated the homes of banished aristocrats or wealthy kulaks was difficult for him to reconcile—although even under the czar there had been censorship and prohibitions. It was an easy mistake to make in the late twenties when, for more than ten years, Russia had been the scene of the most diverse theatrical experimentation in European history, with conflicting theories constantly butting heads with each other.

Politics arrived with a vengeance at the First Studio in the form of Alexey Diky, a former pupil of Vakhtangov, who had become rooted in Marxist doctrine and believed that Chekhov was leading the theater into a miasma that ignored the realities of the new Soviet state. Diky did not start out as a social realist, and his production of N. Leskov's *The Flea* adapted by Evgeny Zamiatin, was one that Vakhtangov, had he still been alive, would probably have approved of. It was boldly expressionistic, laced with irony and racy dialogue, lampooned the Soviet bureaucracy and championed the native intelligence of the Russian people. Despite all this, the production was attacked for its "formalistic nonsense" and ultimately banned—mainly because it was adapted by Zamiatin, who enraged the communist stalwarts and was condemned as "an enemy of the revolution and denigrator of Soviet reality." In the thirties, Zamiatin, like many of the avant-garde artists vilified by the Communists, fled the country and settled in France. But *The Flea*, unlike the morose production of *Hamlet*, was thoroughly entertaining and vastly enjoyed by the public.

Diky, unlike Chekhov, clearly read the signs of the times and methodically began to subvert Chekhov's leadership. The cleavage in the company became clear: there were the "good

Marxists," encouraged by Diky, and the "reactionary idealists," who believed both in Chekhov's talent and the creeds that had been laid down by Vakhtangov.

Little tell-tale signs of disapproval began to appear. When party members journeyed down to the theater, their conversation would inevitably turn to the subject of "the workers." Chekhov would be encouraged to visit the mills and the factories, and to familiarize himself with the working man's problems, tastes, needs and desires. An immersion in proletarian society, the officials implied, would help diffuse Misha's "mystical deviations," and would put him in touch with the true spirit of the Russian people.

After several such innuendos, Chekhov received a letter at the theater from the Commissariat for Education. "It said — still in friendly terms — that my work as the director of the theater was not fully satisfactory," he recalled "and that I must cease disseminating the ideas of Rudolph Steiner to the acting company entrusted to me. Attached to the letter was a list of quotations from Steiner's book. These were meant to illustrate the ideas I had expressed during rehearsals and classes with the actors." The "quotations," it appears, were compiled by two actors from the Diky camp who had transcribed dubious remarks made by Chekhov and then related them to corresponding statements in the Steiner books.

By 1927, the handwriting was not only on the wall, but the wall itself had begun to reveal fissures where shells had started to bombard it. The Department of Agitation and Propaganda, which was attached to the Central Committee of the Communist Party, released a resolution assailing "the activity of anti-Soviet sectors of the intelligentsia, the petty bourgeoisie, and the remnants of the former bourgeoisie." This was a catch-all category that included almost everyone who was not a staunch member of the communist party.

Censorship was dramatically increased. Both form and content was now to be regulated by the party. The pronouncement read: "The organs for controlling the repertory must in every way suppress the attempts to permeate the theater with decadent and other anti-proletarian trends...Supervision by the organs of control must be broadened to include interpretation and staging of presentations, inasmuch as new and unacceptable features have been increased, emphasized, or introduced through them."

Mikhail Bulgakov's play *Day of the Turbines* was immediately indicted because it sympathetically treated those who had fought on the side of the White Army during Russia's civil war. His play *Zoika's Apartment* was likewise attacked because, as Nikolai Gorchakov explained, "it ridiculed the ghastliness of Soviet life." Alexi Faiko's *Evgraf, The Adventure-Seeker* was suspect "because it timidly asked that dreamers and romantics be allowed to exist in the Soviet Union even though they had not yet managed to become 100 percent Bolsheviks." The party developed a new and frightening vernacular by which its enemies could be clearly identified: "bourgeois," "cosmopolitan," "decadent," "alien," "formalist," "aesthetic," "reactionary," and "counter revolutionary." Any one of those adjectives marked its targets for interrogation, inquisition, or liquidation.

A theater showing a preference for classics, or plays lacking propagandistic virtues, was immediately suspect. Even the eminent and internationally acclaimed Moscow Art Theatre came under fire, and Stanislavsky, developing new skills in diplomacy and double speak, was obliged to pacify his Soviet masters. In 1937, on the twentieth anniversary of the October Revolution, he wrote: "How comforting it is to work for one's nation and in close contact with it! The feeling is the result of the education that has been given to us by the Communist Party headed by our dear and beloved Joseph Stalin. He approaches all vital questions so simply and sincerely, and he solves them so directly and so truly! Comrade Stalin is the genuine and solicitious friend of everything living and progressive; [he] always foresees and anticipates everything. How much he had done for us actors! Thanks to him for all of it!"

We know from the testaments of artists such as Shostakovitch, Prokofiev and others that to survive in Stalin's Russia, one had to develop a schizophrenic personality; one had to put forward one face in order to conceal another. Bulgakov's *Molière* may be seen as a play that dramatizes the personal conflicts in the life of the great 17th century playwright, but his depiction of the "cabal of hypocrites," a secret society under the guidance of the Archbishop of Paris, subtextually conveys his attitude toward the Stalinist dictatorship.

Perhaps, in the same way, Stanislavsky's encomium to the "great leader" has its tongue firmly placed in its cheek. Knowing of the humanitarian tendencies of many of these artists, we tend to construct a doubt and then give them the benefit of it. But what is clear is that in 1927–28, with the Communist Party appropriating the minds and threatening the livelihood of many of its most brilliant artists, Moscow was a treacherous place to try to exercise one's dramatic imagination or ply one's craft. (Ironically, in *The Man in the Restaurant*, a film released a few months earlier, Chekhov had played a pathetic waiter harassed by pre-revolutionary forces, and in January, his autobiography *The Path of the Actor* had become a bestseller, making his notoriety greater than it had ever been before.) But ten years into the revolution, the volatility was everywhere. "With increasing intensity," Chekhov wrote, "circumstances were forcing me to reject my philosophy. The struggle was becoming futile. My activity as an actor, director, and head of the theater gradually drew to a halt."

The arrest warrant followed hard upon and Chekhov, who still held a legal passport, traveled to Berlin, where an agent had inquired about mounting a German-language version of his *Hamlet*. From there, he wrote to the Commissariat for Education describing the conditions under which he would return. That letter received no reply—although Chekhov learned afterward that "it had been read, discussed, and even approved."

The year was 1928; Chekhov was 37 years old. The history, culture, and love of his native land coursed through his blood.

He was acknowledged as one of the most exciting and original actors that Russia had ever produced, a peer of major artists such as Kachalov, Moskvin, Lensky, and Davidov. He had been an architect of one of the most dynamic studios to emerge after the 1917 uprising, and a standard bearer for the new generation.

Could those roots be torn up and replanted in another country?

THE
WANDERING
YEARS

Chapter Thirteen

"SEIN ODER NICHT SEIN..."

Chekhov repeated the words of Hamlet's most famous soliloquy in German over and over again. He had already committed the first act to memory and was slogging in the remainder. In Berlin, he felt lighthearted, even festive. The prospect of presenting his *Hamlet* to a German public, many of whom, because of the excellent Schlegel-Tieck translations, believed that Shakespeare was a German writer, was tantalizing. And the famous impresario perched behind his monumental desk had begun their meeting by saying cordially, "It's not every day that a Chekhov arrives here from Russia."

Chekhov demurred the compliment, bowing his head slightly as he had often seen Stanislavsky do when he wished to project a humility he didn't actually feel. The great German tragedian Alexander Moissi, a member of Reinhardt's stable, had brought his Hamlet to Moscow, Chekhov reflected to himself, "and here am I in Berlin. A reciprocal visit, as it were."

"Can you dance?" asked the impresario.

"Me?" asked Chekhov.

"You," nodded the impresario.

But what dancing is there in Hamlet, thought Chekhov. He probably means fencing.

"We will start you out with cabaret," said the impresario. "I will turn you into another Grock, the greatest clown in

Europe. Do you play an instrument? Can you sing? No? Not even slightly?"

"Excuse me," said Chekhov politely. "Actually, I have come to play Hamlet."

"*Hamlet* doesn't matter," said the impresario, brushing aside the play as if it were a troublesome gnat. "The German public has very different demands. Here are my terms: an exclusive one year contract, a monthly salary, and I have the right to choose all your engagements, including film work."

"A whole mass of thoughts ran through my mind," Chekhov recalled, "all in the course of a second. In Russia, the official censors and the political directorate fought me for two years and could not close my *Hamlet*, and here, one man was destroying a dream—without a struggle—with just one word! Where was his power? In money? Is that the capitalist system? My whole life in the theater arose before me with its struggles, its devotion to great artists, its faith in the public. For more than twenty years, Stanislavsky, Chaliapin, and Steiner had fostered my belief in the great mission of the theater; the Moscow audiences had watched *Hamlet* reverentially; the Czech government had asked me to found a Shakespeare company there, a theater devoted to high tragedy and classic comedy…"

"But not everyone can want cabaret?" Chekhov finally blurted out. "Many people *do* want *Hamlet*."

"'Two dozen half-witted Shakespeareans,' scoffed the impresario. 'They'll sit in an otherwise empty theater with their noses in the script to check that you're correctly pronouncing the text. That is not business. Trust me, my friend,' he said as he patted my sleeve in a fatherly way, 'I know the public better than you do.'"

Chekhov and the impresario parted, Misha believing for good. But ten days later, a cable from Max Reinhardt, the doyen of the German stage, reunited them. The maestro, who would be passing through Berlin on his way to Salzburg, had invited Chekhov to discuss a project. Noting the significance of this invitation from the great Reinhardt, the impresario's terms subtly altered—to the agent's advantage—and within days, Chekhov was being ushered into a palatial apartment in one of the most elite sections of the city. Reinhardt greeted him warmly, not withdrawing his hand after their firm handshake, but leading him to a large writing table where the interview began in earnest.

Reinhardt questioned Misha about Stanislavsky's methods and displayed the curiosity that one great director often has about another. He had heard that rehearsals often went on for months and that only two or three productions entered the repertory each season. "We Germans work differently," Reinhardt explained. It was difficult to ascertain whether he was pitying the Russians or the Germans. Finally, he got down to brass tacks.

"*Eine wunbderbare rolle,*" he exclaimed, and one that perfectly suited this comedic Russian performer. The role was Skid, a tragicomic clown in the 1927 play *Artisten* by George Abbott and Philip Dunning (originally produced in New York in 1926 as *Broadway* and subsequently reincarnated on Broadway in 1946 with Bert Lahr as both comic lead and director). The play, described by John Lahr as "the Arthur Hopkins–George M. Watters chestnut," had enjoyed great success in Berlin with Skid played by V.A. Sokolov, and Reinhardt wanted Chekhov to play it in Vienna. Chekhov was to go there immediately, and working with a German assistant, polish up the language and learn clown stunts. When Chekhov managed to squeeze in a reference to *Hamlet* by asking Reinhardt why he didn't stage more classics, the director answered, "The times! The audience doesn't want them right now. But the theater will someday return to the classics." Chekhov wondered whether it would possibly be in his lifetime.

In Vienna, Chekhov met Herr Doctor S., Reinhardt's assistant, who Chekhov described as "a small, square, no longer young man" who greeted him politely but with strict German decorum. He immediately began to correct Chekhov's speech, barking out the correct pronunciations in a loud, guttural voice accompanied by ferocious grimaces. After an hour of drill, Herr Doctor S. had gone from correcting his nouns and verbs to giving him exact intonations and line readings. Chekhov protested. Doctor S. replied, "I repeat, lieber *Tschekoff*, you must, unconditionally, learn to speak *zo!* " and continued fiercely to hammer out exact intonations.

Knowing of Chekhov's association with Shakespeare, Doctor S. thought that might be an easier route into the tuition. Flinging out his arms and constricting the muscles in his face, Doctor S. cried, "*O schmolze doch diese allzu feste Fleisch* [O, that this too too solid flesh would melt]." His face contorted, his throat growled, the blood rushed to his head, he beat his arms against his head and gasped for air. "Maybe I should just go back," thought Chekhov, suddenly remembering that being in exile, there was no "back" to go back to.

After the classes in German diction had been launched, Doctor S. proceeded to teach Chekhov the acrobatics that would be required for the role. This included stunts like jumping over his own leg while holding it in his hand and leaping onto tables from a stationary position. Chekhov yearned for the arrival of Reinhardt, when presumably proper rehearsals would commence. However, when the company finally did arrive in Vienna, it was minus the director. Confronted with the need to master a full German text as well as strenuous acrobatic skills, Chekhov began to crumble. He found it difficult to memorize his text, and the strain of working in a foreign tongue while constantly straining his physical endurance became almost unbearable.

To create an authentic circus atmosphere in the play, Reinhardt had hired a group of clowns and circus artists. On every side of Chekhov, professional acrobats, jugglers, and clowns performed dazzling feats of skill. How paltry, he thought, would jumping over my leg be in the midst of all this breathtaking physical expertise. There were only eight days of rehearsal scheduled before opening night. In the midst of this growing pandemonium, Reinhardt finally arrived. He was as worried as everyone else about the shortness of time, but concealed his fears behind an imperturbable façade of calm and coldness. The priorities were lights, sets, and costumes rather than language and characterization, and most of the maestro's time was taken up integrating the circus performers into his mise en scène. Finally, the full dress rehearsal began and Chekhov started to perform his first stunt, leaping onto a table without the aid of a running start. The actor propelled himself into the air and came crashing to the floor as the actress beside him emitted a blood-curdling shriek. The pain from his skinned knees and elbows shot through Chekhov's body. Reinhardt, inspecting the damage suddenly noticed that the toes of Chekhov's clown shoes were a foot-and-a-half long. He peremptorily cut all of Skid's stunts and the rehearsal continued until dawn.

When opening night approached, Chekhov was in despair, but it was that same despair that caused him to delve even deeper into the psyche of his comedic character. Still, the sense of being ill-prepared was harrowing. "Should I just go out and get drunk?" he wondered, but no, he lacked the will even for that. As the first light cues were called, Chekhov, dully indifferent, lumbered on stage. The audience was regaled by the circus performers, and bursts of applause punctuated the clowns' routines. The first and second acts flew by. In the third act, a central scene for Skid and his beloved actress Bonny, there was a long tragicomic monologue that brought on the play's denouement.

Chekhov recounted his experience of the evening graphically:

> "Skid's first lines sounded strange. Not at all guttural, not German…sincere. And how easily he speaks, not at all like in rehearsal. It must be because I'm not acting. I should make the effort…No, I'll wait; I haven't got the strength…this monologue is so long. As Skid spoke, for

the first time I truly understood the sense of his words; his unrequited love for Bonny, his tragedy. Fatigue and calm turned me into a spectator of my own performance. How right, that this voice should be so warm, so intimate. Could that be the reason for this thrilling atmosphere? The audience has pricked up its ears; they are listening, intently…even the actors are listening…even Bonny. In rehearsal she was only concerned with herself. Why didn't I see before how lovely she is? Of course Skid loves her. I paid careful attention to Skid. Bonny sang a sad song at the piano. I looked at Skid sitting on the floor and I thought I saw his feelings, his excitement, and his pain. His manner seemed strange to me. He would change tempo abruptly, or break off his sentences with unexpected, but very appropriate pauses, or he would accent things strangely. "This clown is a professional," I thought. In my partners I saw, for the first time, a keen and honest interest in Skid's words and in his inner mental state. I was amazed to realize that I could divine what was about to take place in his soul a second from now. His anguish grew. I began to pity him, and instantly tears gushed from the clown's eyes. I became frightened. Sentimental! The tears aren't necessary, stop them! Skid held back his tears and they were replaced in his eyes by a sudden glow of strength. In this strength there was a pain so tragic, so familiar to the human heart…

Skid rose, crossed the stage with a strange gait, and began to dance in clown fashion, using only his legs; moving comically, faster and faster. The words of the monologue—impassioned, articulate, sharp—flew through the auditorium and traveled into the orchestra, the boxes, the balcony. "What's this?" I asked myself. "Where did *this* come from? I didn't rehearse *this*!" My partners moved from their fixed positions and stepped back to the walls of the set. "They never did *that* before!" Now *I* could direct Skid's performance. My consciousness divided. I was in the audience and at the same time, near myself and in each of my partners. I sensed what they felt, what they desired, what they were all waiting for. Tears! I prompted the dancing Skid: "Now! It's all right." Fatigue transformed into ease, joy, happiness.

The end of the monologue approached. How sad, there is so much more that I could express; such complicated, unexpected feelings arose in my soul. The clown's body was so agile, so obedient. And all at once, my entire being, and Skid's, were filled with a terrifying, almost unbearable force. And there were no barriers against it. It penetrated *everything*, and was capable of *anything*. I felt awestruck. Making a supreme effort of will, I again entered into myself and mechanically finished the last few sentences of the monologue.

The act ended and the curtain came down. The audience, Reinhardt, and even Herr Dr. S. rewarded me lavishly for my past torments. I was grateful and moved. I had "found my role," as they say. During the *Artisen* premiere, fatigue, apathy, and a hopeless acceptance of an inevitable failure involuntarily deactivated my personal vanity, fear, and nervousness. As a result, a part of the higher ego was freed, and the conditions for inspiration arose. From then on, I played my clown with great pleasure.

What Chekhov describes here is a sensation very few actors ever experience, but when they do, it is forever memorable. Out of an enormous internal pressure, a liberating duality is born. The actor sees himself *playing* himself. The actor and the role are both divided and united, and, as if through the lens of a movie camera, he pans easily from his inner state to his outer being. In this condition, as Chekhov attests, things happen that were never planned, never rehearsed. The fruits of insights and experiences unconsciously planted in rehearsal suddenly blossom and fall from the tree. If an actor, like Chekhov, has the ability to leave the channels of his creativity unblocked, something truly mystical is forced through them via the pressure of performance. Mystical, in the sense that one cannot gauge exactly where it has come from, but one knows it has come from somewhere beyond their own metabolism. French actors, when they have played extraordinarily well, often say, "the gods were with me," and in a sense, they *have* been the recipients of a kind of unearthly benison. The out-of-body experience that inspiration of that kind engenders is a gift that does seem to derive from supernatural sources, and one needn't be either a mystic or a swami to recognize it.

Chekhov worked closely with Reinhardt for two years. Although highly impressed by his inventiveness and mastery of different styles, Chekhov faulted him for not being able to pass on to others the artistry he possessed. "Reinhardt," he concluded, "did not create a school. He could demonstrate brilliantly—performing an actor's entire role before him, speaking all of his lines for him. But he was unable to give an actor the technical means to achieve the desired result." In retrospect, Stanislavsky rose even higher in his estimation.

The German's method of work was surprising to Chekhov. Reinhardt prepared his production in the solitude of his own study. He worked out staging in advance and included specific details of precisely what should take place on the stage. His *regiebuch* (production script) completed, it was handed on to assistants who did all the preliminary work with the actors. Reinhardt would appear toward the end of the rehearsal period and when he did, things would often change radically. The actors, having eagerly anticipated his arrival, would become energetic and highly attentive. Reinhardt himself tended to be taciturn at rehearsals, but actors came to interpret his glances, his coughs, and even his silences. He didn't merely watch the rehearsals but constantly acted or spoke the actors' lines to himself, as if testing their readings against his own rendition. His remoteness seemed to increase his company's desire for interaction and, as a result, sensing indifference or disapproval, they would try out new things to please the maestro.

Possessing a palpable inner strength and an unmistakable decisiveness, Reinhardt, despite being short and somewhat ugly, always made a majestic impression. When Stanislavsky was to visit Germany and a meeting had been arranged between them, Chekhov began to worry about the effect the imposing Russian master might have on the elevationally challenged Reinhardt. "Stanislavsly, the leonine, white-haired giant, and Reinhardt—who barely came up to his shoulder! What would happen when they stood next to each other? Could the professor bear such a comparison?"

Reinhardt had arranged a banquet in Stanislavsky's honor, the very first meeting between these two great directors. Chekhov became fretful. His affection was equally divided between both men, but the more he thought of the difference in their stature, the more apprehensive he became. The banquet room in Reinhardt's manor, where the reception was to take placc, was vast and opulent. Reinhardt seated himself in a massive armchair with a golden crown high above his head that only exaggerated the smallness of his stature. Silently, Chekhov implored him to stand so as not to be so dwarfed by his surroundings. Stanislavsky arrived. Reinhardt slipped out of the chair and walked very slowly toward the door. Footmen moved the heavy portieres aside and the white-haired giant appeared, glancing about the room waiting to be greeted. Reinhardt, one hand in his pocket, continued his progress toward the door, almost as if in slow motion. As he approached, Stanislavsky recognized him and moved briskly toward his host. Reinhardt's left hand slipped out of its pocket and hung elegantly by his side. His right arm stretched out toward Stanislavsly, causing the Russian to take a step back, creating a slight distance between the two men. Reinhardt raised his head and, like a connoisseur inspecting a Raphael or a Rembrandt, peered intensely into Stanislavsky's face. "My pounding heart counted out several seconds," recalls Chekhov "and then a miracle occurred before our eyes. Still keeping that distance between them, Reinhardt began to grow in stature, becoming the grand and majestic Max Reinhardt. The magician, the wizard had triumphed! He escorted his guest through the spacious chamber. The more Stanislavsky bustled, the slower and calmer Reinhardt became. They were both magnificent; one in his confusion and childlike openness, the other, with the confident serenity of the connoisseur. Everyone understood the tone that had been set by this greeting—*you must be a Reinhardt to appreciate a Stanislavsky!*"

This clash of the titans was probably more in Chekhov's mind than it was in either Reinhardt's or Stanislavsky's. The fact is, Reinhardt's standing in Europe was every bit as imposing as Stanislavsky's, and the two men treated each other with the kind of respect that equals usually show to one another.

At the end of the dinner, which was filled with lively bonhomie and photographers snapping pictures, Stanislavsky was ushered outside of his host's palatial manor and presented with a magnificent motor car, a gift from an admiring Reinhardt. When he saw the splendid glittering chrome and glass object replete with a uniformed chauffeur, a shudder of fear rippled through his body. Not wishing to offend his host, he thanked him politely for the generous gift. At the end of the proceedings, Stanislavsky asked Chekhov to accompany him back to his hotel in the car and there, writhing with anguish, cried out to Misha:

"My God, my God, what am I going to do!?"

"With what?" asked Misha.

"With this…. this motor. It's all very nice and touching, but what do I do with it? It is impossible to take it with me to Russia. And to leave it here would be... somehow... I don't know, dreadful, dreadful! Why did he have to do this?" In a Russia now dominated by the fervent egalitarianism of the proletariat, Stanislavsky knew his gift would appear scandalously counter revolutionary.

When the car arrived at his hotel, Stanislavsky bowed several times to the chauffeur, nervously tapped his hand to his breast several times, and trying to master his confusion, disappeared into the lobby.

Chekhov found Stanislavsky most charming when he was embarrassed or perplexed. The director would often display odd behavior of which he was thoroughly unaware. In Berlin, when Chekhov dropped in on him while the director was expecting a visit from a distinguished count (which, like the automobile, might have compromised him with the Soviet authorities), Stanislavsky said, glancing down at his watch, "Sit down, Misha. Any minute now, I am expecting another idiot."

Stanislavsky was often socially inept when dealing with foreign dignitaries. On one occasion, he sat his honored guest down at the table while he antisocially placed himself several feet away. At a loss for words, and with a vague smile playing on his lips, he met—then avoided—then met again—the eye of his guest. He then rose and bowed low four times, either in greeting or perhaps trying to settle himself comfortably in his chair. Then, after a cough and a pause, he looked lamely at his guest and asked, "Do you want to wee-wee?"

When Stanislavsky left Germany to return to Moscow, it must have been a great wrench for Chekhov. Although he understood the inevitability of his new circumstances, it was difficult to accept the removal of everything he had held dear in his homeland. No matter what new strictures the Soviets were now imposing on their artists, his friends and fondest memories were still in Russia. Attempts were being made on his part, and those of his colleagues, to effect a safe return, but these grew progressively more faint as time went by. He was a fish out of water in Berlin. He went there full of plans to remount his *Hamlet*, and found instead that he was considered merely a boulevard comedian—probably because the news of his rollicking Khlestakov had preceded him.

When the Habimah Theatre came to Berlin for a short tour, his spirits instantly rose. The company wished to add a play of Shakespeare's to their repertory and they asked Chekhov to direct *Twelfth Night*. He agreed eagerly.

Habimah was a Hebrew-language theater peopled with

intense, argumentative, but thoroughly committed actors. It was one of the many ethnic theaters in Russia, and the one that proved to be the most durable. Founded after the revolution of 1905 by N.L. Zemach, who also acted with the company, it had a difficult gestation period and an even more difficult birth. Viciously suppressed by czarist authorities during the Jewish persecution of 1911, the actors managed to resurface after the 1917 revolution, only to be stamped out again. Were it not for the intercession of Maxim Gorky and Stanislavsky, the theater might have vanished altogether.

Vakhtangov's staging of S. Ansky's *The Dybbuk* was its defining moment and in 1925–26, the company toured America with productions such as Henning Berger's *The Deluge*, Penskom's *The Eternal Jew*, and Richard Beer-Hoffman's *Jacob's Dream*, but it was the gaunt and chilling *Dybbuk* that caught the imagination of foreign audiences. Shortly after its premiere in Hebrew, the play was performed in English at the Neighborhood Playhouse in New York, and the company managed to gain the support of affluent American Jews such as Alice and Irene Lewishon. In 1928–29, swept up in the Zionist fervor of that period, Habimah moved to what was then Palestine and established a streamlined new playhouse in Tel Aviv. After the state of Israel was proclaimed, Habimah became the country's leading national theater and has prospered there ever since. The ties to Russia were not only with Stanislavsky, but also with his pupil Gnessin, who led the Hatai Company and was mainly responsible for the successful transplantation to the Middle East.

There is a certain irony in the fact that the style of the company—histrionic, often turgid and heavily melodramatic—in many ways resembled the pre-revolutionary acting that Stanislavsky's influence did much to eradicate. It was not a company known for its lightness of touch. Chekhov immediately grasped that the first problem was to induce levity in performers who were not temperamentally predisposed in that direction.

Believing that a straightforward approach would yield the best results, Chekhov put the problem squarely to the company. What *Twelfth Night* needed was a lightness, an airiness that might well be beyond the capacities of the players. At first, this gentle reproach was met with complete silence. After a while, the natural volubility of the Jewish actors took up the challenge and, gesticulating wildly, everyone started exploring the problem in both Russian and Hebrew. "If lightness is needed, lightness is needed!" said one. Another urged the director "not to settle for anything *but* lightness!" A third turned on Chekhov as if he had intimated that these actors were characteristically grave—which of course, they were. Gradually, the company became obsessed with the new objective: "We *will* be light!" they thundered heavily to one another and to their director. The task that lay ahead absorbed everyone and the collective resolution ended in kisses and embraces, as if the pronouncement of the objective was also its fulfillment. The actors sat down at the long table for a first reading of the play, and a sense of purpose spread like a rainbow over their heads.

Having established the central stylistic need of the play, Chekov proceeded to create exercises to develop the requisite levity. Here, the Steiner disciplines became invaluable. "Habimah," said Chekhov, "strove for lightness stubbornly, fanatically, and gravely. And they succeeded. I have never seen such a capacity for work in any other company. If a miracle can be accomplished by earthly means alone, then it occurred here, before my very eyes. Meskin, for example, was a heavy man, seemingly cast in bronze with a voice so low that when you listened to him, you wanted to clear your own throat. But he scampered about the stage as an airy, pot-bellied Sir Toby, scattering Shakespeare's phrases and jests as if Hebrew had been the author's original tongue. Baratz was a small but weighty man who learned how to balance his weight on his heels, wearing away several pairs of rubber heels in the process. 'Look,' said one to the other, trying to suppress their mirth, 'Baratz, on tiptoe!' With each day, Shakespeare's comedy grew, transforming the actors and revealing the play's humor and charm."

Chekhov learned a great deal about Jewish politics during the course of rehearsals, and about the aspirations of Jews for their own homeland and their own theater in Palestine. He became aware, perhaps for the first time, of the suffering of these people who were passionate about creating a Jewish state, one that would be mercifully free of pogroms and Cossack raids. After rehearsals, the company would sing synagogue chants, folk songs, and wedding songs. The merrier they were, the more they brought tears to Chekhov's eyes, and the more he wept, the more the players laughed at him. But a strong bond of affection was forged between cast and director. It was also, for Chekhov, a kind of reunion with the spirit of Vakhtangov, who had worked so closely with these actors on *The Dybbuk* in the days when both men shared the birth pangs of almost every production they mounted, singly or together.

The premiere was before an invited house overflowing with well-wishers and Zionist sympathizers who understood the cultural significance of recreating Habimah in Palestine. Before the first act, Chekhov, standing in a box in the orchestra, made an introductory speech welcoming the public. The frivolity of the performance was a revelation to those who knew the company only from its more somber Hebrew productions.

In the middle of the first act, reports Chekhov, "a man in a long dark velvet garment made his way to the front row, surrounded by a respectful retinue. He wore a cap of the same dark velvet color. His tall figure and handsome, well-proportioned face with its white beard called up an image of ancient mysteries. He was Rabindranath Tagore, the renowned Indian poet." Chekhov doesn't elaborate on the nature of the interruption or precisely what Tagore said, and so it is impossible to know whether it was to raise an objection or deliver a compliment. *Twelfth Night* was a great success with the public, and gave guest performances both in Berlin and in London. It even garnered a highly upbeat review from Sean O'Casey in the British press. In a private letter to Sydney Bernstein, O'Casey wrote effusively, "The production of *Twelfth Night* by the Habimah Players bewildered me with its joy, rhythm, color, and loveliness. Christ, this is Shakespearean comedy at last! This is the big mind, the big laugh, and the big heart of the poet. Here is the production with which the audience can laugh with Shakespeare, dance with Shakespeare, and sigh with Shakespeare. As God is in the composition and color of a great painting, as he is in the line and column of a great piece of sculpture, as he is in the spirit and sound of a great poem, so is he in the acting of the Habima Players. To think that I could be so moved by a thing done in a tongue I do not understand, and to think of the times I have been moved to a deep shame by the things done in a tongue every word of which I knew too well."

The renewal of old ties with his Russian comrades was a bittersweet experience for Chekhov, as it only served to remind him of the fact that artistically, he was in limbo. But one encounter was not only gratifying but extremely fortuitous.

It was in Berlin that Chekhov first met fellow Russian George Shdanoff, who was to become a good friend and a close professional associate in virtually all of Chekhov's work, particularly when he traveled to England and America.

Originally intending to pursue a medical career like his father, Shdanoff's first visit to a theater as a child sidetracked him into the profession, and despite strong family resistance, he pursued acting, directing and teaching for all of his long life. (He died in Hollywood in 1999.) His fellow Russians' reservations about Stanislavsky's approach, particularly in relation to "emotional memory," created a strong bond with Chekhov. Shdanoff was also an experimental filmmaker. After the Nazis came to power, he made an antiwar film called *No Man's Land* that angered the German authorities and, because they believed it to be subversive of their National Socialist ideals, jeopardized Shdanoff's life. Alerted to the fact that he was liable for immediate detention, he enlisted the aid of Gaston Baty, the illustrious French director, and managed to board a train to France before the Nazis swooped down upon him. All the prints of *No Man's Land* were destroyed.

Shdanoff's first meeting with Chekhov was in June 1928 during the Berlin period. "When I saw him," Shdanoff recalled, "I was amazed at how thin and short he looked—a build very much like that of Fred Astaire. But his big grey-blue eyes were remarkable. There was so much pain and sorrow in them, so many other hidden emotions, so much untold yearning...and his hands were unusually beautiful and expressive." Shdanoff's first question to Chekhov was to ask what he felt about Stanislvasky's view of emotional and sense memory.

"I do not use them," replied Chekhov, "not as tools for preparation of a part nor as exercises. I never liked them and have never used them!" That immediately struck a chord with Shdanoff. "I was greatly relieved, even excited, and jumped up from my chair and grabbed his hands," said Shdanoff. "My rebellion against these and other points in Stanislavsky's method was not unjustified!" It was the beginning of a collaboration that would last some twenty-five years and profoundly influence the direction Shdanoff took as both actor and teacher. Film commitments made it impossible for Shdanoff to join Chekhov either in Berlin or in Paris, but in the spring of 1937, the two kindred spirits would be reunited at Dartington Hall in Devon, where both men would have some of the most creative years of their lives.

Chapter Fourteen

MISHA FLOURISHED IN BERLIN, becoming even something of a matinee idol. When he asked one of his many female admirers what she saw in him, she replied naively, "But you are such a successful man!" That was the last thing that Chekhov felt about himself.

The desire to stage his own *Hamlet* bitterly frustrated under Reinhardt, gradually became an obsession. Chekhov saw the production as the forerunner to his own theater which he was now determined to create. He maintained a childlike belief in his "ideal audience," one that would disdain potboilers and gravitate naturally to classics and works of social significance. His distaste for naturalism grew even more abhorrent. Chekhov enrolled in the Rudolph Steiner School in Berlin, concentrating on eurythmics and their application to dramatic speech. Despite the fact that no producer had come forward with any offers, he conducted private rehearsals of *Hamlet* in his home using sympathetically inclined German and Russian actors. He even went so far as to cut and adapt the play, realizing several of the roles would probably have to be doubled and trebled. "In the depths of my soul," he wrote, "I realized that my idea for a new theater had not yet matured, but the pleasure of idealistic enthusiasm proved stronger than common sense." His intention was to mount a compressed version of the play as a means of raising the funds needed to establish the

new company, but he found "not the slightest interest" in his
Hamlet. The German public seemed to prefer him in trivial
and undemanding comedies. His quixotic nature came up
with the scheme of hiring a circus van and performing
Shakespeare's play on street corners throughout the city, but
his friends dissuaded him.

In Berlin, there was an unexpected reunion with Olga
Chekhova, who at this time was already a star of the German
cinema and an actress whose charisma almost rivaled
Dietrich's and Garbo's. In 1930, she was lured to Hollywood
and made a romantic comedy titled *Love on Command*, but
the accent proved too obtrusive, and when studio bosses
demanded she lose twenty pounds, she promptly hightailed it
back to Germany. A prolific film actress with solid connections
to the UFA Studios at Babelsberg, Olga persuaded Misha to
appear in a silent film appropriately titled *Der Narr Seiner
Liebe* (*The Fool of Love*) directed by herself, which was quickly followed by *Troika*, another "silent" in which she starred and
her ex-husband played a village idiot. It is tempting to believe
there was some vindictive typecasting involved in these efforts
as, in one sense, Olga never quite forgave Misha for being the
only man over whom she had entirely lost her head and the
one who inspired the iron self-sufficiency that sustained her
for over sixty years.

Chekhov's early years in Berlin (1928–29) coincided with
Bertolt Brecht's *Threepenny Opera* and Erwin Piscator's reign
on Nollendorfplatz, where he premiered his controversial production of *The Good Soldier Schweik* (which triggered a crim-
inal blasphemy suit against its designer George Grosz), but
Chekhov makes no mention of these revolutionary developments. He saw only the indifference of the German public to
his particular notion of serious theater and it plunged him into
a fierce nostalgia for both his Russian colleagues and the
Russian audience before whom he had played so happily. His
yearning to return to Mother Russia grew even greater, but
realizing that course was not open to him, his thoughts turned

to France, where in the late twenties, there was a large Russian colony. In Paris, thought Chekhov, he would be appreciated and supported. There, the new theater could be founded, and on a terrain better suited to his tastes and talent.

Despite the advice of friends and colleagues, Chekhov decided to leave Reinhardt, forego the numerous opportunities that had begun to present themselves on the German stage, and move — posthaste — to Paris. But before he could launch his French idyll, there was an unexpected detour that, in a curious way, psychologically prepared him for what he would find in Paris.

An old Ukranian friend of Chekhov's, identified only as C., came to visit him in Berlin bearing an offer from the Czech government, reiterating that country's invitation to establish a classical theater in Prague. C., wearing a gold shoulder strap, shiny copper buttons, and rows of military decorations, offered both his services and his influence in realizing the offer. He spoke of his close association with many of the Czech officials and of President Jan Masryk's personal love of theater. Chekhov was blindsided. He explained that his plan was to move to Paris and establish his theater there, but C. would hear none of it. "Tell me," he said, "what is the chief element of the theater?" "The actor, I suppose," answered Chekhov. "No, no — acting is the easiest part. The most crucial element is the administrator — the man with a brain for financial affairs. And since we already have such a man, half the work is done, don't you see?" "But where is this administrator," asked Chekhov. "Here he is!" said C. spreading out his arms and thrusting forward his powerful chest. "Behind me, you will be as if behind a stone wall. Rest easy, create, don't worry about anything, just work!" Perhaps, thought Chekhov, this Czech bird in the hand may be worth more than two in the French bush.

C. proceeded to formulate a budget for the first seasons and when it was done he presented it to Chekhov. The total was six million crowns, which terrified Chekhov. "Even five hundred thousand is a bit too much, in my opinion," he said, "I'd prefer even less." "Don't you realize, my friend, who you are?" asked C. "How could you ask for anything less than five million? Is that becoming? A cultural undertaking on a European scale! A new era in the theater! Do you think you're coming to beg alms from President Masaryk?"

C. pooh-poohed all of Chekhov's objections and insisted he would personally submit the budget to Mazaryk himself. His concern would be "the business of the theater" and all Chekov had to worry about was "the other side of the footlights." His self-confidence was unshakeable, and Chekhov, although wary, convinced himself this might be the stroke of luck he had been praying for. Neatly folding the pages of the copious budget into a large dossier, C. left for Prague instructing Chekhov not to worry.

Chekhov began to formulate the plays he would mount in the opening season, beginning, of course, with *Hamlet*. He also began sounding out actors to see if they might be interested in joining him in this exciting new venture.

Weeks went by without any word from C. Finally, almost a month later, he received a letter from the president's office graciously rejecting the offer of a new theater in Prague. It pointed out that at the present time, it was impossible to consider supplying the vast amount indicated in the budget.

"I burned with shame and cursed myself for my moral weakness and lack of character," wrote Chekhov. "In the heat of the moment, I wrote C. an angry letter. His reply came back full of loving outpourings, consolation, and even vague hints of a future collaboration. The letter was written with various colored pencils and full of exclamation points, question marks, scribbles on the margins, and underlined phrases such as 'Don't despair, my friend!', 'Avanti, caro!', 'We'll show them!', and so forth. I threw the letter aside without finishing it and speedily prepared for my departure."

The only theater Chekhov had known in Russia was subsidized theater. The pitfalls, deceptions, and false starts of commercial theater were a world in which he wandered like a man

from another planet. Whatever the disadvantages of Soviet theater might be (and by the thirties, they were considerable), the
art form was respected, financed, and devoted to high ideals. In
Berlin, and later in Paris, Chekhov was to discover that the
capitalist stage was rife with impostors and charlatans. For the
trusting Misha, it would be a difficult lesson to learn, and one
that, despite recurring disappointments, he would never
entirely assimilate.

Chapter Fifteen

IN PARIS, Chekhov threw himself wholeheartedly into the quest for a new theater and the audience he implicitly believed would be there to sustain it. Russian émigré actors flocked to him from all sides, drawn by his professional stature and sharing his desire to install Russian culture in a country that prided itself on displaying multinational artistic achievements. Salaries were negotiated and advances distributed. The actors were highly motivated and, right from the start, the theater seemed to have a firm foundation.

It was in Paris that Georgette Boner, a young budding producer and the director of the *Deutschen Bühne*, fell under Chekhov's spell. She had studied acting with Max Reinhardt, but found her talents for administration were more fulfilling. She soon became an active collaborator, helping to raise funds, negotiate contracts, and smoothe Chekhov's way through the morass of French theater politics. Boner, like Chekhov, had a strong interest in fairy tales, and together they researched mythological source material that would resurface prominently in Chekhov's later work. It was a relationship that would endure long after the Parisian period extending into Latvia and Dartington Hall.

Since the difficulties of mounting *Hamlet* seemed too ambitious for a first production, Chekhov decided to start with a stage adaptation of *Don Quixote*. A small theater in Montmartre (the Atelier) presented the perfect venue. A secretary was hired, filing cabinets began to fill up, and letters were sent and received with fervent regularity.

To acclimatize himself to his new society, Chekhov attended French theater almost daily. With each performance, his ardor for his own work grew. Everything was so superficial, he told himself "so banal, that a new theater is *vital!*" Only the work of Louis Jouvet impressed him. "He had lightness that never turned into lightheadedness."

Instead of recruiting the leaders of the Russian émigré community and creating an audience base for the new theater, Chekhov spent a lot of time with the kind of useless people who always swarm around a new project, offering lip service but essentially pushing personal agendas. Eventually, the French press were alerted and interviews, articles, and other forms of publicity began to appear about the displaced Russians and the theater they were zealously putting together.

There were countless meetings with potential backers, often old Russian dowagers who were fulsome in their praise for Chekhov and maudlin about their memories of "old Russia." Foreign millionaires were mustered into service by Russian well-wishers, but disappeared almost as quickly as they arrived. Outstanding French celebrities were pursued by self-styled promoters for the cause. An alleged close friend of Charlie Chaplin joined the movement, confident that the film star, a proclaimed Socialist, would become an eager backer. Nothing came of it.

One morning the secretary knocked at Chekhov's door. "Wake up!" he cried. "The company is going to America! Congratulations!" A meeting was arranged at an elegant hotel between Chekhov, the secretary and his newfound American millionaire. After an elaborate description of their plans, it transpired that the American had no interest whatsoever in theater. When the secretary took umbrage at being so rudely misled and protested loudly, the millionaire had both men firmly escorted from the hotel.

Someone suggested that Chekhov approach Baron Rothschild with the model and sketches for the first production, and somehow an interview was arranged. Rothschild studiously examined the colorful sketches and ingenious set designs of the artist Masutin and concluded they were brilliant. "We have triumphed," thought Chekhov, "at last!" The next morning's post contained a rejection letter from Rothschild.

Despite these rebuffs, Chekhov decided to begin rehearsals on *Don Quixote*, persuading himself that once the production was in place, finance would follow. Not relying on fate, the secretary and other key members created the "Society of Friends of the Theatre" and began soliciting contributions. On the first day, the Vysotsky family, well-off émigrés living in Paris, sent 250 francs. The founders were delighted, but in the days that followed, no other contributions appeared. Once word got out that the financial foundation of the new theater was decidedly shaky, earlier donors began to renege. Chaplin's bosom buddy mysteriously disappeared. On one occasion, Chekhov watched as the secretary, pretending to order costumes for the show, pressed his finger down on the telephone cradle breaking the connection, but shouted into the receiver, "Varya, drop everything and speed up the order for *Quixote*." Exiting hurriedly, he called after Chekhov, "All right, the costumes are all set!" As the weeks wore on, disillusioned actors began to fall away. Even the eager secretary had vanished. Mercifully, the Vysotsky family once again came to the rescue with a small sum. "It was not enough to finance the expensive production of *Don Quixote*, wrote Chekhov, "so I decided to stage a pantomime based on Russian fairy tales. The absence of dialogue would make the show immediately accessible to French and Russian audiences so that, if successful, we could expect good attendance."

The pantomime was hastily prepared. Behind it, there was a growing desperation that, after all the initial hoopla, *something* had to be presented if even a shred of credibility was to survive.

During rehearsals, the musicians developed a strong
antipathy for their young conductor; far too young, many of
them thought, to try to tackle even a show as modest as this
one. The conductor was not inclined to be conciliatory and
the atmosphere grew even more acrimonious. On opening
night, to avenge themselves, the musicians tore one page out of
each orchestral part. Chekhov describes it:

> The overture was playing, the curtain rose, the act began.
> The audience watched attentively and waited. After a few
> minutes, the orchestra stumbled—a violin scraped sadly,
> the flute whistled once, then just stopped. Everything
> went quiet. A laugh from the back of the stalls broke the
> tense silence. The conductor, like a mad marionette,
> raised and lowered his hands, but no sounds issued from
> his orchestra. The laughter began to crescendo, aug-
> mented with whistles, hisses, and insults directed at the
> musicians. The innate cruelty that can be found at the
> heart of all audiences began to surface. The helpless con-
> ductor, terrified by the jeers and whistles, fled the scene.
> The musicians clumsily tried to retrieve the lost sheets of
> music. Onstage, the actors waiting for their musical cues
> were frozen in *tableaux vivants*. Finally, all the sheets
> were assembled and the music resumed, but only to be
> interrupted again a few minutes later. By intermission, all
> of the pages had been properly assembled but it was too
> late. The performance has been irreparably ruined.

Masochistically, Chekhov announced a second performance of his pantomime. He dismissed the young beleaguered
conductor and spent the remainder of his funds hiring new
musicians, but word had spread fast, and at the second performance the auditorium was virtually empty. Writhing
inwardly with despair and wounded pride, Chekhov addressed
the dozen or so people scattered around the stalls. He told
them that he and his company were "idealists" and in no way

troubled by the minuscule house. He urged them to draw closer to the stage, and assured them the company had the
warmest regard for the people who had gathered and would
perform energetically for them. A few people in the gallery
rushed downstairs and sat themselves in the front row. The
others remained where they were. The company, standing in
the wings, felt humiliated by their director's address. A performance of sorts was carried out, but after that, the pantomime simply vanished both from sight and memory.

After the fiasco, Chekhov thanked his loyal actors and told
them they were released from any further obligations to perform, but they were all aware the theater had been leased for
the entire season and had to be paid for. In spite of the funere-
al atmosphere, they refused to play dead only to be buried. Post
mortems were disallowed. A discussion was begun and suggestions flew from every side. Why not present something with
proven worth like *The Deluge*, which had been a success in
Moscow? Why not show the Parisian audience the very best of
what the contemporary Russian theater had to offer? Chekhov
was doubtful. Apart from being spiritually spent, he was physically exhausted as well. But the growing ardor of the actors
would not be denied. The eternal optimism that makes actors
believe in miracles even when they are knee deep in calamities
was gradually gathering force. The decision to proceed with
The Deluge was unanimously agreed upon. The Russian newspapers that had cruelly slated the pantomime considered the
new production simply a "change in the repertoire" and react-
ed favorably. The word of mouth for *The Deluge* grew steadily,
and miraculously, a Russian audience of sorts began to
emerge. To maintain their interest, Chekhov brought back
some of the most popular items from the Second Moscow Art
Theater: *Eric XIV*, *A Chekhov Evening* and *Twelfth Night*.

The need to maintain the theater's momentum involved
slapdash rehearsals and a number of painful artistic compro-
mises. Chekhov grew progressively discouraged. He had to
face the fact that the Russian audience resident in Paris was

simply too small to support a permanent theater; a fact that could have been ascertained by a minimal amount of research beforehand had Chekhov been a businessman rather than an idealist. The future looked bleak and there was nowhere else to go. "There is no point in imagining an 'ideal theater,'" wrote Chekhov after the experience "in France or in Germany. I finally acknowledged the error of my Don Quixote idealism and I also recognized how undemanding theater audiences really are. The farther from Russia he went, the drearier life became for the Russian actor. We completed our first season and half-heartedly contemplated the next."

It was in the summer of 1931, while Chekhov was struggling in Paris, that Meyerhold, still at work in the Soviet Union, directed Yuri Olesha's play *A List of Assets*, ostensibly a *drama à clef* dealing with Chekhov's decision to forsake his homeland. The play ends with the central character (Chekhov) being assassinated by a White Russian émigré in Paris. Whether this was a perverse piece of flattery or wishful thinking, it is difficult to say. But previously, Meyerhold and members of his theater, had visited Chekhov in Paris in an attempt to persude the actor to return. Like so many such overtures from various quarters, this one also came to nothing. (Zinaida Raikh, Meyerhold's wife, would subsequently accuse Chekhov of being a traitor to the Russian people. In 1940, after her husband's arrest, her mutilated body would be discovered in their Moscow flat. Although officially attributed to "thugs," it is generally believed the crime was committed by Stalin's Secret Police.) One year earlier, Chekhov had written to Lunacharsky offering to return to Moscow if he could be given the directorship of a theater devoted entirely to classical plays and not obliged to purvey Soviet propoganda. Obviously, three years into Chekhov's exile, his political naiveté remained perfectly in tact.

By 1932, Chekhov was forced to acknowledge that since his departure from Moscow, and despite a brief commercial success in Germany, his life was in limbo. He was overcome with a crippling apathy. Chekhov hobnobbed with Russian émigrés in Paris but it became too painful to be constantly reminded of his homeland. His only pleasurable diversion became chess. He attended all the Paris tournaments and played privately with experts such as Alkehine and Bernstein, two recognized chess masters of the day. His only link with theater was his leadership of the amateur theater group into which he had reluctantly been drawn during the heady phase of the Paris season. He gradually became aware that, more through osmosis than design, he had acquired many of the skills that had been handed down from Stanislavsky, Sulherzitsky, and Vakhtangov. His own theories had been forged in his work both in Russia and in Germany, and he was surprised to find himself articulating beliefs and developing techniques that he was unaware he possessed.

It was during this period that he experienced another of his epiphanies; this one at a dance marathon that was taking place in a giant circus tent in the center of the city. It had been going on for almost a week when Chekhov stumbled upon it. Eight or ten couples were still participating, dancing nonstop, without sleep or rest, while maniacal revelers on the sidelines urged them on. Money was being tossed at the dancers. The first prize of 25,000 francs would be awarded to whichever couple "died" last. By the fifth day, the survivors consisted of only three bedraggled couples and one lone female who, a few days earlier, had lost her partner. The howls of the audience stunned and sickened Misha. Despite his disgust, he found himself merging with the crowd, and, like them, looking forward to the next collapse and predicting the marathon's next victim. One of the male dancers fell to the floor with a thud, smacking his head against the wooden dance floor, his right hand grotesquely twisted behind his back. The crowd whooped and whistled. Bystanders fought with one another, tore the hats off their heads and tossed them toward the dancers. The crowd, sensing some imminent fatality, grew in size. They were pushed back by burly ushers, but spilled over

the human barricade, hungrily gaping at the handful of half-
dead dancers that remained. The music of the tinny band
never flagged for a moment.

Wrote Chekhov:

> I came to myself and suddenly felt a sharp, burning
> hatred—not of them, but of myself, of my idea of a new
> theater, of my dream of an ideal audience, and of that
> loathsome twin of mine whom I had christened Don
> Quixote. The beast that the atmosphere of the dance
> marathon had awakened in me stalked its prey. I wanted
> to destroy, to murder, and I *did* murder; the fatal blow
> landed on the knight with the barber's basin on his head,
> my alter ego, Don Quixote. All of my groundless dreams,
> all of my passionate but empty idealism, all of my smug
> self satisfaction—everything that lived within me, all van-
> ished, stopped, died. I ran out of that circus tent and
> found myself back on the boulevard. My emptied soul
> waited for something, and shortly, something began to
> rise from its depths. I did not yet know what it was, but I
> felt this was real, this was something I could not live with-
> out, that I could not face the future without. It was suf-
> fused with both tranquility and strength. I divined that
> that this was the birth of my philosophy—not only in my
> mind but now lodged within my entire being, in my
> heart, and in my will. What I had called anthroposophy,
> which I knew and cherished as a grandiose system of
> thinking about the world and man, was now becoming
> an *independent, living being.* Let me not lose this new
> unity that I had never felt before, I pleaded with myself,
> this "I," so serene and strong, this new person growing
> within me. And let me not sink back into this pathetic
> man shuffling along the boulevard who was now alien to
> me, but whom I had previously thought of as my*self.*

In the midst of these cathartic thoughts, Chekhov claims

he was approached by an old woman—short, dried up, and wearing a wide-brimmed black straw hat that concealed most of her face. She loomed before him like something out of a bad dream, and in a low, muffled voice said, "Your fleeing Moscow resulted in the arrest and exile of several members of the Anthroposophic Society. If you had any decency you would return at once. Only your return to Russia can save them!"

"I followed her with my eyes," writes Chekhov, "without will, without thought, feeling guilt, melancholy, and pain. The 'great new being' I had just experienced faded away completely. The old woman walked slowly, never turning back; her black straw hat glinted under each street lamp as, one after the other, she disappeared beneath them. I stood for a while and then went to the nearest bistro and drank cheap, acidic wine. Only the first few glasses were unpleasant."

That Misha was prone to hallucinations has been observed by many of the people who knew him most intimately. That he often behaved oddly, seemed not to be in the real world, has also been reported by friends and co-workers. That he inherited alcoholism from his father would appear to be an undeniable fact, and one that he himself had acknowledged on numerous occasions. But before one attributes visions like the one described above to the excesses of liquor or the mental meanderings of an unstable personality, one has to remember that mystical beliefs—both Christian and metaphysical—were bred in Chekhov from a very early age, and became an integral part of both his philosophy and personal experience. There is a distinction to be drawn between the clinical psychotic who hallucinates in a state of delusion and the man who has been weaned on religious and paranormal conceits in an ordered and intellectual fashion. For people who hold such beliefs and can rationally defend them, the supernatural state is not so much an aberration as it is a plane of consciousness as legitimate as the mental sphere in which a mathematician or nuclear physicist resides. Their frame of reference, due to their education and experience, is rarefied and very different from ours, but it would be an act of rashness to relegate them to a state of dementia.

In Chekhov's case, his epiphany in the streets of Paris caused him to confront the impractical and quixotic nature of his immediate past. It was a sobering experience that cleansed rather than muddied his perceptions. He himself acknowledged the change in his perspective. "What did I lose in Paris?" he wrote afterward. "Money and excessive ambition. What did I gain? A certain talent for self-criticism, and an inclination toward fully thought-out actions. As was often the case, my life now changed, both internally and externally. A period of good fortune began."

He received an offer from Riga in Latvia to organize a tour of *The Inspector General*, playing Khlestakov and directing. Riga, during the thirties, consciously tried to emulate Paris. It was steeped in its own culture, curious of others, and anxious to be thought of as something of a burgeoning European capitol. Its clubs, bars, and restaurants patterned themselves on French bohemianism. In this stimulating cultural milieu, Chekhov was immediately renewed. He ate, drank, caroused, signed autographs, danced Russian dances (as well as the recently imported fox trot) and lost himself in a whirlwind of social activity with women, poets, politicians, and intellectuals. Regularly recognized in restaurants, he would often be invited to the tables of complete strangers and immediately drawn into revelry. On one occasion, he was confronted with a bare-breasted girl wearing a gold cross around her neck. The symbol brought tears to his eyes and he bent down and kissed the crucifix.

The rehearsals for the Gogol, unlike those in Germany or France, were conducted in reverential silence, full of commitment and enthusiasm, like those he had known in Russia. Due to the foreign celebrity in their midst, the actors were acting better, and with greater discipline, than ever before. Tickets for the performances were sold out in two days. The entire atmosphere was eager, expectant, and respectful; a welcome change from Paris. These were people who, as Stanislavsky would have said, "loved art—and not themselves in art."

The performances went off with great élan; Riga accorded his Khlestakov a Moscow-like reception. Two performances were particularly memorable. At one, Max Reinhardt arrived and strongly approved; at another, Fyodor Chaliapin attended, and a great buzz went through both the company and the audience. Afterward, Chekhov and the singer dined together. After praising his performance, Chaliapin proceeded to regale Chekhov by parodying the antics of bad opera singers, which brought tears of laughter to Chekhov's eyes. Chekhov assumes Chaliapin's praise was sincere, since some time later his son, Fyodor Fyodorovich, confided to him that, alluding to Chekhov's acting, his father had said, "He spins lace, the son of a bitch."

Riga had been a refreshing diversion, but after the tour Chekhov reluctantly returned to Paris where he was prepared to idle away his time playing chess and contemplate a barren future. Behind the scenes, his friends Georgette Boner, the Reinhardt pupil who had now become a fulltime acolyte, and Viktor Gromov, his Russian assistant, had been negotiating to arrange a niche in the Baltics. Within a matter of weeks, an offer came from the Latvian State Theatre and the Russian Drama Theatre offering permanent positions at both venues. He packed his belongings, and he and his wife Xenia moved permanently to Riga.

Chapter Sixteen

THE WORK IN LATVIA involved both acting and directing—which was fine for Misha, as he had now developed a number of ideas in both areas and was anxious to try them out. His plan was to mount a new production of *The Death of Ivan the Terrible* to run in tandem with *Hamlet*. Chekhov would perform in Russian while the other members of the cast played in Latvian—which was not as outré as it sounds, as most Latvians both spoke and understood Russian. Since the beginning of the century, Latvia had been occupied by either German or Russian masters.

In Moscow, Misha had been prevented from mounting a projected production of *Ivan the Terrible,* as the Communist authorities feared a sympathetic portrayal of Ivan might vindicate czarism for the public, many of whom were still sympathetic to the murdered Romanoffs. Subterraneanly, the performance of *Ivan* had been shaping itself in Chekhov's subconscious since the early days at the Moscow Art. When he came to stage it, he was astonished to find how quickly it all fell into place, as if the character had simply been waiting to be reclaimed. He had never played it in Moscow, although he had been closely associated with the celebrated production in which the eponymous role was performed by A.I Cheban, a charismatic Russian actor of the old school. But Chekhov's conception was so far removed from Cheban's, there was no fear the memory of it would influence his interpretation.

Sensing a profound affinity with the ambitious ruler, Chekhov simply watched as Ivan's characteristics coagulated within himself. As before, he carefully melded together complementary traits; in this case combining the extremes of cruelty and childishness. As it turned out, the Soviet authorities were right to be wary of the play, for Chekhov's Ivan did manage to vindicate the malevolent czar and gain the sympathy of the audience. Chekhov put Stanislavsky's rule to good use: "When you play an evil character," he had said, "search for his goodness." The closer the tyrant approached death, the more goodness Chekhov found in him. The more horrible his appearance became, the more his soul yearned for redemption and the more the audience's sympathy grew. With Ivan's death, Chekhov managed to retard the progress of time like a musician slowing down a metronome. His body became transparent; his eyes, like those of a frightened baby, simultaneously widened and clouded. The rallentando toward death was experienced not only onstage, but in the entire auditorium. Time palpably slowed down, then came to a stop, and Ivan expired.

The organic connection between Chekhov and his interpretation of character could not always be summoned on command. "My subconscious was not always ready to assist my creative work," Chekhov admitted. "At times, the connection with the subconscious would be broken for long periods. There were times when this higher awareness would ignite only at the dress rehearsal, or even during the premiere itself. In *The Deluge* and in *Eric XIV*, for example, I struggled to create the roles during the entire period of rehearsals. Vakhtangov, who directed these productions, was in despair. After the final dress rehearsal of *Eric* he even considered canceling the previously announced, sold-out premiere. But he understood all of my spiritual peculiarities, took a risk, and was vindicated. During the opening night, my subconscious creative powers broke through and before the audience, to

Vakhtangov's indescribable joy, they created an image of the mad king such as neither Vakhtangov nor I had ever anticipated."

It was clear that by the time Chekhov was performing in Riga, he had honed his inner technique to such a point that he could conjure up precisely those effects he wished to create. But that always meant collaboration with the higher realms of his imagination. The "technical actor" rehearses assiduously in order to perfect every detail of the performance he wishes to convey. The "chekhovian actor" realizes that the extra dimension that makes the difference between a competent and an inspiring performance depends on a quotient that cannot be drilled into being, but must arrive from some sphere beyond cognitive control. To the extent that an actor can consciously summon those subconscious resources to bring this about, Chekhov had begun to master that art.

The Inspector General and *The Deluge* played in repertory at the Russian Drama Theatre and were eventually joined by a less successful production of *Selo Stepanchikovo*. At the Latvian State Theatre, *Hamlet* and *The Death of Ivan the Terrible* alternated with one another. Riga was getting a rich diet of Russian classics. Its pretensions toward Parisian cosmopolitanism were rapidly being realized.

While in Latvia, Chekhov irritated many of his colleagues by casting a young, relatively untried actor in the important role of Boris Godunov; a practice that was unheard of in continental theater. He felt the actor, who had been little more than an opera super, had been suppressed in the stultifying atmosphere of the State Theatre and needed a chance to spread his wings. Chekhov saw this as a renewal of the nonconformist spirit he himself had experienced when he first joined the Moscow Art. He recalled an instance when Stanislavsky was directing Molière's *The Imaginary Invalid* and Chekhov was a new and relatively green member of that company. Chekhov had convened a meeting with the lowlier, supporting players in the men's lavatory and began to hector them about their slavish obedience to the powers of the dictatorial management. "It is shameful," he railed at them "that you allow yourselves to be oppressed, to be treated like lowly peasants, like operatic spear carriers. Where is your human dignity? Where is your artistic pride? The great Kachalovs and Moskvins play whatever they want, they grab the best roles for themselves — and you remain silent and meekly bow to them as they pass you in the corridor. Wake up! Protest!"

In the midst of this agitprop harangue, the door of one of the stalls opened with a sharp snap of its bolt and the six-foot-six Stanislavsky suddenly loomed before the actors. An ominous silence fell upon the lavatory conspirators. Stanislavsky, staring down at the undersized Misha from his great height took the actor by the scruff of his jacket and hoisted him into the air. When their eyes were level with one another, he heaved a great, exasperated sigh and said, "You are the plague of this theater." He then dropped Chekhov to the floor and stalked out of the lavatory.

Chekhov admitted that for many years after that incident, his own rebellious spirit had been somewhat crushed, but suddenly, in a position of authority himself at Riga, it had been rekindled and mustered into the service of the lowly super whom he raised from the anonymity of the company's lowest ranks. The choice was apparently judicious. The actor performed admirably in the role of Godunov, and thereafter his career blossomed.

While in Riga, Chekhov was approached by the Lithuanian State Theatre to participate both as actor and lecturer to the company in Kaunas. Since the offer had come from his old Moscow Art comrade A. M. Zhilinsky, he readily accepted, even though it meant commuting between Latvia and Lithuania two or three times a week. With the aid of assistants, he managed to fulfill his duties to both theaters. In Kaunas, he directed Zhilinsky in the role of Hamlet. Since they had both been pupils of Stanislavsky and Nemirovich-Danchenko, they shared the same frame of reference and worked together harmoniously. Devoid of any sense of professional rivalry, Chekhov was delighted with Zhilinsky's interpretation of the role, which was very different from his own. "His Hamlet was astonishing," wrote Chekhov. "His soul scudded past the events that encircled his life, seemingly *above* them. At the same time, his entire being—with its flaming, passionate heart, sharp wit, and all-penetrating eye—was here on earth, with the king and queen, Ophelia, Horatio, and old Polonius. How did Zhilinsky do this? How did he achieve such an effect? That is a secret known only to his own creative soul."

Actually, Zhilinsky, a tall, handsome, erect figure with a deep resonant voice and a confident manner, was in many ways a much more conventional Hamlet and closer to a matinee idol than Chekhov, and so the difference between Chekhov and Zhilinsky would have been quite striking. But when Zhilinsky went on to play Sir Toby Belch in *Twelfth Night*, the actor transformed himself into a roly-poly little man girded round with an enormous paunch, all vestiges of the heroic Hamlet eliminated. "I always considered the ability toward total transformation a sign of talent," Chekhov explained, "a gift from God to the actor. And it is one of the chief attributes of the Russian actor. But a time will come when the Western actor will understand how meager his life on the boards is, spending all of his life portraying only *himself*."

Chekhov, like Barrymore, Olivier, Guinness—like many European actors and very few American stars—was a firm believer in the actor's duty to metamorphose with each role, and like them, he dredged highly contrasting personae out of his own being. Eric XIV was as far removed from Khlestakov as Khlestakov was from Skid or Skid from Ivan the Terrible. As has been said, the sin of the actor is not "playing oneself," but "not having enough of oneself to play." When people met Chekhov socially for the first time, he appeared to be a short, snub-nosed, unprepossessing, and unremarkable person. That such a small vessel could contain such vast and hidden treasures always produced a startling reaction.

His time in Riga and Lithuania was perhaps one of Chekhov's happiest periods, and certainly one of his most productive. He was not only acting, directing, and teaching, but through a reunion with the artist M.V. Dobujinsky had renewed his interest in drawing and painting. In addition to Russian classics and Shakespeare, he also staged Wagner's *Parsifal* at the opera house in Riga and began assembling the notes that would eventually become *On the Technique of Acting* and *To the Actor*. He had begun to filter the influences he had absorbed from Stanislavsky, Vakhtangov, and Sulerzhitsky, but perhaps more important, he had traced the connections between Steiner's philosophy and the exigencies of dramatic art. In so doing, he had begun to craft a theory of acting that transcended the commonplace rules of technique and actually became a *weltanschauung*. Not only an organum of art, but a theorem for life.

But the idyll in Riga was too good to last, and after his return from Lithuania, the first cracks began to appear.

At Riga, one of Chekhov's most zealous protégés was an actor identified by Chekhov only as SH. He began as an assistant to Chekhov and was soon attending many of his classes as an observer. Chekhov began to notice how, sometimes in a corridor or a dark corner of the studio, groups of students would gather around SH. Their voices would be low and one could never quite make out the tenor of their remarks. Frequently, SH would nervously glance around to make sure that his whispers were not being overheard. His presence at Chekhov's classes became much more prominent. When students put questions to Misha, SH would reply in Latvian. Once, when Chekhov was casting a program of student performances, SH demanded that the female roles should be played by certain students he had preselected. Chekhov rankled at this impertinence and refused to accept his suggestions. SH then fixed Chekhov with a fierce glare, as if trying to alter his decision by means of hypnosis. Chekhov brushed SH aside and registered the fact that he would have to be wary of this man in the future. Little by little, SH began to increase his influence at the school, clearly subverting Chekhov's authority and quietly casting aspersions on his abilities. "He blossomed into a magnificent flower," said Chekhov, "telling unfunny anecdotes, laughing in a high raspy voice, slapping people on the back who were of higher status than himself, appearing where he was not invited, joining into conversations, laughing too much, drinking, eating and visibly gaining weight."

There was one man in Riga that most people in the theater feared, and SH was particularly wary of him. That man was Janis Karlinch, a brilliant but acerbic theater critic who was blunt, truthful, and intrepid. His columns were respected throughout the country, and his perspective on plays was invariably unique and original. He was a small man with a ready smile, in his early forties, modest, and inconspicuous despite the power he wielded in theater circles. Janis became something of an unofficial patron of the theater school and took a direct interest in its affairs, thus dismantling many of SH's stratagems that were directed against Chekhov. It was Janis who suggested Chekhov tackle *Parsifal* despite Misha's protestations that he had no experience in the field of opera. "That's all right," said Janis soothingly. Two days later the offer came to mount the Wagnerian production with unlimited rehearsal time and magnificent material resources, an offer that Misha found impossible to resist.

No sooner had he had begun to stage *Parsifal* than Chekhov was felled by a sudden heart attack. With Chekhov hospitalized for a month, SH, his malevolent assistant, was installed as acting director of the theater school. Even more distressing to Chekhov was the fact that he had staged only two scenes of the opera before his attack. Janis Karlinch, a regular visitor to the hospital, assuaged his fears both about the school and the opera. He was keeping a wary eye on SH and there was nothing to worry about there. As for the opera, Karlinch arranged for Chekhov's assistant to sneak into the hospital after hours and, by the dim light of the corridor, map out the scenes that were scheduled for rehearsal the following day. In this way, though often keening with pain, the production was furtively assembled despite Chekhov's absence.

When the final dress rehearsal came around, Misha demanded he be released from the hospital so he could attend the performance. Somehow, with Karlinch's politic assistance, a temporary release was arranged. Sitting crouched at the back of the auditorium and gulping pills, Chekhov watched the entire opera unfold. Last-minute notes were relayed to the singers, and when the gala premiere took place the following day, Chekhov again managed to be in attendance. No late-comers were permitted to be seated and the performance itself was enveloped in a charged silence. No applause greeted the ends of acts, no bows were taken between scenes, and the intense silence sustained itself right through to the final cur-tain—at which point the audience's explosive ovation rocked the very foundations of the old opera house. There were end-less curtain calls and the spectators refused to leave the the-ater. An exhausted but euphoric Chekhov was helped back to his hospital bed.

After he was discharged from the hospital, Chekhov's life was entirely turned around. He could no longer perform, and was in no condition to shuttle to and from Lithuania. He visit-ed the theater school whenever possible, gave a few odd les-sons, and tried to attend as many meetings and conferences as his health permitted, but they were few and far between. One night, returning from an extended meeting at the theater, he noticed the streets were empty and uncharacteristically quiet. A curious atmosphere hung over the city, one that brought back troubling memories of Moscow in 1917. Suddenly, an army truck roared past carrying a horde of soldiers with rifles on their shoulders. This was followed by a second truck, and a third, then the ominous, all-pervading silence returned. Chekhov hurried back to his apartment.

The next morning he learned that a bloodless revolution

had taken place, but unlike the Bolshevik takeover in 1917, this one had placed a fascist regime in power; a government headed by Karlis Ulmanis. The Latvian parliament had been dissolved and all political opposition banned. Ironically, it was Ulmanis who led the movement against the occupying German forces in 1918 to establish the first independent Latvian republic. Now, sixteen years later, he installed an open dictatorship with himself as leader. Within five years, after the so-called Molotov-Ribbentrop pact between Russia and Germany, Latvia would be handed over to the Soviet Union as one of the Baltic states under its ever-widening sphere of influence. Similar coups had already transformed other Baltic countries such as Lithuania (1926) and Estonia (1934). Five years later, all of Europe and America would be plunged into war.

With Ulmanis' assumption of power, SH's moment had also arrived. Suddenly, the conspiratorial directorial assistant was a man of immense political influence, and in one anonymous editorial after another he agitated for the removal of Chekhov from the now "reformed" country of Latvia. Even the formidable drama critic Janis Karlinch felt the impact of the sudden power shift. His influence evaporated as SH's grew. Chekhov lost his positions at both the theater and the school, and repaired to the countryside where again he took refuge in the writings of Rudolph Steiner. It was as if the iron fist that had caused him to flee Russia in 1928 had stretched out beyond the borders of his homeland to place him, yet again, in its grip.

The flight from Moscow had taken Chekhov westward—first to Berlin, then to France, with a brief detour to the Baltic states. Now he would be pushing even further westward. By the end of 1934, he would be in America, then in England, where despite his failures and the frustrations, one of the most creative and influential phases of his life was about to begin.

FROM
BROADWAY
TO BLIGHTY

Chapter Seventeen

SOL HUROK (née Gurkov, 1888–1974), the international impresario who was responsible for importing the finest specimens of high culture to America—most notably the Ballet Russe de Monte Carlo—was in reality something of an illiterate slob. A short, thick man with pudgy hands, he pronounced "ballet" as "ballot" and always referred to himself in the third person. He started his sentences with "Hurok wants" or "Hurok needs" creating the impression that he was servicing some foreign potentate whose name happened to be Sol Hurok. Like Sam Goldwyn, he often minted epigrams that were nonsensical "If people don't want to come," he once said, "nothing will stop them." Maligning a critic who had given one of his ballet companies a bad review, he exclaimed, "He has a mind like a clap-trap." But it was Hurok that brought the American contralto Marian Anderson back to America from Europe where, under his management, she had her greatest triumph. He also reintroduced Arthur Rubenstein to stateside audiences after a lapse of fourteen years, arranged Jan Peerce's debut recital at Town Hall, and created a concert series at Carnegie Hall that included a groundbreaking appearance by Benny Goodman.

In 1935, Hurok offered Chekhov a tour of the United States at the helm of a company he christened the Moscow Art Players, which he hoped would be mistaken for the Moscow Art Theatre. (In 1923, Hurok's arch rival, Morris Gest, had caused a sensation in New York by presenting Stanislavsky's company to great acclaim.) Chekhov, who together with Georgette Boner was ready for yet another change of direction, rustled together as many worthy Russian émigré actors as they could find in Europe, and the company headed to Broadway.

No sooner had Hurok announced the season than the Soviet government threatened to cancel plans to bring Moscow theater companies to America if the Moscow Art Players were allowed to perform on Broadway. Chekhov, his pessimism recharged, held his breath. Hurok's Slavic ire at the proclamation was aroused and he vigorously proceeded with the announced tour.

The season at the Majestic Theatre opened with *The Inspector General*, with Chekhov reprising Khlestakov; Henning Berger's *The Deluge*, Gogol's *Marriage*; and an *An Evening of Anton Chekhov Sketches*, which, being performed by the great Russian playwright's nephew, gave the evening a firm stamp of legitimacy. Later, the season included Ostrovsky's *Poverty Is No Crime* and two new plays by Soviet playwrights. On the whole, the reviews were rhapsodic, but more important, an excitable buzz began to circulate among the theater community, which occasionally happens in New York and which tends to confer a réclame quite distinct from good notices.

Brooks Atkinson's *New York Times* review began, "Now that Michael Chekhov and P. Pavlov [he played the mayor] are in town, it is possible to understand why Gogol's *Revisor* or *The Inspector General* is considered the funniest prank in the Russian language." (Four seasons earlier, there had been a tepid adaptation directed by Jed Harris, which had raised snickers but no laughter.) "The visiting Russians," Atkinson continued, "who troupe under the somewhat ambiguous trade name of the Moscow Art Players, know how to act this brawl of a satire and buffoonery. They are immensely entertaining. Nothing is much more cheering in this penny-plain world than a band of actors who can fling themselves headlong into

Chekhov, circa 1928,
before emigrating from
Russia.

Xenia Karlovna Ziller,
Chekhov's wife for 37
years.

ABOVE: Chekhov with Beatrice Straight at Dartington. LEFT: Xenia Chekhova before the departure to America. OPPOSITE PAGE: Chekhov at Dartington Hall, circa 1936.

Chekhov with three of his closest friends.

TOP: Chekhov teaching at Dartington. British actor, Paul Rogers behind him by window; Deirdre Hurst du Prey, left of Chekhov; Beatrice Straight, left of du Prey. BOTTOM: Dartington Hall, Devon, in the 1930s when Chekhov first arrived.

Chekhov as Frazier in
The Deluge (1915)
revived on Broadway in
1935.

Chekhov as Khlestakov
in *The Inspector General*
(1921).

Chekhov as the title
character in *Eric XIV*
directed by Vakhtangov
(1921).

Chekhov as Ivan in
*The Death of Ivan the
Terrible* in Riga (1932).

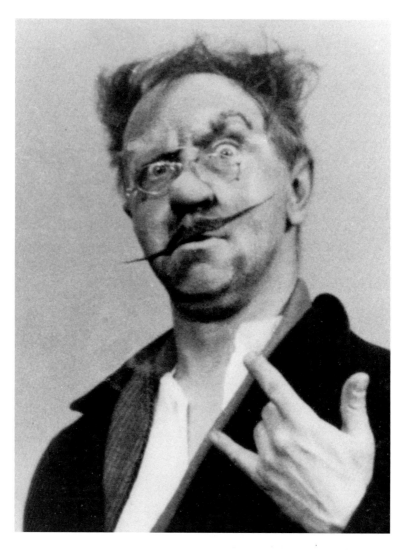

Chekhov in *The Drowned Man* sketch by Anton Chekhov (1935).

Student in *Rendezvous*
sketch by Anton
Chekhov.

Chekhov in the sketch
I Forgot by his uncle
Anton Chekhov
(1942).

Chekhov (right) as Khlestakov in *The Inspector General* at the Majestic
Theatre, Broadway (1935).

TOP: Ridgefield production of *Twelfth Night* directed by Chekhov. Hurd Hatfield, back row far right. Yul Brynner, back row far left. Ford Rainey (bearded) third from left. BOTTOM: Ridgefield production of *King Lear* (1939). Left to right, Mary Haynesworth, Beatrice Straight, Yul Brynner, John Flynn.

Ford Rainey as King Lear, Ridgefield 1939.

The cast of *The Inspector General* (1946) produced by the Actors' Lab at Las Palmas Playhouse, Hollywood California. Morris Carnovsky (center, left of table) played the mayor.

ABOVE: Chekhov in his first Hollywood film, *Song of Russia* (1943)
directed by Gregory Ratoff. Screenwriter Paul Jarrico was later blacklisted.
OPPOSITE PAGE, TOP: Chekhov with Ingrid Bergman in *Spellbound*
directed by Alfred Hitchcock (1945). The film earned him an Academy
Award nomination. OPPOSITE PAGE, BOTTOM:Ida Lupino, Paul Henreid,
and Chekhov in the film *In Our Time* directed by Vincent Sherman (1944).

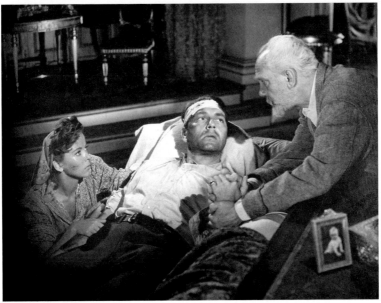

TOP: Judith Anderson and Chekhov in *Specter of the Rose* (1946) written, directed, and produced by Ben Hecht. BOTTOM: Vittorio Gassman, Elizabeth Taylor, and Chekhov in his last film, *Rhapsody* (1954) directed by Charles Vidor.

a whirligig of fooling." Atkinson also gave a graphic account of the look of the show. "Their costumes bulge with merriment," he wrote, "their wigs are fantastic, their stomachs groan with rotundity, and their putty noses and bushy sideburns are ripe for clowning. Having the capacity to play with great gusto, they have built up *The Inspector General* into something extraordinarily hearty by all kinds of extravagant stage business—hysterical heel clicking, frenzied crowd sallies around the stage, pompous military ceremonies, fanfares of the band and cheers from the crowd outside. If this is not the whole gamut of theater, it is certainly theater liberated from bonds of self-consciousness and imitations of life, and it is gloriously refreshing on that account. Every man of intellect knows that the ideal of the theater is a drama entirely populated by low comedians."

The tenor of the notices created a buzz of interest in the visiting Russians, and early ticket sales were brisk. Nothing, not even some qualifying notices, could dampen the furor. The Russians were dispensing wild, anarchic comedy, and it was drawing the town.

Among those who caught the Chekhov productions at the Majestic was Robert Lewis, an alumnus of the Group Theatre who, having proven himself both as an actor and a director, became one of America's most respected acting teachers. On the strength of what he saw that night, he became a great champion of Chekhov. Because of his erudition and background in straightforward Stanislavsky methodology, his first-hand account of the performances in his memoir *Slings and Arrows* is worth quoting in full.

> All eyes were opened to what could, for once, accurately be described as "total" acting. By that I mean each part Chekhov assumed was minutely executed from the point of view of physical characterization—the walk, the gestures, the voice, the makeup—all were meticulously designed to illuminate the character he was playing.
>
> Even more remarkable was that, at the same time, his

emotions were full, all equally chosen and experienced according to the minds and hearts of the personages he acted. Here was the supreme example of the complete "inside" coupled with the complete "outside" each deriving from the other. Never again could one willingly accept the proposition that emotion was all-important and that if one felt truthfully, characterization would take care of itself. Or, conversely, that the delineation of the physical behavior of a part, coupled with intelligible line readings, was satisfactory without the inner life, thought and feelings being experienced by that particular character.

His Khlestakov in the Gogol play was a prime example of total acting. To create the characterization of an arrogant fop, Chekhov, himself a short man, stretched himself taut as he pranced three steps forward and two back. In his hands he held gloves in such a way as to elongate his fingers. All his sounds and movements were musicalized. Yet so forceful was Chekhov's inner momentum in his phantasmogoric drunk scene at the curtain of one act, that we Group actors staggered up the aisles of the theater, having caught his intoxication.

The Deluge by Henning Berger was a sort of morality play, and in it Chekhov demonstrated, in one unforgettable moment, what he called "psychological gesture." The play was set in a bar peopled by a bunch of disreputable characters. Chekhov played an American businessman named Fraser. In the second act, when all the patrons waited, terrified for the approaching waters of a broken dam that would surely wash them all away, Chekhov was sitting at a table with a business colleague he had bilked some time before. In an attempt to purge himself of guilt before dying, Chekhov confessed to the man that the terrible circumstances of life had led him to cheat and that actually he felt only affection for the man personally. As he acted this speech, Chekhov kept digging his hands into the area of the man's heart as though trying to become one with him, creating a powerfully revealing "psychological gesture" of the nature of love.

The evening of Anton Chekhov sketches was a kaleidoscope of fascinating roles, tragic and comic, each one perfect in terms of physical characterization plus internal truth.

The brilliance of the Russian actor's work was not lost on Stella Adler and other senior members of the Group Theatre who were desperately trying to rejuvenate the company after the resignation of Lee Strasberg. Here, many felt, was the perfect solution to the group's aesthetic problem; an actor with a Stanislavsky-based technique who could revitalize a tired, trouble-wracked ensemble.

During the performances of the Moscow Art players, Chekov became the object of a curious kind of rival courtship; the most formidable of these courtiers was Stella Adler, the doyenne of the Group Theatre and wife of Harold Clurman. Both Cheryl Crawford and Lee Strasberg had left the group, and despite the recent success of Clurman's production of Clifford Odets' *Golden Boy*, the company was foundering. Strasberg had been the artistic spine of the company and its revered (occasionally despised) mentor. Now there was a void that needed to be filled. Adler, who had been enthralled by Chekhov's performances and previously alerted to his brilliance by Stanislavsky, with whom she had studied in Paris, saw Chekhov as the man who might revitalize the lagging organization.

Another enthralled spectator in the audience at the Majestic Theatre was Beatrice Straight, the daughter of Dorothy and Leonard Elmhirst, who had been alerted to the Russian's arrival by Edith Isaacs, the editor of *Theatre Arts*. Seeing Chekhov in the Gogol, wrote Straight, "was a pure inspiration, a kind of magical style of acting I had never dreamed could exist, least of all, had ever seen or heard, even if it was in Russian. He was like a dancing light on stage, but completely believable."

Straight was looking for a director to head up the Dartington Hall company her parents had recently established in Devon. The two actresses often found themselves huddled together at the stage door after the performance. "There was Stella Adler," recalled Straight, "a famous actress in her thirties, wrapped in furs and black velvet, and I, who was twenty-one, barely out of school and in my English tweeds. How could I ever persuade [Chekhov] to come up to an unknown island and set up a theater school in an unknown language?" A task made even more difficult by the fact that, at this stage, Chekhov spoke no English, so all conversations had to be relayed through a translator.

In the twenties, Rudolph Steiner had attempted to create a model community along similar lines, gathering together members of the faithful to apply the principles of anthroposophy. He felt, if it was to succeed, it was important for such an experiment to be removed from the hurly-burly of the big cities and allowed to evolve as a self-governing commune in natural surroundings. And, of course, the First Studio of the Moscow Art had a similar arcane origin when it was formed as a subsidiary to the mother company. Both of these facts inclined Chekhov toward the Dartington Hall project. The knowledge that it was to be bankrolled by Dorothy Whitney Elmhirst, one of the wealthiest women in England, no doubt also played a part.

The arrival of the Moscow Art Players was more a *succèss d'estime* than a resounding commercial success. After its initial four-week run, the company toured Philadelphia and Boston, but the language barrier was a serious disincentive to audiences and Hurok probably lost money on the venture. The impresario says virtually nothing about the Chekhov season in his memoirs. But whatever character defects Sol Hurok may have suffered from, he is owed a great debt of gratitude for introducing Chekhov to America. It was from these Broadway productions that the American theater became aware of the genius of Michael Chekhov, and everything that followed in the next decade can be traced back to the impact of that season.

Beatrice Straight's Elmhirst proposal was accepted within weeks of her offering it, and the wheels were put in motion for a theatre studio at Dartington Hall. For the first time in his life, Chekhov was being afforded an opportunity to put his theories into practice with an ensemble of actors of his own choosing on a firm financial basis and, as it turned out, in an idyllic setting.

Chekhov sensed that this was a blessing. But would it, like Germany, like France, like Latvia and Lithuania, also become a curse?

Chapter Eighteen

AS ONE APPROACHES the great stone arch that leads into the Dartington Hall Estate, one is confronted by a great swathe of green, like a verdant tablecloth spread out for a gigantic outdoor feast. On either side of this green square are stone cottages that serve as guest accommodations and, at the far end, an ancient tower house that dates back to the twelfth century.

In 1388, King Richard II granted the site to one of his most loyal followers, John Holand, the Earl of Huntington. Twelve years later, after an unsuccessful rebellion against Henry IV, who one year before had usurped the throne from Richard II, Holand was beheaded by the bailiff of Cirencester and his severed head tossed into a basket.

For the next six centuries, passing through the hands of royalty, clergy, and gentry, Dartington survived a variety of historical changes, most of them bloody. In 1925, Dorothy and Leonard Elmhirst purchased the estate, determined to make it a rural center for arts and crafts in the Devon countryside. It was a social experiment founded on agriculture, forestry, and manufacturing with its own ideological system of education. It rapidly became a nexus of recreational activity.

In the mid thirties, Walter Gropius, founder of the Bauhaus in Germany, was brought to Dartington to redesign parts of the Dartington Hall structures, particularly the Barn Theatre. In 1934, Kurt Joos, the choreographer and ballet director whose ballet *The Green Table* had caused a sensation in Paris, was offered refuge by the Elmhirsts at Dartington. The Nazis had demanded that he purge the Jewish dancers in his company, and Joost had steadfastly refused. Hitler had made it impossible for him to remain in Germany. When Beatrice Straight persuaded Michael Chekhov to found his theatre studio there, Darington was already simmering with musical, dance, and theatrical experimentation. By the time Chekhov had relocated to America, Benjamin Britten and Peter Pears were contemplating turning Dartington into the site for both a music festival and a summer school. The Elmhirsts became a little anxious about the scope of Britten's ambitious plans for creating a home for chamber opera, and eventually Britten himself came to believe Aldeburgh might be a more suitable site for the small-scale musical center he had in mind. Britten and Pears maintained good relations with the Elmhirsts and often returned to Dartington Hall both to visit and to perform. From the moment the Elmhirst family acquired it in 1925, the air of Dartington had been charged with the spirit of artistic enterprise and this was largely due to the drive and personality of Dorothy Whitney Elmhirst.

Dorothy Payne Whitney was the daughter of William C. Whitney, a capitalist buccaneer in the early twentieth century who was instrumental in creating companies such as British American Tobacco and Consolidated Edison. Her early life was dogged by tragedy. Her mother died when she was six years old and her stepmother, with whom she had forged a very close relationship, was killed in a riding accident when Dorothy was twelve.

Dorothy was only sixteen when her father died suddenly. She found herself not only bereft of a father, but left vulnerably independent, the mistress of a great fortune, and obliged to hew out a future entirely on her own. At eighteen, she threw herself into social work, laboring in the slums of New York, where the poverty was insidious and almost irremediable. She worked in settlement houses, in relief work, and in trying to improve the caliber of the inner-city schools. For a time, she was also involved in a children's court. The more she worked with destitute immigrants and families that lived in the grip of crippling poverty, the more she became aware of the underlying social causes behind their plight. She found herself being drawn to feminist issues and became active in the Woman's Trade Union League, the Woman Suffrage Campaign, and the Workers' Education Association. This daughter of one of the wealthiest families in America gradually became radicalized, and her outlook, by her own admission became "more and more left wing."

In 1911 Dorothy married Willard Straight and the newlyweds went off to China to view, the social conditions in that country firsthand. She had three children, Whitney, Beatrice and Michael, but remained actively concerned with international developments and worsening economic changes in America. Together with Willard, she founded two journals, the *New Republic* and *Asia* magazine. When World War I broke out, Willard went immediately into military service. He died of pneumonia in France just as he and Colonel House were preparing the plans for the Peace Delegation. He and Dorothy had been married only eight years.

In 1925, Dorothy remarried, to Leonard K. Elmhirst who, although born to be a typically British "sahib" developed rapidly into an "antisahib." As a young man, he fell heavily under the spell of the Indian poet-philosopher Rabindranath Tagore, from whom he was inspired to create small, self-sufficient communities in India. Elmhirst postulated a fresh and innovative approach to education, declaring, "To release the imagination, to give it wings, to 'open wide the mind's caged door,' this is the most vital service that it is in the power of one human being to render to another." Together with Dorothy, Leonard began implementing his plans for an ideal society in India and it was here that the seeds of the Dartington Hall experiment were sewn.

The period that followed was extremely hard for Dorothy.

"In the intensely emotional, unreasoning, partisan and cruel attitude following the war," she wrote, "I found myself isolated and, had I not held a very strong position, I would have been persecuted by the super-patriots, the strongly entrenched right wing in the U.S. I learned a great deal during those seven years from 1918 to 1925. I knew where I stood, where I belonged, and what I believed in—the importance of the individual, the rights of free speech and a free press, the redistribution of wealth, democratic institutions, tolerance, an interacting spirit, [and] a world brotherhood." The words could be those of a Wobbly or an ardent socialist, yet they were the heartfelt sentiments of the daughter of one of the most privileged families in America.

When Dorothy first met Leonard, it seemed to her that their lives "converged and belonged together." It took a Herculean effort for her to summon up the courage to leave America, but in 1925 the couple relocated to England. "In my small world—in my trivial life," she wrote, "I seem to be following some pattern that I see clearly now in the life of my father. Of course, there are many differences, and mine are small in comparison with his, but certain things were necessary to him and they seem to be necessary to me. His hunger and thirst after beauty brought a balance to his life. For me, it is the same; the arts are essential for any completeness."

Since the age of twenty, Dorothy had harbored a passion for theater. She had never seriously considered yielding to that passion; it seemed somehow trivial compared to the weightier issues that consumed her time and energies. However, after Chekhov had been brought to Dartington and the Theatre Studio was up and running, Dorothy found herself actively drawn into the work. Little by little, her passion became manifest.

"One day I went over as a visitor to his class," she explained. "Several people were sitting with me on the little balcony, and I watched an exercise. Mr. Chekhov was showing the different qualities of emotion in the way we approach someone. He walked across to a student in one tempo, and then in another, taking her hand and saying, 'How are you.' It was a simple exercise, but it was such a revelation to me that I knew I had met the man who was for me, the master. Then Beatrice urged me to join the group for an hour a day. I did with certain misgivings, but soon it was two, three, four, five, six hours a day and even more. I hardly asked myself where I was going; I only knew that the work opened up new vistas of life for me."

Dorothy became a regular member of the Theatre Studio, and when *The Possessed*, a play cobbled together from the works of Dostoyevsky, was being readied for Broadway, Chekhov urged her to be part of the company. Although she accepted his offer, once war was declared in 1939 and life in England became dangerously unpredictable, she felt she had to forsake the production and return to Dartington.

One can only speculate on how skilled an actress Dororthy Elmhirst actually became under Chekhov's tuition, but what is beyond doubt is that exposure to the work of the Theatre Studio added a dramatic dimension to her life that greatly enriched her. Like Chekhov, she was attuned to spiritual qualities, and despite her immersion in thorny social and political issues, she shared her mentor's belief in what she described as "a different sense of time." Chekhov's letters to her are filled with both love and gratitude. He recognized that the Dartington Hall experiment that she made possible enabled him to purge the frustrations of his "wandering years" and put into practice the idealized theater that he had carried inside of himself since forsaking Russia in 1928.

Chapter Nineteen

ALTHOUGH DOROTHY ELMHIRST was the guardian angel of Dartington Hall, it was her daughter Beatrice Whitney Straight who was unquestionably its moving spirit. It was Beatrice who immediately sensed that Chekhov could be the *élan vital* behind the theater studio in Devon, and I believe it was due to her charm and ebullience that Chekhov was persuaded to forsake New York and consider founding a serious theater in the wilds of the English countryside.

Beatrice, born in 1914 in Old Westbury, New York, and transported to England when she was eleven, began her acting career as a teenager at Dartington Hall in the twenties, just as the hall was going through its most experimental gestation period. While still a student, she won great critical acclaim for her performance in Ibsen's *A Doll's House*, and acting quickly became the ruling passion of her life. Once the Chekhov studio was established there, she naturally gravitated to important roles, including Viola in *Twelfth Night* and Goneril in *King Lear*. Her Broadway debut was in 1935 in *Bitter Oleander*, and she went on to a highly respectable, even enviable, career, taking over from Wendy Hiller in the role of Catherine Sloper in *The Heiress* and playing Lady Macduff in Michael Redgrave's *Macbeth*. It was during *The Heiress* that she met and married her co-star, Peter Cookson.

During the war, Beatrice produced, directed, and acted in

a series of radio programs entitled *Report on the Underground*, dramatizations based on confidential information from underground fighters in Nazi-occupied territory, which commanded rapt listeners during the critical months of the European resistance. In 1950, she played the lead in *The Innocents*, based on Henry James' *Turn of the Screw* and produced by Cookson. In 1953, she won a Tony for her portrayal of Elizabeth Proctor in Arthur Miller's *The Crucible*. During those fervid, red-baiting days, because of her involvement in the Miller play she was suspected of Communist sympathies and was in serious danger of being blacklisted. With the aid of highly placed attorneys and the expenditure of a great deal of money, she managed to elude the clutches of the House Un-American Activities Committee and continue working. She segued into film and television and, in 1978, won an Emmy nomination for her role in the miniseries *The Dain Curse*. She also played Lynda Carter's Queen Mother in the seventies' *Wonder Woman* television series. Her most prominent film achievement was probably *Network* in 1976, for which she earned The Academy Award for Best Performance by a Supporting Actress.

Biddy (a childhood nickname that stuck throughout her life) attended some of the most exclusive private schools in the land, but despite her elevated social position was a thorough egalitarian. On tour, she lodged with all the other actresses in the same, often bedraggled, rooming houses. She was always the mother hen of her companies, making sure that cast members got sandwiches and coffee when rehearsals extended far into the night, and always attentive to fellow players' personal problems; a caring and empathetic person who turned newcomers wary of her wealth and status into close friends. "Biddy," as one of her close collaborators put it, disregarding gender, "was always a mensch." Dorothy had brought her up to be morally upright, politically aware, and artistically courageous. She was, for Michael Chekhov, a cheerful kindred spirit, and together they created an atmosphere of aesthetic experimentation that made Dartington Hall unique among theater schools of the thirties.

Several of the first students accepted to the Chekhov Theatre Studio were auditioned in New York by Tamara Daykarhanova, a friend of Chekhov's from Russia and an outstanding drama coach in her own right, but the majority of them were then vetted by Chekhov himself. It was a mixed crew consisting of six Brits, three Canadians, one German, one Welshman, three Americans, two Australians, one Norwegian, two Latvians, and one Lithuanian. Among that first bunch in 1936 there were performers such as Alan Harkness, Blair Cutting, Terence Morgan, Eleanor Faison, John Sheperly, Felicity Cummings, Deirdre Hurst, Paul Rogers, and of course, Beatrice Straight. (Paul Rogers was to become a leading actor in England and a prominent member of the Royal Shakespeare Company.) In the second year, they were joined by Sam Schatz, John Flynn, Mary Haynsworth, Woody Chambliss, Daphne Moore, Erika Kapralik (who later became Mrs. Chambliss), and Hurd Hatfield (whose career never quite recovered from playing the Apollonian lead in *The Portrait of Dorian Gray*).

The regime at Dartington Hall was rigorous, usually lasting ten hours a day. The students were lodged in Redworth House in the town of Totnes, which was only about fifteen minutes from Dartington Hall. (The house itself had been built for Isadora Duncan by one of her affluent lovers who had been a singer, and it was rumored that something of mad Isadora's personality still lingered in the air.) Each morning, a uniformed driver arrived in a station wagon to escort the students up the hill to where the studios and theater were located.

The morning was devoted to work on concentration, imagination, atmosphere, objectives and psychological gesture. Improvisation was ubiquitous and constantly being varied; scenes were often based on short stories by Gogol, Poe, and Anton Chekhov. The ensemble work, weather permitting, would be conducted on the sumptuous outdoor lawns of the

Dartington grounds. There, students were urged to decipher the "gestures" that trees and vegetation were making all around them, that clouds were shaping above them. Films of the students clad in uniform blue leotards, the women in flowing dance skirts, all wearing simple, calfskin sandals, capture the joy and untrammeled liberation these exercises engendered.

The classes dealt with fundamental Chekhovian staples such as the "sense of ease," the "sense of beauty," the "feeling of the whole," and the "feeling of form." Almost all the work was ensemble work—each student intimately interacting with the others to create tableaux, choreograph patterns, or improvise as a group. The assumption behind all these exercises was that everyone was potentially an artist, and the object of their efforts was to reach, mold, and convey the artistic substance of what was hidden deep within their natures. As was customary in England, work stopped sharply at 11:00 a.m. and 4:00 p.m. for tea breaks; an interregnum that Misha enjoyed as much as everyone else.

Chekhov, unlike Strasberg, did not believe in negative criticism. He felt that harsh observations only forced the actor to take refuge in himself and discouraged future creativity. When results came up short, he would find a way of reconsidering a scene, a speech, or an exercise to see if it could be approached by other means. As a result, the group developed an enormous sense of confidence and self-worth. Whether, in the long run, this was the most useful approach to acting training may be disputable. Beyond the confines of Dartington Hall, in the less coddling atmospheres of the real world, there would be critics, directors, and members of the public who would be more judgmental of the trials and errors of neophyte actors.

Like the earliest days of the nascent Group Theatre at the Brookfield Center in Connecticut, Dartington became a crucible in which all the hopes, aims, ideals, and ambitions of a close-knit group of actors were mixed together and vigorously stirred. Spearheaded by Chekhov's idealism, everyone felt that, beyond the routinized, predictable and vulgarized contemporary theater that surrounded them, there was an ideal theatre that could be discovered through hard work, experimentation, and dedication, and the person who believed this most passionately was Chekhov. Searching for values that were richer and more durable than those that had been bequeathed to him both in Russia and the West, Chekhov conducted in-depth investigations of theories, notions, and hunches that had been coagulating in his brain during his days with Vakhtangov and his brief period of experimentation in Latvia. Dartington was the laboratory in which a melee of wild hypotheses could be put to the test in order to finally discover what acting was all about and how it could be conjured up out of the human psyche.

There were experiments with silence, shrieks, tempo, and rhythm. The nature of pauses was assiduously examined. What happens if an actor pauses *before* a speech; what happens if he pauses *afterward*? What kind of inner content must a pause contain if it is not to be simply a stretch of empty silence? When does a facial expression become a grimace? When does a grimace become a mask? When is a mask legitimate? When is it excessive and unnatural? How is "contact" established between actors? Is there a palpable vibration that is sent from one to the other—like a message on a telephone line that can be received and answered? Or is it a quality that grows out of an atmosphere? Out of conscious attention or unconscious intuition? How can one integrate text without losing the personalized color that belongs to actors and that gives text its meaning onstage? Is style something bestowed by the playwright, concocted by the actor, or imposed by the director? When does naturalism become realism and when does expressionism become surrealism, and how does one gauge the steps in between?

These questions are almost never dealt with in conventional theater training programs, and in some countries like England, where the virtues of technique are revered and intellectualism disdained, they are scoffed at and ridiculed. What Chekhov instilled in his actors was an awareness of *potentialities* beyond what were commonly considered acting skills. The irony is that by questing after these potentialities—even if nothing was ever found—conventional skills were strengthened.

Chekhov had set out nine aims for his Theatre Studio. Like many documents of the time, they read like a manifesto for a new utopian order. Briefly, they can be summarized as follows: 1) To probe more deeply into the playwright's work; to go beyond the obviousness of naturalism; 2) To reevaluate the actor's approach to his art and more deeply internalize his technique; 3) To apply the laws of musical composition to productions so as to create the kind of unity one finds in symphonic forms; 4) To encourage the actor to master a series of performance tasks (clowning, fencing, acrobatics, dance, etc.) not usually associated with his conventional skills; 5) To persuade the theater to accept the responsibility of dealing with, and offering solutions to, overwhelming social problems; 6) To lure theater away from "morbid or unbalanced' works and concentrate on "the heroic in performance" rather than the "defeated," and to emphasize "the greatness of the human spirit in its age-long struggle with adversity"; 7) To make humor a key element in all its work; 8) To encourage the acting ensemble, through improvisation and other techniques, to develop the means to create its own plays; 9) To coalesce the established relationship between the actor and the audience so as to concentrate on those problems that were common to both.

A cursory glance at these aims reveals that, in many instances, they contain the same kind of precepts that influenced Sulherzhitsky and Vakhtangov in the First Studio, not to mention the master plan drafted by Stanislavsky and Nemorivich-Danchenko for the original Moscow Art Theatre. The fact is the mission statements and credos of almost every new theater tend to sound like every other. There is a great deal of unanimity about the theater's major artistic and social objectives. How, and by whom, they get applied makes all the difference.

A good deal of time at Dartington was spent on fairy tales, which was a way of coming into contact with archetypes and also a way of finding a path away from naturalism. Fairy tales remained for Chekhov an indispensable tool for developing the sense of child's play that he felt was at the root of all acting. He had begun this work with Georgette Boner during his sojourn in Paris, but at Dartington it grew considerably, even to the extent of creating a fairy tale "committee" that tabulated every fairy tale they could find and then categorizing them according to subject matter. Ultimately, he hoped to create a fairytale company that would play exclusively for children, although he felt the advantages that would accrue to actors would be equally as great.

Throughout, intellectual analysis was consistently discouraged. When an actor began to articulate a concept, Chekhov would say, "Show me, don't tell me!" (An odd contradiction in a man who was steeped in dialectics and immersed in philosophy.) He was also opposed to demonstrating effects to actors. When asked to show what he meant, he would insist, "I do not demonstrate; you must find your own version of these things." No doubt, the memory of Stanislavsky's demonstrations—with exact inflections and mimicked gestures—was still fresh in his mind.

Besides acting, there were classes in dance conducted by Lisa Ullman, a member of Kurt Joos's ballet company, and lessons in which painting and music were creatively intertwined, which were given by the notable American painter, Mark Tobey. The relationship between terpsichore and fine art was regularly inculcated, and actors were made to feel that all the arts conjoined in acting and could foster one another. Chekhov's own preoccupations with painting and caricature remained with him throughout his life, and were particularly productive during the Dartington period, when all of his creative faculties were most stimulated.

The physical training was always *psycho*physical; using the body to find and express movements that originated from within. "We try to develop this ability to have our psychology as bodily expression," Chekhov wrote, "and to have bodily expression as our psychology—so that these two waves—bodily and psychological waves—will merge together and become one." He encouraged his students to ask how, not what. Straightforward calisthenics or repetitive physical exercises were almost never employed. If the body was not linked to the psyche, there was nothing for it to do. Chekhov was not concerned with simply building muscles or performing aerobics. The Steiner approach to eurhythmics was regularly utilized, as was Steiner's theories on speech. (No apparent reference was made to Emile Jacques-Dalcroze, who actually invented eurhythmics in 1897. The difference seemed to be that Dalcroze's aim was simply a performer's kinaesthetic response to rhythm, whereas in Steiner's case, eurhythmy is an attempt "to make music and/or speech visible to an audience through movement.") Alice Crowther, the studio's speech teacher, fostered the notion of diaphragmatic breathing, instilling the idea that breath was not there to be conserved but expelled; that breath came to the actor of its own accord; that the *in-breath* of intention would constantly renew itself once the *out-breath* found its true purpose.

In those heady Dartington days, acting was practiced as a science, esteemed as an art and revered as a creed.

Chapter Twenty

WHEN THE CHEKHOV STUDIO THEATRE began its work at Dartington, Chekhov knew that before long he would have to obtain plays for the company to perform. Rather than rely on established works, he believed he could persuade certain notable writers to join the company and take part in fruitful collaborations between actors and playwrights. The play would, in a sense, be evoked by the inventions of his actors, altering and integrating their work with that of the playwright's. At the end of the process, the ensemble, rather than a single detached writer, would be responsible for the final product. It is an idea that has been tried before but never with outstanding success. The ensemble might enjoy shaping and influencing the arc of the material at hand, but the playwright was far less inclined to cede final authority to actors and directors, no matter how gifted, which might veer away from his original vision.

Naively, Chekhov wrote to several leading playwrights proposing that they provide root material that would then be collectively developed. R.C. Sheriff, whose *Journey's End* had been a great success when produced by a theatrical partnership spearheaded by Dorothy Elmhirst, expressed initial interest, but ultimately declined. T.S. Eliot, according to his secretary Anne Bradley, was "pleased and honored" by the suggestion, but "regretted that he is not free to consider anything of the kind as he is under contract with Mr. Ashley Dukes for any plays that he may write."

James Bridie, the Scottish playwright whose works include A *Sleeping Clergyman, Tobias and the Angel, Mr Bolfry* and *Daphne Laureola*, was more forthright. "The idea of building up a play bit by bit in the workshop over two or three years," he wrote "is of course, fascinating, but I foresee friction, saturation, rivalry, and in my own case exhaustion long before the finish. I have not met Chekhov but he must have sublime gifts of tact and masterfulness if he is going to achieve something coherent with a dramatist who will not be content to regard his as the final word. He must catch a young and humble writer who has not grown arrogant and obese and avaricious."

The unflappable Dorothy Elmhirst took this rejection letter as a tentative foot-in-the-door and followed it with another, urging Bridie seriously to reconsider the suggestion. He replied, "To begin with, the dramatist must be the boss. The present lamentable state of the arts is due to their forgetfulness that they are the handmaidens of the Muses. They dress up in their mistresses' clothes and are surprised that nobody takes them for ladies." But despite a certain wariness about concocting a "synthetic" play, Bridie had a notion of "what it might and ought to be if it takes a dramatic form" and ended by saying he would "like to have a talk with Chekhov about it."

Despite Dorothy's persistence, nothing ever came of her suggestion. Playwrights, no matter what degree of eminence, found it hard to relinquish the sacred act of personal authorship. As it turned out, it was the "good lieutenant" George Shdanoff who cobbled together an adaptation of Dostoyevsky's *The Possessed* for the company, and no new playwright ever emerged from the work of the Chekhov Studio.

One has to note in passing that the two writers most closely associated with a permanent ensemble, Anton Chekhov at the Moscow Art and Clifford Odets at the Group Theatre, created their plays in the unassailable ivory towers of their own imagination and then passed them down to the dutiful directors and actors who proceeded to realize those plays in the customary way. Neither is there any evidence that Burbage, Kemp, or Condell ever assisted Shakespeare in any of *his* literary endeavors—although I'm sure he appreciated the natural chemistry that made the Lord Chamberlain's Men so well suited for interpreting his work. A worthier goal, it would seem to me, would have been to create an ensemble intelligence so dramaturgically sensitive that playwrights could be eliminated entirely—along the lines of The Living Theatre and Theatre du Complicitè. But in the hamstrung thirties, it was highly courageous of Chekhov to give joint ownership a try.

At the beginning, Chekhov firmly believed that the work with his Dartington group could be transferred to London; a city which, in the thirties, was culturally undernourished. In contemplating professional West End productions of the Chekhov Studio Theatre, Beatrice Straight wrote to Hugh "Binkie" Beaumont, head of H.M. Tennent, then the leading commercial producer in England, feeling him out on Chekhov's idea for an extended rehearsal period of two or three months to perfect the production. Mentally, Chekhov was still in the world of the Moscow Art Theatre where for example, Stanislavsky had once rehearsed a play for eleven months and then, deciding it was not stageworthy, simply canceled the entire project. "No actor of his acquaintance," wrote Beatrice to her mother, conveying the gist of Beaumont's reply, "would be willing to entertain the idea of rehearsing more than four or five weeks. An approach such as Misha's has never occurred to them, and they would regard it as fantastic." Day by day, Chekhov was learning that theater in the West was a very different creature than it was in the heyday of the Russian Revolution when heterodoxy was the rule and the wilder the experiment, the more it was appreciated by the proletarian public.

● ● ● ● ●

For some time, Chekhov and Shdanoff had been brainstorming a version of Dostoyevsky's *The Possessed* that would incorporate excerpts from other Dostoyevskian novels. The international malaise in the mid-thirties, it seemed to Chekhov, was spiritual in nature. The world had lost its faith, and in its place, the Soviets had offered dialectical materialism that was enervating an entire population. For Chekhov, Dostoyevsky's work, and particularly *The Possessed*, contained a message worth disseminating as much in the West as in the USSR. He actively began improvisations and scene work based on the material Shdanoff had begun assembling from the great Russian writer's work. The Dartington Hall actors immediately immersed themselves in recent Soviet history. Chekhov drew on his most personal and traumatic experiences in fleshing out the background of the world the company was to create. Beatrice Straight and her mother, Dorothy, were mustered into the project and sopped it up wholeheartedly.

But two years into the first term's work, the situation in Europe had become so turbulent that the Elmhirsts and Chekhov himself had begun to consider a move out of Devon and into the safer confines of the United States. In 1938, Beatrice traveled to America to scout out a new location for the studio. After several fruitless quests, she came across a large, disused schoolhouse four miles from Ridgefield, Connecticut, which she felt could be converted into a comfortable new home for the company. The site spread over 150 acres of land, with enough buildings to accommodate large studios, a library, recreation rooms, dormitories, and a theater. The rural setting was reminiscent of Dartington, and its close proximity to New York—only 55 miles away—was a strong incentive. Letters between Dorothy and Biddy flew between England and America, and it was quickly decided that the premises should be purchased and renovated, and the entire operation transported to Ridgefield.

It was something of a hurried decision, but one that political neccesities forced upon them. Chekhov mustered an enthusiasm for the move, feeling that in many ways America offered far greater opportunities for the acting company, specifically those students who had graduated into the last phase of their training and were ready to play professionally. Biddy, characteristically, was optimistic about the new start. Xenia, on the other hand, who was just beginning to assimilate life in Devon, was flustered by the prospect of leaving Europe altogether to reassimilate in yet another new land. Some part of her always believed that, despite everything, there would be a return to Russia. Many of the students, particularly the English ones, felt that such a move represented a retreat from their threatened homeland and refused to go. Dorothy was very much of two minds about the move in regard to herself. She had been happily rehearsing the role of Nicholas Stavrogin's mother in *The Possessed*, which Chekhov was anxious for her to play, but the idea of abandoning Dartington when the future of both England and the estate itself seemed so precarious, weighed heavily on her. Ultimately, and much to Chekhov's chagrin, she decided she had to stay on in Devon and hold down the fort.

On the brink of their departure in November 1938, the students and teachers prepared a farewell performance at Dartington's Barn Theatre. Students mounted three scenes from Gorky's *The Lower Depths*, Hurd Hatfield played a short sketch entitled *The Old Jew*, and Dorothy Elmhirst performed Ase's death scene from *Peer Gynt*. It was a bittersweet end to a venture that had begun only three years before with such heady exhilaration. On December 17, Dorothy wrote, "Beloved Misha and Xenia: You have opened a new life for me that neither time nor separation can destroy. My heart is too full of gratitude to speak. Nothing can diminish the power of love I feel for you. Life is forever different because you came."

Chekhov always regarded the move to Connecticut as simply a temporary change of plan and had coolly announced that the company would eventually return to England after hostilities ceased. But many died in the war, and the lives of many others were so radically transformed by the conflict that they wandered off into different directions. Chekhov, who had become accustomed to false starts, refused to believe that this, the fulfillment of his life's greatest ambition, would not reincarnate on foreign soil and ultimately realize itself.

He had to believe that. He couldn't go on if he didn't.

Chapter Twenty-One

THE RIDGEFIELD THEATRE was officially launched in December of 1938. New members (among them Yul Brynner) were brought in to replace those that had not made it to Connecticut, and they were integrated with the more experienced students who had undergone the studio's work in England. Unlike the ambitious nine points, which had preceded Dartington Hall, Chekhov framed four rather modest aims for the new theater in America:

1. To apply a method of training that will develop emotional flexibility and body technique.
2. To develop a technique for the approach to the form and construction of plays.
3. To give the actor a practical opportunity to enrich his abilities through a knowledge of the methods and problems of the director.
4. At the end of this training period, to form a professional company.

At Dartington, a number of trustees in conjunction with the Elmhirsts footed all the bills, so Chekhov was subject to no great economic pressure. This was no longer the case at Ridgefield. The bulk of the financing would come from student fees ($1,200 per year), and, it being a new set of premises, those costs became considerable.

The other major difference had to do with expectations. At

Dartington, there was unlimited time to workshop plays through experimentation and improvisation. It had been an hermetically sealed community, literally in a world of its own. But at Ridgefeld, there would be preparations for a forthcoming Broadway production of *The Possessed*, and so time had to be more strictly allotted and objectives more clearly focused. Underlying all these new drives was the hope—and it became more and more pressing—that the forthcoming production would generate revenue to help sustain the work of the new studio. Many of the studio's highly touted staples, such as fencing, clowning, choral singing and dance, had to go by the board. The aim now was to concentrate efforts on the play that would eventually open in New York. To streamline efforts at Ridgefield, several of the senior members of the studio, most notably Beatrice Straight, Deirdre Hurst du Prey, and Blair Cutting, began teaching the incoming students what they had been taught by Chekhov. They were issued certificates recognizing them as official teachers of the Chekhov technique. (This was, in fact, the beginning of the Chekhov Industry, and today, there are official and unofficial Chekhovians scattered throughout the world.)

In 1939, a new producing company called Chekhov Studio Theatre Productions was formed that would act as the impresario for the company's future offerings in New York. The immediate plan was to open *The Possessed* in the fall, and shortly afterward, to follow with a version of Charles Dickens' *Pickwick Papers* entitled *Adventures of Samuel Pickwick*. The Lyceum Theatre was quickly booked for the first production. For Chekhov, this was a "consummation devoutly to be wished": a company he had selected and trained, a project derived from Russian masterpieces such as *Crime and Punishment*, *The Idiot*, and *The Possessed*, an adaptor/collaborator with whom he had worked for more than a decade, and a play that, it seemed to him, dealt directly with the madness that was rapidly overcoming Europe, and was uppermost in the minds of every thinking person both in America and England.

On October 24, there was a distinct buzz in the air as a throng of glitttering first-nighters, many of them drawn from the ranks of the Four Hundred, settled into their seats at the Lyceum Theatre in New York.

Chapter Twenty-Two

"THE POSSESSED" had a devastating effect—not only on the audience and critics who saw it, but on Chekhov himself who was fairly poleaxed by its reception. The *Daily Worker*, the Communist paper that one might have expected to be sympathetic to a Russian-orientated company dealing with the works of Dostoyevsky, was particularly scathing. Clearly, word of Chekhov's low standing with the Soviets had preceded him to New York.

"Exactly what transpires in the mind of a man of the theater who twists life to suit his own conclusions is revealed at the Lyceum Theatre this week, where Michael Chekhov, nephew of the great Anton, does things to Dostoyevsky," wrote the *Daily Worker* critic identified only as G.B. "To most of the audience, the big event of the premiere was the appearance of Beatrice Straight in a leading role. Miss Straight has, among other things, plenty of Whitney millions, for she is the daughter of Dorothy Whitney, and thus the Lyceum was cluttered with Vanderbilts, Cuttings, Van Volkenburgs, and sundry princes and princesses of White Guard persuasion." The anonymous critic proceeds to annihilate the political implications of Shdanoff's free adaptation but cannot resist returning ambivalently to Mrs. Whitney's wealthy daughter. "...The play is really an awful bore. Except when Miss Straight is on the stage. It is impossible to believe that anyone so beautiful could be so rich. It just isn't fair to all the poor little actresses of Broadway. If Miss Straight were a homely person who had to buy her way on the stage—that would at least be in keeping with the fiction. But this gal with a lovely voice ought to get out from under the weight of turgid, czarist, decomposed corpses and go on the stage."

Miss Hope Hampton (either with or without her jewelry in tow, it is not made clear) was heard to comment to her escort Monsieur Brulatour: "Cette piece est sombre, n'est ce pas?" To which John Mason Brown, who overheard the remark, wrote: "It was impossible not to see Miss Hampton's point." Walter Winchell, then a reviewer for the *Daily Mirror,* admitted that he "fled after the first act" and concluded: "The sets and costumes, routine matters, are by M. Dobujinsky. *The Possessed,* it is safe to wager, will be among the 'dispossessed' almost immediately, so tedious is it."

The unkindest cut of all was probably the notice in the *New York Times* by Brooks Atkinson, who three years before had led the cheering section for the Moscow Art Players. "In the last act of *The Possessed*...a saintly philosopher declares that a wave of triumphant laughter roaring around the world will destroy tyranny and despotism. Probably a wave of laughter going around this town might have a salutary effect on the people involved in this fiercely stylized production....It is played under the direction of Michael Chekhov, one-time member of the Moscow Art Theatre, by students in his school and company. Excepting one brilliant mob scene representing a revolutionary meeting, it comes close to being a travesty on the humorless manners of the Russian intelligentsia. Excepting that one scene, it conveys none of the spontaneity of a work of art...What despotic dictatorship has done toward destroying the spirit of human beings in Russia, Mr. Chekhov has done to his actors here. Ironically enough, he has done it in a play that pleads the cause of the free man."

The most thoughtful and balanced review came from the aforementioned John Mason Brown, who wrote: "Ultimately,

The Possessed turns out to be elementary enough. In fact, its final point as to the choice faced between Christ or a man-god created by the destructive forces of mob worship is so simple that the only wonder is that it should ever take so long to make....The plea for moral rearmament comes much too late. Before that, the powers of darkness reign, the script wanders in and out of revolutionary meetings showing, in highly debatable and grotesque terms, how those interested in destruction are finally possessed by the forces of destruction. What is offered in the place of immediate comprehension is a play frightened by a macabre ballet that deals in baffling and pretentious terms with temptation, wickedness, the lust for power, misery, murder, indecision, and revolutionary organizations in czarist Russia. Suddenly, the midnight sun appears, and the light it casts very briefly makes you feel as if, after a very bad dream, you had been awakened to be told that two and two makes four. For suddenly *The Possessed* begins to preach, and preach not only with a pointer in hand but with the aid of some contemporary overtones that ought to add to its interests, even if they do not."

Although Chekhov and Shdanoff had to bear the lion's share of the blame for this failure, I suspect the real villain here is Rudolph Steiner, whose simplistic notion of a Christian brotherhood and redemption through Christ runs pulsatingly beneath the Dostoyevsky material and, more likely than not, was what inspired Misha to offer it to the world.

The company had worked long and hard on *The Possessed*, and the demoralization was felt all round. In a letter he wrote soon after the debacle, Chekhov poured his heart out to Dorothy: "I know I promised to write you, dear Dorothy, after the performance, but I could not and can't. The things have turned so unexpectedly in *every* way that I am crushed and depressed indeed! I was prepared for the worst but not for the plain, banal, huge, shameless dishonesty that above all became terribly contagious! I am helpless, like a beaten dog. If you would be here, Dorothy, you would not speak about style, translation, etc. You would see it from the other point of view and first of all would see what sort of plays have success on Broadway. You would understand where the real cause lies. But all these things here are insignificant and everyone gets what he deserves."

The note of self-pity is uncharacteristic of Chekhov, who over the years had learned to roll with the punches, but *The Possessed* represented the fruits of two years at Dartington Hall, the first sampling of the theories and practices he had instilled into the fledgling company that, like its director, had become attuned to theater as a higher calling that dealt with significant themes. Clearly, Chekhov's sensibility was not attuned to the Broadway ethic. When critics like Sidney Whipple in the *New York World Telegram* can compare Verkhovenski's "checked box coat and small brown derby" to comedian Bobby Clark, it should have been clear that Broadway's frame of reference was a million light years away from Dostoyevsky. It is not that *The Possessed* was misunderstood; it wasn't. It probably *was* mawkish, preachy, and dramatically overheated by a relatively young, inexperienced cast, and as intolerable as the reviewers declared it to be. But part of its failure was due to the fact it was being foisted in a context where frivolity, amusement and escapism were at a premium. In 1939, one month after Europe exploded into World War II, the last thing a Broadway audience was prepared for was a treatise on the triumph of spirituality over power politics. Chekhov's other miscalculation was to believe that a company of young, inexperienced actors could hold their own in the cut-and-thrust world of Broadway, which, whatever its vices, was the mecca of professionalism. I doubt that the reaction to *The Possessed* was dishonest, as Chekhov claimed. If anything, it was an aggressively honest reaction by hard-bitten New York theatergoers who resented being preached to or fobbed off with serious intentions projected by an unseasoned company of relative newcomers. In the USSR, of course, the Dostoyevskian credo and political discourse would have been understood and probably cheered. But then, in a nation in the stranglehold of Stalin's totalitarianism, it would never have been produced.

Ford Rainey, an experienced and highly self-contained actor, had joined the company in 1939. He was subsequently to tour in two of its Shakespeare productions. Some time after his period with the Chekhov troupe, he wrote a reminiscence of his tenure there, and as it is a firsthand glimpse of the Ridgefield period from someone intimately connected to it, I quote some of its more salient sections.

> When the Chekhov Studio came to New York from England, I auditioned for Michael Chekhov on the stage of the Lyceum theater…I started out with a bravura soliloquy from Lynn Rigg's *Roadside*. After about two lines of this and before I could really get into it, Mr. Chekhov said, "Well, enough of that! What else have you to offer?" Thrown for a loop, I began one of Orlando's speeches from *As You Like It*. I went up on my lines and was allowed to struggle on through the whole painful speech. I've forgotten what else I did, or was allowed to do, but I walked out [of] the audition kicking myself around several blocks. It was no·comfort when I later learned that Gregory Peck had been turned down too, and that they were looking for "special qualities."

Rainey was given a walk-on part in the mob scenes of *The Possessed*, and, he said, he "was very impressed with the acting of most of the members of the group, but appalled by the acting of some others. Privately, Biddy, and Ronald Bennett in particular—and what ever became of him I wonder?" Rainey was then asked by Chekhov to double with John Flynn in a forthcoming production of *King Lear* and to understudy Woody Chambliss as Sir Toby Belch in *Twelfth Night*. When Chambliss left the studio to follow his wife Erika to Hollywood, Rainey automatically inherited the role.

Writes Rainey:

> Early on, after one of our private workouts on *Lear* in a
> scene in which Mary Lou Taylor was playing Cordelia,
> Mr. Chekhov asked Mary Lou if I liked him or not. He
> said that when a director worked with an actor as closely
> as we were working on *Lear*, it was like a father-son rela-
> tionship. I assured Mr. Chekhov, by way of Mary Lou,
> that I loved working with him and appreciated the oppor-
> tunity to work on such a great role under his guidance,
> and that I certainly had a great affection for him. I did
> and do, but I think what he felt was that I was still my own
> man. I believe one of the great pitfalls at the studio was a
> blind worship of Michael Chekhov.... Each actor has to
> create and form his own method from what he has drawn
> on before and based on the material at hand. Just as
> Stanislavsky and Michael Chekhov kept moving ahead,
> changing and reformulating their methods, so each per-
> son must move ahead. It must never become dogma.

At the Los Angeles Theatre Center, I had the opportunity to
direct Rainey in both an Ibsen and a Shakespeare. He is a talented, self-possessed actor and, in his nineties, still very much
his own man. It is interesting that he was the only member of
the original Ridgefield troupe who ever expressed any frank
criticism of Chekhov. The problem of becoming enveloped by
a charismatic teacher to the exclusion of objectivity and personal discrimination is one that besets many teacher-student relationships. It had serious consequences for Lee Strasberg and
Jerzy Grotowsky, both of whom acquired guru status with
many of their disciples. Rainey's cool-headed attitude to acting
tuition is both refreshing and admirable. Interestingly, he also
suggested another reason for the failure of *The Possessed* in
New York. "The critics were ready to kill before each production of the studio because the publicity was so bombastic. *They*
were going to show America how it should be done. There was

nothing subtle or humble in the publicity, and people resented that. There was always this attitude of "we are going to show you great acting."

It was during the preparations for the Rainey *King Lear* that everyone at Ridgefield suddenly had a terrible fright

● ● ● ● ●

Chekhov was always highly impressionable in regard to women. "From my earliest years," he admits "I was constantly falling in love. The very first time I would meet a girl, regardless of her appearance, I would firmly resolve to marry her. I know that I loved deeply, for my whole life. Girls with snub noses, girls with freckles, with braids, each and every girl whom fate sent my way, fled from my declarations of love and from my proposals for a speedy wedding." This helplessness before the fairer sex never entirely left him, and in Ridgefield, it reached critical proportions.

In Dartington he had been enamored with Erika Kapralik, a Viennese actress who had auditioned for the school in German, despite the fact that Chekhov frowned upon accepting students with foreign accents. Erika was a young, powerful actress who, unlike many of the American or British students, was capable of playing in an "epic" style. During the audition, as she was crouching on the stage floor performing her speech, Misha bent over and looked into her face and she instinctively drew him into the scene. That was probably the moment he got hooked. She was immediately accepted and from then on, Misha showered fulsome compliments on her that produced a certain amount of squirmy embarrassment among the others in the class. As the term progressed, his further attentions were tactfully rebuffed by Erika.

She was followed by an actress named Tammy Faulkner, with whom Chekhov also became besotted, praising her beyond her merits and again causing gossip and discomfort in the company. Despite the fact that she was a first-year student

and normally not eligible for roles in the company's more professional productions, he seriously considered casting her in a
lead role in *The Possessed*. As there was little reciprocation, the
infatuation soon faded.

But these were puppy loves compared to what he felt for
Margaret Draper, a short, plump girl who joined the company
in Ridgefield. This was an infatuation that turned into an
obsession. Like the others, it began simply as a flirtation, but
perhaps because it was subtly encouraged, grew exponentially
from day to day. Chekhov cast her as Maria in the forthcoming
production of *Twelfth Night* saying she was the only woman in
the company who could possibly do justice to the role. This,
despite the fact that other, more experienced actresses were
already being considered for the part. Chekhov's loss of equilib-
rium in regard to Draper was noticed by all, including Beatrice
Straight, who, playing Viola and being in a senior position
with the company, began worrying about its effect on the general morale. She also knew that Chekhov was about to start
rehearsals for a difficult production of *King Lear* with Ford
Rainey in the lead role, which was to go on an extended tour
through southern and midwestern states.

One night, well past midnight, when everyone was in bed,
Chekhov was seen standing under Draper's window in a
bathrobe and slippers and it was felt by many that this time
Misha's romantic fancies were going too far. A few embarrassing skirmishes had already taken place during rehearsals, and
as a result, the ruling came down from above that Draper was
forbidden to have any personal contact with Chekhov. But one
night, Xenia, following up a rumor spread by a gossipy student,
went up to Maplewood Hall, where the members of the company were housed, and discovered Misha in Draper's room.
The tirade against her husband reverberated through all the
corridors of the house, causing doors to fly open on every side.
Words like "harlot" "whore" and "slut" were interspersed with
untranslatable Russian invective. The racket brought many of
the students out into the corridor, and, escaping from the wild

Xenia, Misha fled into Mary Haynsworth's room at the end of the hall. There, according to Haynsworth, "he promptly lay down on the bed and had a real—or fake—heart attack—it was hard to tell which—while Xenia stood over him screaming 'Go ahead, die, die!!'—It was quite a scene."

Misha recovered quickly, suggesting the "attack" was feigned rather than real. The gossip took a few days to die down, but gradually, the crisis subsided.

King Lear and Don Quixote were the two roles Chekhov most wanted to play. He had been cogitating Lear for many years and was full of mystical and fanciful ideas about Shakespeare's tragic monarch. For Ford Rainey, it was a plum part for a young man who had just completed his tuition at Dartington and was looking forward to cutting his teeth on real audiences.

The rehearsals for *Lear* had gone on for only a week or so when Misha disappeared. One day he simply did not appear at rehearsals and was nowhere to be found. It turned out he had holed himself up in the "Babushka," a retreat in upper New York state that belonged to Eugene Somoff, his Russian administrator at Ridgefield. The *Lear* company was sorely distressed and Shdanoff was shocked and depressed by the news. When Misha's whereabouts became known, Rainey and Hurd Hatfield sought him out in the rustic lodge to discover why he had abandoned the production. It became clear that Chekhov's withdrawal was the result of a traumatic rebuff he had received from Draper. They tried desperately to persuade him to return. "It doesn't depend on me," Misha told them petulantly. "It depends on *her*."

Hatfield and Rainey met with Draper to see if she could resolve the crisis, but, unaware of how deeply Chekhov's feelings ran, she was simply bewildered by the turn of events. Back in Ridgefield, it became clear that if the company's commitments were to be honored, Misha had to be replaced. Alan Harkness, who was playing the relatively small role of Duke of Albany in the production and who had been a valued acting instructor at Ridgefield, was called, drafted into service as director and rehearsals were reconvened. Beatrice Straight gently but firmly asked Draper to leave the company. Rainey adjusted to the fact that the elaborate *regie* that Misha had discussed with him would have to be abandoned, and Harkness' more practical approach substituted; an alternative which, given Rainey's harried state of mind, was in many ways preferable.

On the day *King Lear* was scheduled to open in Albany Chekhov appeared at the theater, commandeered the rehearsal, and in Rainey's words, "tried in one day to coach me into his conception of the character of King Lear. I was, of course, totally flummoxed."

As it turned out, *King Lear*, in tandem with *The Cricket on the Hearth*, enjoyed a healthy tour but for some, Chekhov's juvenile disintegration in the face of a failed romantic imbroglio shook confidence in their director. Xenia, understanding Chekhov's volatile character, was, to her credit, more forgiving than others, and in time the incident blew over. Many years later, when Rainey suddenly appeared at one of Chekhov's classes in Hollywood and explored the possibility of reviving *Lear*, it couldn't help but bring back sour memories of the Draper affair.

Chapter Twenty-Three

UNDAUNTED BY THE POOR RECEPTION for *The Possessed*, Ridgefield soldiered on, somewhat shaken but still determined to realize its high aims. *The Adventures of Samuel Pickwick* was summarily canceled, and Chekhov now concentrated his energies on preparing a professional company tour of *Twelfth Night* and another Dickens adaptation, *The Cricket on the Hearth* (which he had played successfully in 1914 with the First Studio). The plan was to book the shows in university theaters along the East Coast. These performances proved to be an unqualified success, with good houses and excellent notices at virtually every site.

Misha wrote to Dorothy from Ridgefield on October 25, 1940:

> It seems to me that our star begins to rise upon the horizon. The *Twelfth Night* and *Cricket* (especially *Twelfth Night*) performances had real and true success among a most varied audience. Each time when I attended the performance, which I did constantly up until now, I was full of doubt and fear and suspicion of not being able to eliminate entirely the experience on Broadway, but each time the audience itself awakened me from my heavy dreams, and through the audience rather than my own desire, I enjoyed the success quite objectively. The expe-

rience with these two productions, and your kind cable, encouraged me to a great extent, and I never doubted that sooner or later we would appeal to the audience. I feel myself now so free, so happy and so willing to go on creating with our group that I even dare to think of acting *King Lear* myself, if my struggle with the English language will be finally successful.

Chekhov was now bursting with ideas for new projects, which he poured out in letters to Dorothy. These included: "A play about Don Quixote where the background will be that of the Spanish Inquisition." And a play about Francis of Assisi, "where in Italy, certain parts were overwhelmed by the Germanic people and the Italians tried to resist them." He felt so strongly about the St. Francis project that he asked Iris Tree, daughter of Sir Beerbohm Tree and a member of the Ridgefield troupe, to begin hammering out a script.

He was gradually becoming aware of Beatrice Straight's extraordinary development—both as an actress and a person. "My impression is more and more that her angel is near to her, not only in art but in life. One could not radiate as strongly as she does, one could not have such a strange and mercurial personal destiny if one was not ready for it; if the angel did not lead her, as if hastily, to a certain definite aim. One couldn't bring so near to each other the life and the art as Biddy does if there were no close guidance from above. In our conception of the theater, we have to find the connection between the life and the art, and that is what I see arising in Biddy."

Dorothy had no problem identifying the seraphim that Chekhov described. By then, she was as metaphysically tuned in as her mentor, but an unshakeable practicality tended to guide her day-to-day decisions. Chekhov continued to urge her to come to Ridgefield, join the company, and fulfill the promise she had shown at Dartington, but in England the war was growing grimmer each day, with Churchill desperately trying to coax Roosevelt into an Anglo-American alliance against

Hitler. Although *Lear* would soon join the repertory, it was Ford Rainey, and not Chekhov, who would play the king.

Emboldened by their success on the tour, and particularly with the audience reaction to the Shakespearean comedy, Chekhov decided to try Broadway again.

The Chekhov Theatre Studio's production of *Twelfth Night*, directed jointly by Chekhov and Shdanoff, which opened at the Little Theatre on Broadway in July of 1940, did not duplicate the success of the Hurok season, nor did it resemble the calamity of *The Possessed*. The reviews were, on the whole, respectable, but devoid of the heady euphoria that greeted the Moscow Art Players five years before. Sam Schatz, who played Malvolio, was considered "amusing" although the more discriminating theatergoers silently wondered what Chekhov himself might have made of the role. Beatrice Straight was a "lovely and youthful" Viola, Hurd Hatfield, "a comical" Sir Andrew Aguecheek and Yul Brynner's perform-ance was described by George Freedley as "effective and funny" which must have buoyed the spirits of the future King of Siam in this, his first stage role in New York.

Freedley's review danced gingerly around the show. "There is much that is good," he wrote, "and much that is bad about it all...The production moves smoothly, but the mechanics of the play seldom have seemed more creaky." The actors were referred to as "talented amateurs" who "seem more like stu-dents undertaking a task with hope and enthusiasm than actors playing their part." But, in the best critical tradition of blowing hot and cold, Freedley continued: "Yet at the same time, there is a fresh approach to playing that is both amusing and heart-ening. It is a confusing presentation that has a good deal to offer those who are interested in modern Shakespeare revivals," which clearly Mr. Freedley wasn't.

Richard Watts Jr., whose reviews also tended to shuttle between sweet and sour, didn't mince his words. "The almost inescapable fact about *Twelfth Night*," he wrote, "is that its fes-tive antics have become unbearably tedious to most of us, but that a certain dewy, youthful charm that sings gracefully of the morning of the world clings to it and gives it its surviving value of beauty and sweetness. When a production forgets the loveliness to concentrate on the highly questionable comedy, it is throwing away the virtue of a classic to give us its frailties. The story of Viola and her love still has something sweet about it; the tale of the baiting of Malvolio is now just a bore, and an embarrassing sort of bore at that. As for those scenes of hilarity between Sir Toby Belch and Sir Andrew Aguecheek, they are almost especially unfunny."

Brooks Atkinson in the *New York Times* was, on the whole, pleased, but pointed out that "...the frolicsome style also has weaknesses that the Chekhov Players have not altogether escaped. The improvisations are often too studied and thus lack spontaneity. The tone of the performance is sometimes precious and ingrown. There is a certain tea-table flavor to scenes of artifice." But, ever the provider of useful blurbs, he concluded: "This version of *Twelfth Night* has both weight and gaiety, and it is wholly delightful...directed with dash and good humor." Atkinson felt it was Ford Rainey's performance as Sir Toby Belch that "emerges as the hero." That must have rung curiously in the ears of the actors playing Malvolio, Viola, and Olivia.

Although he regretted a certain archness and wasted motion in Chekhov's *Twelfth Night*, Stark Young writing in the *New Republic*, said, "I have never, in a long list of *Twelfth Night* productions, seen certain motifs and themes of the play turn out so clear; I have never heard a reading that made them so reckless and irresponsible, as they should be, but yet so exact to the play's intention." He had words of praise for Ford Rainey's Sir Toby and Hurd Hatfield's Sir Andrew, and preferred Beatrice Straight's Viola even to that of Helen Hayes. "On the whole, however," he wrote, "the best thing about the performance is.....the ensemble playing. Ensemble—that sounds like the simplest thing in the world. But run over in your mind the Shakespeare performances you have seen these past few years. They may have their good points, but these do not apply to ensemble. They have not had the training, the rehearsing, the playing together, the company organization, for proper results—take the banquet scene in Mr. Maurice Evans' *Macbeth*, for example, in which, save for Mr. Evans and Miss Anderson, the rest are mere paper dolls."

"Finally," Young concluded, "there is a baroque element in this Chekhov production of *Twelfth Night*. This is what is really new and fresh about the whole occasion, though it should not be so, since the very soul of the play's whole style lies in the baroque impulse." Young was a good friend of the Elmhirsts and it was probably difficult for him to maintain complete objectivity, but he was a rigorously honest critic and, in recent seasons, there had been a lot of torpid Shakespeare around on Broadway. This time around, Chekhov's training had clearly paid off.

Chapter Twenty-Four

BY THE EARLY FORTIES, with World War II hotting up in Europe and the U.S. draft claiming all able-bodied men and seriously attenuating the company, the Dartington experiment at Ridgefield was beginning to reveal fissures. The draft was the most immediate cause, but there were others.

Previously, the Elmhirsts provided a weekly stipend to all the actors for travel and hotel expenses; money that was usually given in advance and then forwarded by the married men to their wives. Now that the tours had been included in standard Equity touring contracts, the actors received normal wages only after their week's work was over. The largesse associated with the "good old Dartington days" rapidly came to a close. This was explained to members of the company by Beatrice Straight and the lawyers acting on her family's behalf. It outraged actors such as Sam Schatz and John Flynn, both married men who had become accustomed to the payment of expenses in advance. At the meeting at which the new rules were set out to the company, both actors angrily walked out of the room and subsequently resigned from the company. Woody Chambliss, who had been obliged to be apart from his wife Erika, felt the strain on his marriage imposed by the constant travel and he too left the company; Blair Cutting and Alan Harkness quickly followed suit. Chekhov, who felt the underpinning of the company rapidly giving way, made a passionate

speech to the actors about commitment and the need to maintain the integrity of what had been built up both in Devon and
at Ridgefield. But the draft continued to decimate the male
members of the company and before long it became clear that
the experiment that had begun six years before was cruelly
unraveling. Even the ever-optimistic Beatrice Straight seemed
to be reeling under the burden, and the rapid loss of key actors
such as Flynn, Chambliss, Schatz, Cutting, Harkness, Taylor,
and Rainey felt like nails being hammered into a coffin. In
1943, Ridgefield was abandoned and the Chekhov players went
their own way. Beatrice Straight, now married to political
activist Louis Dollivet and financing his magazine *Free World*,
moved to New York; Chekhov began contemplating
Hollywood.

The final appearance of the Chekhov Studio took place in
the fall of 1942 at the Barbizon Plaza Hotel as a benefit performance for the American-Russian Committee for Medical
Aid to the Soviet Union. It consisted of two one-act plays based
on stories by Anton Chekhov, *The Witch* and *I Forgot*, that
Chekhov had first performed when Hurok brought the company over from Russia in the thirties. This time they were played
by Chekhov in English and represented his last performances
on an American stage. The other short pieces were of *Happy
Ending* with Deirdre Hurst du Prey and David Heilwell, *After
The Theatre*, with Penelope Sack, and *The Story of Miss N.N.*,
featuring Beatrice Straight.

The Ridgefield company's final productions, *The Cricket
on the Hearth*, *Twelfth Night* and *King Lear*, had augured a
bright future in America, but they were to be the last professional productions directly associated with Michael Chekhov's
name.

Toward the end of the war, a small nucleus of Chekhov
actors, including Hurd Hatfield, Alan Harkness, Iris Tree,
Daphne Moore, Mary Lou Taylor, Sam Shatz, Ronald
Bennett, and Woody and Erika Chambliss, created the High
Valley Players in Ojai, California, which, because of their prior

association with Chekhov, was often touted as being an off-spring of the Dartington Hall/Ridgefield experiment; a connotation that irritated Chekhov, who had no direct association with the group and felt his ex-students were trading on his name. Beatrice Straight would begin a successful Broadway career in New York. Twenty-five years after Misha's death, she and Robert Cole would found the Michael Chekhov Studio in Manhattan.

In those troubled last days when it became clear that the plug was about to be pulled on Ridgefield and the entire Dartington experiment, Chekhov felt somewhat betrayed—but there was nothing he could do to prevent its dissolution; too many key members had already jumped ship. But ironically, in 1943, just before it closed, several remarkable things were in the works.

Chekhov and Shdanoff had begun conversations with a poet-playwright who was working as a waiter in a Greenwich Village club. They were both impressed by what they had read of his material and were planning to incorporate him into the work of the studio. His name was Tennessee Williams. At around the same time, a young Russian émigré had applied to become a resident playwright with the company, and the studio was considering offering him a moderate salary. His name was Vladamir Nabokov. The plan was for him to write a dramatized version of Chekhov's beloved, and constantly deferred, *Don Quixote* which Misha was eager to direct. There were several planning sessions between Chekhov, Shadnoff, and Nabokov just before the studio shut down. Had it continued, and had the likes of Williams and Nabokov come on board, there is no telling what might have developed. The likelihood is that other projects like *The Possessed* and *Twelfth Night* would have moved from Connecticut to New York, and instead of spending the last decade of his life in Hollywood, Chekhov might have ultimately developed a presence on the Broadway stage.

Dartington-cum-Ridgefield was destined to fade into legend, affectionately revived in conferences and alluded to in theater journals, but not providing a living heritage that anyone could point to. It would be some thirty years before stage aficionados would begin to reflect on happenings in the wilds of Devon or the purlieus of Connecticut and realize that something rather significant had taken place there.

A call from the actor-producer Gregory Ratoff, who was preparing a film about the Russian resistance against the Nazis, was about to move Chekhov forward again; this time, on to his final journey.

HOORAY FOR HOLLYWOOD

Chapter Twenty-Five

IN THE EARLY FORTIES, Los Angeles was a tightly packed Pandora's box filled with graft, gang violence, labor disputes, war jitters, and a rapidly expanding émigré community. Germany's invasion of Poland in 1939 had created bitter divisions between those who felt Nazism must be resisted, and that larger, more vocal majority of citizens who believed that foreign entanglements were essentially Europe's affair and need not concern America.

Immigrants escaping Hitler's Germany poured into America, many of them making a beeline to Hollywood, where the movie business was one of the few American industries that was flourishing. Bertolt Brecht, Thomas and Heinrich Mann, Igor Stravinsky, and Arnold Schoenberg joined émigrés such as Fritz Lang, Joseph von Sternberg, Billy Wilder, Salka Viertel, Franz Werfel, Leon Feuchwanger, Dmitri Tiomkin, and Max Steiner, who had already put down stakes in Hollywood.

The studio chieftains—Irving Thalberg, Louis B. Mayer, Harry Cohn, David O. Selznick, the Warner brothers—ran their companies as if they were fiefdoms, although in terms of finance and international influence, they were virtually empires. By 1939, Hollywood had proven itself with pictures such as *Gone With The Wind*, *Ninotchka*, *Wuthering Heights*, and *The Wizard of Oz*, while films like *Citizen Kane*, *Casablanca*, and *The Maltese Falcon* were just around the corner. A West Coast business financed largely by East Coast banking interests, Hollywood privately acknowledged that its major output was shlock, but the tacit assumption was if it wanted to produce quality goods, it had the means to enlist first-class talents such as Ernest Hemingway, F. Scott Fitzgerald, William Faulkner, Aldous Huxley and Nathaniel West. However, the industry never acknowledged that the expedient nature of its operation was such that even the finest writers and intellectuals found themselves mercilessly ground up by the inexorable crunch of its commercial machinery. Because of its pride and affluence, the industry sought out celebrities (Samuel Goldwyn offered Sigmund Freud $100,000 if he would advise him on a film depicting scenes from the famous love stories of history, and was flummoxed when Freud not only declined the offer but also refused to meet with him), but the gap between mass-produced commodities and cinematic art was only occasionally bridged.

Hollywood's sense of noblesse oblige extended to members of the acting profession. The studio bosses were dimly aware that the migration from Europe had landed a large number of outstanding actors on their shores, but if they were known at all, it was only by reputation. European quality was appreciated in the abstract, but people like Cohn, Mayer, Selznick, and the brothers Warner had no firsthand knowledge of the talents that now surrounded them.

Apprehensions about the coming war contributed to the political paranoia that was sweeping the country. It began with the House Un-American Activities Committee under Congressman Martin Dies in 1938, and reached something of a climax in 1940 when Dies turned his venom upon Hollywood, which he claimed was "a hotbed of Communism." After casting vague aspersions on several well-known celebrities (even including the ten-year-old Shirley Temple), he succeeded in shutting down the WPA's Federal Theatre project, where Orson Welles and John Houseman had conspicuously begun to revolutionize the American theater. That accomplished, Dies resolutely turned his guns toward the West. "Forty-two or

forty-three prominent members of the Hollywood film colony"
he brayed "either were full-fledged members of the Communist Party or active sympathizers and fellow travelers." He cited
no names but alleged that Communist propaganda could be
discerned from films such as *Juarez, Blockade* and *Fury*.
Capitalizing on the anti-Semitism that was rife in Hollywood
during this period, Dies capped his denunciation with the
"fact" that "most of the producers are Jews."

Eventually, specific stars were singled out, the most notable
being Humphrey Bogart, James Cagney, Frederic March,
Franchot Tone, and Melvyn Douglas. The liberals countered
with protest meetings and salvos fired from some of their
biggest guns. Dorothy Parker, at a public meeting at the
Philharmonic Hall, accused the congressman of wanting to
destroy the Hollywood progressive organizations "because
you've got to control this medium if you want to bring fascism
to this country." But Dies insisted all he really wanted was to
investigate. Cagney, Bogart, March, and others furnished
books and records for the committee's inspection, and Dies
reluctantly conceded that they "are not or never have been
Communist sympathizers." The furor died down and Dies
went off to investigate organizations such as the TVA and WPA.
Liberals heaved a sigh of relief, but a decade later, roundly
impressed by the national headlines the Dies Committee had
managed to garner, Senator Joe McCarthy would revive the
call to purge all subversives, and Hollywood and the country
would suffer a paroxysm of paranoia from which they would
not easily recover.

It is hard to say how much of all this penetrated the consciousness of Michael Chekhov. He had had his run-ins with
aggressive officialdom in Moscow and could immediately recognize the pungent aroma of witch burnings when he smelled
it. But within a matter of months, Pearl Harbor would be
attacked by the Japanese, the country would be hurtled into
war and an entirely new set of priorities would be rapidly put
in place.

Chapter Twenty-Six

THE CHEKHOVS had been invited to Hollywood by the Russian actor-producer Gregory Ratoff and installed at Selznick studios through the influence of Serge Rachmaninoff, who insisted Misha be given a contract. (Russians such as Rachmaninoff and Arnold Schoenberg behaved imperiously with studio heads, who were often more docile with them than they were toward their celebrity actors.) Misha began giving classes twice a week in a makeshift studio on Harper Street and occasionally in his modest Tudor house in Benedict Canyon. Before long, the word was out. One of the most charismatic actors of the Russian stage, a close collaborator of both Stanislavsky and Vakhtangov, was now living in Hollywood and disseminating the ideas that had revolutionized some of the most notable theaters in Europe.

Between 1944 and 1945, Chekhov's classes enrolled an A-list of actors, including Yul Brynner, Ingrid Bergman, Leslie Caron, Gary Cooper, James Dean, Rex Harrison, Sterling Hayden, Jennifer Jones, Gene Kelly, Marilyn Monroe, Patricia Neal, Paul Newman, Jack Palance, Gregory Peck, Mala Powers, Tyrone Power, Anthony Quinn, Robert Stack, John Abbott, Beatrice Straight, Robert Taylor, Arthur Kennedy. Many of them were nominated for, and several of them won, Oscars for performances coached by Chekhov himself or his trusty lieutenant, George Shdanoff. Some, like Anthony

Quinn, Leslie Caron, and Jack Palance, gravitated to Chekhov after rejecting the ego-bruising training of Lee Strasberg. Others, like Mala Powers, Marilyn Monroe, Robert Stack and Patricia Neal, had their first real acting instruction under Chekhov and remained with him until the end of his life. Chekhov, working closely with Shdanoff and his wife Elsa Schreiber (a brilliant teacher who developed her own slant on the Chekhovian technique), coached some of the most notable stars to emerge in the fifties.

Anthony Quinn described the anticipation that he and many other Hollywood actors had felt at their first encounter with Chekhov, who was touted as a kind of "Russian hero" by his expatriated countrymen. "I was just a young kid at the time" recalls Quinn, "and from all I'd heard, I expected a six-foot, seven-inch man to walk in, very imposing with this great booming Russian voice. Instead, in came this tiny little man, very frail, with a high-pitched, breathy voice. *This* is the great Russian actor?!" Once the classes began, Quinn's view of Chekhov took a 190 degree turn. The "tiny little man with the high-pitched breathy voice" grew larger with every appearance.

The number of students that attended classes would vary from a hardcore dozen to forty or fifty. There were many transients—actors such as Joseph Schildkraut, who would come when he was about to undertake a specific role fraught with difficulties; or Ina Claire, who regularly commuted from San Francisco when she was about to come out of retirement to play opposite Claude Rains in T.S. Eliot's *The Confidential Clerk* on Broadway. There were also one-offs such as Montgomery Clift, who had a longstanding professional relationship with the Russian coach Mira Rostova; and Marlon Brando, who essentially belonged to Stella Adler but was urged by her to acquaint himself with Chekhov's ideas. There was also a large sampling of California flakes, young and ambitious contract players who, being more committed to stardom than to study, irritated Chekhov. They were often tardy, and their attendance irregular. In order to tactfully divest himself, Chekhov would explain that since he was about to take part in a Hollywood film, classes had to be temporarily suspended, and students would be contacted when they resumed. He made a point of not contacting the flakes so a natural attrition would occur. Debbie Reynolds was a fastidious student; Robert Wagner, often absent because of his busy work schedules. Gary Cooper, who at that time was heavily into his affair with Patricia Neal, also attended classes, and although an unlikely disciple, was extremely earnest in his desire to learn.

Anthony Quinn tells the story of how Chekhovian technique came to Cooper's aid in one of his last films. At one of the classes Cooper attended, Chekhov had demonstrated an exercise in centering. The actors were asked to imagine there were tubes running from their feet down to the middle of the earth below. Then to imagine these roots rising upward—little by little—from the cavernous depths to where the actor was actually standing, gradually becoming empowered by the connection. Once the energy from below had transferred itself up from the bowels of the earth to where he stood, the actor was urged to transmit this power through his body and into his voice; radiating as it were, from the subterrestrial force from which he could now draw enormous strength.

While in Mexico shooting *Blowing Wind* with Anthony Quinn and Barabara Stanwyck, Cooper had a fairly lengthy speech to deliver to Stanwyck that he simply couldn't master. According to Quinn, the lanky Cooper had made twenty takes and spoiled every one of them. The director, as exasperated as Cooper himself, suggested the company break for lunch. Quinn saw Cooper disappear behind a tree and strenuously apply the centering exercise he had been taught in Chekhov's class. He rooted himself to a spot directly behind the sprawling oak and tried to imagine the power of the middle earth sending its energy up through miles of rock and soil into his feet and, once there, distributing its force throughout his body.

After lunch, with cast and crew wary of what the afternoon

might hold in store, the same shot was set up again. Cooper successfully brought off the scene in one take. The director, the cast, and the entire crew were astonished by the transformation.

Chekhov himself had a similar problem in a scene from Hitchcock's *Spellbound* where he was supposed to strike a match and light up his pipe while having a brief conversation with Ingrid Bergman about her husband's alleged troubled state of mind. Take after take, the coordination between the lines, the match, and the pipe simply would not jell. When the frustrated director suggested they skip that scene and move on to the next, Chekhov implored him to permit one more try. As the cameras rolled, he delivered the lines and brilliantly improvised an irritable scattering of all the matches in his matchbox as he testily lit his pipe and began to puff. Here, Chekhov managed to incorporate his own vexation at fluffing the moment by using an improvised piece of business directed against the root of his problem—the recalcitrant matchbox—spontaneously enhancing the scene.

One of the remarkable aspects of Chekhov's portrayal of the psychoanalyst in this film is that it required nothing more than a piece of studied naturalism. Chekhov chose black-rimmed, rounded spectacles reminiscent of those worn by Sigmund Freud, and adopted the authoritative manner of the psychiatrists who, at Stanislavsky's bidding, had examined him all those many years in Moscow. He was nominated for an Oscar for Best Supporting Actor in *Spellbound*, using a style of acting that he had personally renounced thirty years before and that, because of his tutelage at the Moscow Art, he could do, if necessary, standing on his head.

● ● ● ● ●

Chekhov had sometimes brief, sometimes extended, encounters with a number of Hollywood stars. One of the earliest was Jennifer Jones, an actress who using her given name of Phyllis Isley had started in quickie westerns but whose career dramatically escalated after she caught the eye of one of Hollywood's most powerful producers.

Jones' professional career began as a Seventh Avenue fashion model in New York, a past she forcibly tried to obliterate. Her dark sultry looks and the fact that her father owned a chain of movie houses in the East won her a six-month contract from Republic Studios, where she appeared in forgettable films such as *New Frontier* with John Wayne and *Dick Tracy's G-Men*.

A shy, insecure girl from Tulsa, Oklahoma, Jones used acting therapeutically; it was a way of manifesting parts of her personality which had become deeply suppressed. In 1939, she married a fellow student, actor Robert Walker, and bore him two sons. Walker, like his wife, was anxious, introverted, and vulnerable; the union gave both of them a kind of anchor in life. When they were hard-pressed and living in Greenwich Village, Phyllis Walker uncharacteristically mustered the courage to walk into David O. Selznick's office and ask to be auditioned for *Claudia*, a film she had heard was in the works. During her reading, she dissolved into tears and simply could not continue. Her vulnerability and helplessness made a strong impression on Selznick who, uncertain as to where he might use her, nevertheless signed her to a contract.

What followed was a gradual but total appropriation of the fragile actress by the self-assured producer. He renamed her Jennifer Jones and proceeded to take full control of her life, falling in love with her in the process. While Jones was working with her husband on the film *Since You Went Away*, Selznick continued to tighten his grip on the young actress. During a farewell scene with Walker in the picture (which obviously augured events in their present relationship), Jones again burst into tears and entirely fell apart. Selznick was summoned to the set and coaxed her back to the camera.

After a slow but steady publicity campaign, Selznick cast her as the leading lady in *The Song of Bernadette*. On the day she was handed the Oscar for her performance in that role, she

sued Walker for divorce and almost immediately became the
second Mrs. David O. Selznick.

Walker, although he had begun to achieve recognition in
films such as *See Here, Private Hargrove*, *Strangers on a Train*,
and the aforementioned *Since You Went Away*, was shattered by
the sudden desertion of his wife. Sensitive and insecure at the
best of times, he turned to the bottle and became progressively
unstable and violent, so much so that he was persuaded by
MGM to sign himself into the Menninger Clinic. There he
received intensive psychotherapy and a regular diet of sodium
amytal. One of those injections, administered after a heavy
bout of drinking, killed him at the age of thirty-two. "My personal life," he had told the recently hired contract player June
Allyson, "has been completely wrecked by David Selznick's
obsession for my wife. What can you do to fight such a powerful man?" Obviously, the answer was, beat a shameful retreat,
which, in Walker's case, turned into a rout.

Selznick wanted his discovery to have the best acting coach
that Los Angeles could provide, and from the inquiries he
made around town, he determined that the ex-director of the
Second Moscow Art Theater was by far the most skillful and
the most prestigious. He arranged for a studio limo to collect
Chekhov at his home in Benedict Canyon and deposit him at
the Zanuck estate, where he would be ushered to an upstairs
room to work with Jones. She would invariably greet him cordially, but always wearing dark sunglasses. When the session
was over, the same limo would bring Chekhov back to his
modest home on San Ysidro Lane. "In all those many months,"
Chekhov recalled "I never once saw Miss Jones' eyes."

Later in her career, after the actress' daughter Mary
Jennifer had committed suicide and Jennifer herself had
attempted to take her life, the star attached herself to several
mental health causes. No doubt, an actress with such a troubled temperament would find a sympathetic mentor in a man
like Chekhov, who in his earlier life had been beset with similar problems.

Chapter Twenty-Seven

IN THE LATE FORTIES, Marilyn Monroe had begun a close working relationship with Natasha Lytess, a drama coach at Columbia Pictures, but the starlet was still acutely aware that her acting abilities were more potential than manifest. Shortly before her contract at Columbia expired, she confided her insecurities to Jack Palance, who had befriended her at the studio. He too had been shopping around for a coach who could widen his orbit as an actor and free him from the psychopathic heavies into which he was regularly being cast. He strongly recommended Michael Chekhov, who he felt was providing some of the most stimulating acting instruction in Hollywood, and in the fall of 1951, Marilyn eagerly signed up for the Chekhov classes.

Almost immediately, she found herself playing Cordelia to Chekhov's Lear and marveling at the transformations her new acting coach could effect. "I was out of the room for seven seconds," she told an interviewer for *Redbook* magazine. "When I came back in, I saw a king before me. Mr. Chekhov did it without changing a costume or putting on makeup or even getting out of his chair. I never saw anything happen so fast in my life. So little was done in so short a period of time that I really became Cordelia." Whether at this stage of her career Marilyn's transformation was quite as finite as Chekhov's is somewhat doubtful, although Chekhov's wife Xenia recalled afterward that Misha was genuinely struck by Marilyn's sensitivity.

Marilyn juggled both Natasha Lytess and Michael Chekhov simultaneously—never telling one about the other. Both Lytess and Chekhov had been firmly grounded in classical theater. Lytess, who had been through the Max Reinhardt School in Berlin, was deeply immersed in Hollywood's community of displaced German intellectuals, and Chekhov spent much of his free time with Russian émigrés. The exemplars that were held up to Marilyn would have been Shakespeare, Gogol, Dostoyevsky, Ibsen, Hauptmann—the great European dramatists—even though the work in which she was actually involved consisted of perishable potboilers such as *Ladies of the Chorus, A Ticket to Tomahawk,* and *Love Happy.* But the exposure both to Lytess and Chekhov goes a long way to explain her ambition to tackle serious roles, which inspired only sneers from journalists who saw her simply as a sexy airhead.

Marilyn Monroe's personal insecurity has been laboriously chronicled. She was forever finding father substitutes or ostensible strongmen who would help her navigate the rapids of her life and steer her toward the right career choices, even when the men themselves turned out to be somewhat rudderless and their advice was, in any case, blithely ignored.

At first Chekhov, who had a full roster of students, was reluctant to take on another, particularly one that was considered a studio starlet, but Palance managed to persuade him to at least meet with Marilyn before rejecting her. After their first meeting, Misha, who was as vulnerable to feminine beauty as he was to inchoate talent, agreed to take her on for one session a week. She fell quickly under his spell and gave her new mentor an engraving of Abraham Lincoln, a hero that had been glamorized for her by Arthur Miller a decade before the two became romantically involved. "Lincoln was the man I admired most all through school," she explained to Chekhov, "now that man is you."

Admirable as he was to her, Marilyn was still Marilyn and her penchant for lateness and absenteeism was as much in evidence with Chekhov as it was soon to become a regular irritant on the film set. Chekhov, brought up on the strict discipline of the Moscow Art, was seriously vexed by her unreliability. He suggested that perhaps it would be a good idea to give the classes a rest for a while. Marilyn, who had rapidly come to feel Chekhov was awakening a part of her that had lain dormant for years, scrawled off a desperate note: "Please don't give up on me yet. I know (painfully so) that I try your patience. I need the work and your friendship desperately. I shall call you soon." She dutifully did, and the classes continued.

The real bond between teacher and pupil was that both of them, in their own way, and for different reasons, shared a profound dislike for the brittle commercialism of the film industry. Marilyn wanted to escape from the sexy, dumb blonde image that had turned her into a cash cow for 20th Century Fox. She genuinely felt the desire to tackle challenging roles in meaningful projects and acquire the artistic dignity that would enable the real Marilyn, as opposed to the titillating captive of the studio bosses, to emerge. Her marriage to the politically involved Arthur Miller could be construed as a subconscious impulse in that direction, as could her subsequent involvement with Lee Strasberg and his ambition to turn the Actors' Studio into a major American theater company.

For Chekhov, Hollywood after Moscow, Berlin, and Paris was simply unreal. It was a pasteboard world in which all questions of art were subordinated to considerations of commerce. He shared Marilyn's distress at the kinds of roles she was offered in flimsy and inconsequential films. Perhaps, having been a sublime comedian himself, he might have changed his attitude had he lived to see his pupil in Billy Wilder's *Some Like It Hot* or *The Seven Year Itch* but in the early fifties, the Plasticene Age, both teacher and pupil had good cause to feel discontented with their Hollywood lot. His own creative instincts encouraged Marilyn's desire to acquire quality in her professional life. He thought she should be doing better things and, considering his own cameo appearances in films such as *Cross My Heart* and *Texas, Brooklyn and Heaven,* he felt the same was also true for himself.

During one of their private classes when Marilyn was working on a piece from *The Cherry Orchard,* Chekhov abruptly broke off the rehearsal and asked her if she were thinking of sex while playing the scene. Marilyn was astonished by the question. No, she said, she was not thinking of sex; she was focusing entirely on the matter in the play.

Chekhov paced the room for a few moments then sat down and carefully explained that throughout the scene he had been receiving strong "sexual vibrations" from the young actress which led him to believe that it would be best to discontinue the session. This observation caused Marilyn to burst into tears and, as she did so, a light snapped on in Chekhov's brain and he began to elucidate that insight to his pupil. It appeared that unintentionally, and almost without her knowledge, Marilyn was emitting a kind of sexual aura over which she had no conscious control. Audiences, particularly its male members, had instinctively begun to respond to that aura and the studio bosses, made aware of the phenomenon, had decided to market it for general consumption in one film after another. There was no real concern about her either as an actress or a person. What interested and excited them was the eroticism that emanated from Marilyn and made her desirable to the public. "Sex appeal" was the commodity they had determined to package and disseminate to audiences; the cinematic context was almost negligible. It was enough, Chekhov explained, simply to train the cameras on her and let nature take its course.

This interpretation of her personality and its effect on others incensed the actress. Fighting back bitter tears, she totally rejected that kind of relationship with the public. She was not an "aphrodisiac" and didn't want to be marketed as such. In the beginning perhaps, there was some delight in being desired by men, both privately and professionally, but that was not the Marilyn that had sought out Chekhov in order to develop her skills as an actress. That was the remains of "Norma Jean," not Marilyn Monroe. The conversation between them was cathartic and triggered a resolve on Marilyn's part to assert an independence that had been bubbling up in her for many months. It was after this exchange with Chekhov that Marilyn instigated her campaign to take charge of her own career and choose her own film properties. Misha's perception of the *studio's* perception—and perhaps the *world's* perception—of Marilyn Monroe was not Marilyn's perception of herself, and it all crystallized for her during that revelatory conversation.

But was Chekhov's impression all that valid?

Long before there was a Marilyn Monroe, there was a Theda Bara and a Clara Bow and a Jean Harlow—actresses who exuded a certain sexual availability and whose physical allure was polished, packaged, and marketed for general consumption. Art and sex have been joined at the hip since art and sex first came into the world. If you have someone with physical attributes as striking as Marilyn Monroe's, and an instability and insecurity that inspires men to gravitate to them, is it exploitation to place those qualities into films that project them to a mass market? Does it make sense to cast such actresses as Medea or Jocasta, Lady Macbeth or Hedda Gabler? The secret of casting is to line up the attributes of the character with the attributes of the actress and, although occasionally one comes across a performer with the versatility to move easily from soubrette to diva or from ingenue to character lady, what is more common is to match type to type; to create a harmony between a given personality and a fictitious one that closely resembles the other. We never did see Marilyn's Grushenka or Lady Macbeth, but we did see her winningly comedic Sugar Kane in *Some Like It Hot*, the girl upstairs in *The Seven Year Itch*, Cherie, the torch singer in *Bus Stop*, Lorelei in *Gentlemen Prefer Blondes*, as well as the touchingly fragile Roslyn in *The Misfits* (a role patterned especially for her by Arthur Miller). We also saw her disastrously miscast as a mentally ill babysitter in *Don't Bother to Knock*, and a storm-tossed survivor in the Candian western *River of No Return*. It would appear from her film oeuvre that her talent was best realized as a comedienne, the daffy blonde with an unexpected streak of cunning. To set aside those traits and construe her as a soulful character actress in the works of Anton Chekhov or Fyodor Dostoyevsky seems, from this vantage point, a bizarre contradiction of her natural endowments.

Another way of interpreting her coach's curious insight into her psyche is to remember that Misha was ever the ladies' man; a helpless romantic who frequently responded to feminine beauty with excessive emotions. In a closeted rehearsal situation with one of the most voluptuous women ever to grace the American cinema, it may well be that the "sexual vibrations" were more in Misha's head than they were in Marilyn's subconscious.

Marilyn's attachment to Chekhov and his wife Xenia was deep seated. She consulted him on all her roles, and his unvarnished criticism of her work played directly into her own assessment of her inadequacies. She was never satisfied with any of her screen performances—except perhaps Roslyn in *The Misfits*, which, ironically, never really satisfied the critics. Conscious of her meager education and always feeling something of a fraud, she was buoyed by Chekhov's meticulous appraisal of her work and genuinely felt her inner technique improved as a result of his advice. As she desperately needed a man in her life to fill in for the father she felt she never had, she also required a mentor to shape the artistic longings that accompanied her burgeoning career. Chekhov, in Marilyn's eyes, was a seer—almost a guru—who acquainted her with a level of artistry to which she had always aspired. After his death, that need was satisfied by Lee and Paula Strasberg, and it is interesting to compare the differences between the two discipleships.

Chekhov devoted himself to the fulfillment of the actor's personality—not only in the profession but also in their personal lives. George Shdanoff, in one of those melancholic Slavic moods to which both he and Chekhov were prone, once asked him, "Misha, what are we doing here in Hollywood? We didn't become involved in the theatrical profession to make better actors for Louis B. Mayer!" Chekhov paused for a moment before he replied, "We are *not* making better actors for Louis B. Mayer. We are helping people to grow spiritually—to become better human beings." Behind his training, there lurked the Steinerian principle of attaining the higher life. It was, at base, an unselfish motivation: to make better people so as to make them better actors.

When Lee Strasberg replaced Chekhov as Marilyn's dominant artistic influence (it was Cheryl Crawford, one of the founders of the Group Theater who arranged the introduction), he spent a lot of time encouraging her to view her film career as a stepping stone to more worthwhile achievements on the stage. Since severing his ties with the Group Theater and being installed as leader of the Actors' Studio, Strasberg always contemplated a triumphant return to the New York stage; a kind of delayed conquest that would put his problematic productions of the early Group Theater into a new and more positive perspective. Both he and Paula were conscious of the power they wielded over the preeminent screen actress of the fifties. Strasberg had instilled in Marilyn the belief that she was capable of towering achievements, and that her motion picture work barely scratched the surface of her latent and untapped talent. Paula became an immovable fixture on the film set, sitting just beyond the lights and camera, nodding approval or disapproval of each take and driving film directors to distraction. During the shooting of *The Prince and the Showgirl*, Laurence Olivier, who both starred in and directed the film, complained that Marilyn's constant consultations with Paula were driving him out of his "squeaking mind." He insisted that Paula be removed, and the producers, aware of how rattled he had become at being constantly second guessed, finally obliged. But Paula could never be excised from Marilyn's life. She had put down deep roots there and was constantly on call when Marilyn became flustered, frantic, or depressed.

Strasberg realized that if there was ever to be a revival of his theatrical career, Marilyn could be its catalyst. His praise for her performances at the Actors' Studio seemed, to many observers, excessive to the point of sycophancy. During those sessions, Strasberg had been known to demolish the egos of actors whose talents seemed to be wanting, but with Marilyn he was always solicitous, always encouraging. "It was almost as if she had been waiting for a button to be pushed," Strasberg reflected, "and when it was pushed, a door opened and you saw a treasure of gold and jewels. It is unusual to find the underlying personality so close to the surface and so anxious to break out, and therefore so quick to respond." This, he concluded "was typical of great actors." None of the stage productions they ever contemplated came to fruition. In the 1963–64 season, the Actors' Studio company presented *The Three Sisters* under Strasberg's direction. It received mixed notices in New York and fiercely negative ones in London. Marilyn, who had died in 1962, was spared the pain of having to reassess her mentor's artistic credibility.

To an extent, Marilyn had inflated the personae of both men. It was her tendency to shore up her own weakness by exaggerating the strengths of the men she lured into her life. If there is any distinction to be drawn between her tutelage with Chekhov and Strasberg, it is that in one case she received disinterested assistance in her sincere desire to become a better actress and in the other, a reassuring friendship that may have been tied to a secret agenda.

In the early fifties, by which time Marilyn Monroe had become an avid student of Chekhov's, she and Xenia developed a strong affection for one another. Mrs. Chekhov was not only a shoulder to cry on, but also a source of old world wisdom to which Marilyn often turned for advice. After Misha's death, Monroe set up a $100,000 trust fund that was designated to provide $5,000 per annum for her mother and $2,500 per annum for Xenia, described in her will as her "friend and former mother." Xenia told a reporter for *Life* magazine in 1963, "She decided to keep me without worries until I die." By 1965, taxes had consumed both trust funds, and despite the fact that Marilyn had grossed some $200 million over twenty-three films, there was nothing left. All personal effects and clothing were bequeathed to Lee Strasberg to be distributed by him "in his sole discretion among my friends, colleagues and to those to whom I am devoted." Upon Marilyn's death, among several creditors, Paula Strasberg claimed to be owed $22,000 for "coaching."

Chapter Twenty-Eight

DESPITE HER INSOLUBLE ATTACHMENT to Chekhov and his work, Xenia never entirely emigrated to America. She prepared the meals, she provided moral support for her husband and his circle of new American friends, but she was rooted in the Russian émigré community. Xenia was never happier than when she was speaking in her native tongue to people with whom she could recall the memories of life in Moscow, both before and after the revolution. Chekhov himself would often complain after a hard day of teaching that he was exhausted "talking in English," a language he never entirely mastered. It was a comfort after dealing with actors, some of whom were zealous and others clueless, to return to the Russianness of Xenia and their small Tudor house in Benedict Canyon, and simply be himself. "I don't want to become an accent clown here in Hollywood," he once confided to Jack Colvin, an actor who had become his protégé at the Hollywood classes.

Unfailingly cast as a sweet little old man in one film after another, Misha was painfully aware of the disparity between his film personae and his true self. In Hollywood, he told Colvin, "I think they hire me only for my beard. If they need a Russian old man with a beard, I am there." Eventually, to avoid the endless hours of daubing on spirit gum, he grew his own Van Dyke. Affable, cuddly, and always genial, the anguish of thinking in one language and trying to communicate in another wore him down. Xenia was his mainstay. She reminded him of the Michael Chekhov he had been, and the world from which they had both been cruelly banished.

In 1946, there was another sharp reminder of his Slavic past. It involved a rare and not very satisfying return to the stage, this time only as director, in a city where theater was often looked on as a kind of aberration amidst the frantic film activity that engulfed it.

When the Group Theater was disbanding in the East, several members of the company journeyed to Hollywood in the late thirties and early forties. Spearheaded by Group regulars such as Roman Bohnen, Morris Carnovsky, Phoebe Brand, and Art Smith, they were soon joined by Ruth Nelson, Jules Dassin and Harry Bratsburg (later rechristened Henry Morgan, of *M.A.S.H.* fame).

Among them, and one of the prime movers of the group, was Phil Brown, one of the last actors to have been accepted into the Group Theater before its demise. Together they created a company called the Actors' Lab, which, like the Group, was politically motivated, left orientated, and devoted to formulating a practical acting aesthetic. Their premises were directly behind Schwab's drugstore on Sunset Boulevard, the legendary hangout where Lana Turner was first discovered. It was an appropriate geographical location for an offbeat, anti-establishment company; directly behind the trysting place where Hollywood hopefuls and wheeler-dealers met to quaff coffee and huckster their way into the major studios.

Because the area was not zoned for public assembly, its audience, like its artists, had to become members of the Lab; a legal ruse frequently resorted to in those days to circumvent the zoning laws. The nucleus group was soon joined by established film actors such as Lee J. Cobb, Norman Lloyd, Vincent Price, Hume Cronyn, Larry Parks, and Sarah Allgood. Joe Mankiewicz served on its board.

The Actors' Lab received government funding to assist returning G.I.s, who made up a considerable portion of its membership, and the studios were soon sending young starlets and contract players to the Lab to hone their acting skills. They were almost all unknowns (among them a shy and gawky actress named Marilyn Monroe). But after a while, recruits included people like Tennessee Williams and Jessica Tandy, who collaborated on a one-act play called *Portrait of Madonna* that Williams later developed into *A Streetcar Named Desire* and in which Tandy, already a star in England, established her American reputation. In addition to its work in Hollywood, the Lab sent out touring productions to army camps throughout the country; one of these was a production of *Volpone*, which *Life* magazine described as containing "some of the finest acting to be seen in America today."

There was a dearth of theater in Los Angeles at this time, and the Actor's Lab was one of the first and most prominent of the little theater groups that began to fill that void. Forty years later, there would be more than a hundred waiver theaters in Los Angeles; that is, theaters where professional actors waived their normal union salaries in order to take part in productions of classics, revivals, and new plays. The hope, then as now, was that they would get discovered by casting agents and leapfrog into lucrative film and television work. The Lab gave a jump-start to the careers of performers such as Lloyd Bridges and Shelley Winters, and because of the illustrious past of its founders, attracted a breed of actor that endowed it with a sleazy kind of glamour.

Stella Adler and Harold Clurman, who both vividly remembered the Moscow Art Players' performances on Broadway, suggested to the Lab directors that they tap Michael Chekhov, who was now working and living in L.A., to conduct some acting workshops and perhaps stage a production with their members. In 1946, the Lab contracted Chekhov to stage an American production of *The Inspector General*.

There was a great buzz of excitement at the prospect of being directed by a man who had now become something of a legend in American theater circles. The company, including people like J. Edward Bromberg, Jules Dassin, and illustrious members of the board, congregated in the back room of the Lab awaiting Chekhov's arrival. "Chekhov strode into the room," Phil Brown recalled, "looked over the assembly, pointed his finger at me, without ever having heard me even speak, much less read for the part, and announced, 'You are Khlestakov!' And that was it. Everyone in the room was flabbergasted, including myself!" Afterwards, after having seen photos of the productions at the Moscow Art, Brown speculated that the reason he was chosen is because he strongly resembled Chekhov.

But the collaboration was not fruitful, and sixty years later, the memory of it still stirred bitter memories for Brown:

> I really received very little direction from him. I was miserable, having been accustomed to the methods of the Group where we discussed and wrestled over every little nuance of a part for weeks before feeling we had achieved our goal. The whole experience was, for me, quite uncomfortable. I felt completely at sea. I just played it as best I could. Chekhov approved of everything I did. Chekhov didn't give one much of an opportunity to get close to him as a man. And as I've said, there was very little direction.

The reaction of the Russian émigré community was enthusiastic. They, after all, knew who Chekhov was and had either seen his work in Europe or been privy to the glowing reports from Berlin and Moscow. The L.A. *Times* on October 9, 1946, reported:

> Approached with more calm by its interpreters last night, *Inspector General* might have been the classic it should have been in the Actors' Lab presentation at Las Palmas Theater. As it was, this satirical comedy by Gogol was so whipped and lashed about the stage at times that the vio-

lence of the proceedings must have evoked a confused reaction from the first audience. Doubtless their work will become more unified and better balanced with further performances, and certainly there are the elements to portend an auspicious revival in this locality.

The reviewer thought Carnovsky as the Mayor "could be less stentorian," and Phil Brown "might give a better shaded and less mincing impersonation of the government clerk." Mealy mouthed throughout, the critic was obviously trying to put the best face he could on what was clearly a disappointing performance. After praising the Lab's previous show *Home of the Brave*, he concluded: "*Inspector General* should be a caricature; in last night's proffering it was too much the comic strip."

The company had taken out a six-month lease on Las Palmas Theater, but after the poor reception of the Gogol, which was the last show of the short season, no other productions followed. The Lab remained a beacon for ambitious, Stanislavsky-oriented actors, but the incongruity of a serious, socially relevant theater company never quite jibed with the helter-skelter, catch-as-catch-can world of Hollywood in the forties. Although other directorial projects were discussed and even planned (*The Cherry Orchard* among them), Chekhov's Hollywood life remained confined to teaching and occasional film roles.

One can only wonder what Chekhov might have felt revisiting the play that had dynamically established his career in his native land and was then successfully transferred to Broadway, only to be brusquely dismissed in Hollywood a scant ten years later. Was Gogol simply too old fashioned for postwar American audiences? Would he, along with Dostoyevsky, also have to be tossed into the dustbin? Or did Chekhov have the clarity of mind to realize that a scratch production of a great Russian classic simply couldn't compare with a lovingly prepared, deftly produced ensemble production directed by

Konstantin Stanislavsky and spearheaded by an actor as luminous as Michael Chekhov?

Had it been any other play, it might not have left so bad a taste in his mouth.

Chapter Twenty-Nine

IN HOLLYWOOD, Misha often found himself reunited with old students from Dartington Hall, which invariably prompted fond recollections. Looking back to the creativity and autonomy of Dartington Hall and comparing it with his meandering status in Hollywood always stirred bittersweet memories.

Yul Brynner was an early disciple from Ridgefield. After winning an Oscar for Best Actor in *The King and I*, he had a hypnotic Hollywood presence in the fifties. He was born in Vladivostok, Russia, to a Swiss-Mongolian father and Russian mother, the daughter of a successful doctor. He led a nomadic life, attending school in China and then settling in Paris in 1934. Not enamored of the academic life in the exclusive Lycee Moncelle, Brynner became an itinerant musician, playing guitar among Russian gypsies who were the first to give him a real sense of family. He mixed with surrealists such as Jean Cocteau and Andre Breton, and became a fixture of the bohemian life in St. Germain de Pres. Gradually, he began to get the itch to give up his nomadic existence and devote himself to the stage. His stepmother, Madame Kornova, who had been an actress in Chekhov's Second Moscow Art Theatre, told him, "If you really want to become a serious actor, you must go to America, where the great actor-director and teacher Michael Chekhov is the artistic director of his own theater organization. You must study with him."

During his stay in Paris, Brynner had seen Chekhov perform when his company had toured with *Inspector General*,
Eric XIV, and *Hamlet*. It had been a cathartic experience for
the young actor, who felt that only through association with
Chekhov could he realize "in a concrete and tangible way, a
mastery of the elusive thing that one calls the technique of acting." When he heard about the opening of the Chekhov
Studio in Dartington, he tried but failed to join the new company. When he heard the school had moved to America, he
left for the States immediately, as he has written in his preface
for *To the Actor*, "with the sole purpose of at last working with
[Chekhov]." There, along with actors such as Hurd Hatfield,
Ford Rainey, Mary Lou Williams, Daphne Moore, Blair
Cutting and Beatrice Straight, Brynner threw himself into the
whirlpool of the Chekhov technique.

His English was not yet polished enough to undertake
roles, so he was relegated to the job of driving the company
truck. At the end of each performance, he loaded sets and
costumes into a decrepit van, and while the exhausted company crept into their hotel beds, drove most of the night
toward the company's next booking to set up the following
day's performance. Billed as "Youl Brynner," his first speaking
role was as Fabian in *Twelfth Night*, which he played both on
tour and on December 2, 1941, when the company opened
the show in New York. The same year, he was cast in the
early TV series *Mr. Jones and His Neighbors* and ricocheted
from there into a plum role in *Lute Song*, starring Mary
Martin. A few years later, he made his film debut in *Port of
New York*.

It was Martin who recommended him for the lead in
Rodgers and Hammerstein's musical *The King and I*. He
immediately won great acclaim, and when he repeated the
role in the film version, garnered the Oscar for Best Actor. He
made close to fifty films and died of cancer in 1985. His cobra-
shaped bald pate, robust physique, and searing eyes made him
irresistible to women. The fact that he had a hot and heavy

affair with Marlene Dietrich, if anything, only heightened his sex appeal.

When, in the mid-fifties, Chekhov learned that Brynner was to play the lead in a forthcoming film version of *The Brothers Karamazov*, he tried strenuously to interest his former student in having Marilyn Monroe considered for the role of Grushenka, a role he had already idealized for Marilyn in their private work together. Influential as Brynner was in Hollywood, he could not persuade studio heads to seriously consider her for a role of such magnitude. When the news got out, the idea of Marilyn as a Slavic heroine was roundly mocked by the media; Billy Wilder quipped he would be happy to direct Marilyn in "a whole series of Karamazov sequels, such as *The Brothers Karamazov Meet Abbott and Costello*." At the time, Marilyn was still under contract to 20th Century Fox and they made it clear they had no intention of concealing those adorable, golden locks behind a babushka.

Brynner, like Chekhov and other European émigrés at work in Hollywood, had come to realize there was a temperamental divide between classics and the Hollywood mentality. Although Brynner starred in films such as *Taras Bulba* and *The Brothers Karamazov*, he was more often to be found in grandiose epics such as *Solomon and Sheba* and *The Ten Commandments*, or occasionally, well-crafted Westerns like *The Magnificent Seven* and *Invitation to a Gunfighter*. But in all of his work, whether it was trivia or hollow spectacle, he assiduously applied the techniques he had acquired under Chekhov's tutelage. When *To the Actor* was published in 1952, he contributed a preface that was a touching encomium to his "dear professor."

But, while Chekhov was refining his notes on the complexities of acting and the dedication due to high art, he, like so many Russian émigrés, was beavering away in lusterless movies that would have made Stanislavsky turn pale and Vakhtangov hang his head.

Chapter Thirty

CHEKHOV'S FIRST HOLLYWOOD FILM *Song of Russia* is riddled with ironies, many of them cruel. It was shot in 1943, based on a story by Leo Mittler called "Scorched Earth," and released one year later.

The film was made during the period of the Popular Front, when the USSR was America's ally against the Nazis. It includes a laudatory tribute to Joseph Stalin, with the heroic leader actually making an appearance to urge his people, in concert with the allied forces, to resist the fascist onslaught of Hitler and his hordes.

Chekhov, who had been hounded out of Russia at the risk of his life, plays the hardworking paterfamilias of a collective farm, whose loyalty to the Soviets is unshakeable. The plot concerns a successful orchestral conductor, played by Robert Taylor, who while making a goodwill tour of the Soviet Union, falls in love with a disarming rustic groupie played by Susan Peters. She persuades him to visit her remote village (called Tschaikovskya, in honor of the great Russian composer whose thunderous and sentimental music hounds almost every frame of the film). They fall in love, marry, and the war parts them, but the conductor braves the invading German forces to try to find and rescue his wife. When they are finally reunited, a staunch Communist warrior, played by John Hodiak, persuades Taylor and Peters that they would do more good performing the work of Russian masters in the West than assisting with the "scorched earth" policy that the peasants are energetically pursuing in the countryside. The film concludes with a maudlin call-to-arms voiceover by Hodiak, obviously intended to gird up the loins of all those nations opposing the German conquest of Europe.

Three years later, Robert Taylor, roundly attacking the red subversion in Hollywood, stood before the House Un-American Activities Committee and zealously tried to suggest he was tricked into making this pro-Soviet film. He testified that White House pressure "by Roosevelt aides" had conspired to delay his Navy commission until *Song of Russia* was completed. Louis B. Mayer explained to the Committee that he simply wanted to make a film about "Russians, not Communists," and had suggested to Frank Knox, then Secretary of the Navy, that *Song of Russia* might help the war effort, as the successful *Mrs. Miniver* had done, if Taylor were allowed to complete the film before going off to military service. But the rumor persisted that Roosevelt somehow had a hand in spawning it.

The Committee couldn't comprehend how such a film could even be contemplated, let alone made, conveniently forgetting that at the time, alliance with the Soviets was the official Washington line. When the *Song of Russia* was released in 1944, it received surprisingly positive reviews. The *New York Times* found it "really a honey of a topical musical film, full of rare good humor, rich vitality, and a proper respect for the Russians' fight in this war." Bosley Crowther wrote, "it was very close to being the best film on Russia yet made in the popular Hollywood idiom." The Committee then solicited Ayn Rand's opinion on the matter, despite the fact that her only credentials as a Soviet expert were that she was born in St. Petersburg in 1904, though she admitted she had not been in Russia for more than twenty years. She assailed the film's utter distortion of Soviet life, which created the impression of a happy, smiling, contented populace instead of the bleak captives of a slave state. Trying to get Ms. Rand to admit that in 1943, there was some justification in supporting our partner in the war against Hitler, Ms. Rand would

have none of it. "I think we could have used the lend-lease sup-
plies that we sent there to much better advantage ourselves."

Otto Freiderich, in his incisive book *The City of Nets*,
pegged it neatly when he wrote:

> What Miss Rand could not seem to understand, what the
> House Committee could not seem to understand, was
> that *Song of Russia* was rubbish not because of any politi-
> cal purpose, subversive or otherwise, but because MGM
> was in the business of producing rubbish. That was its
> function, its nature, its mission. It hardly knew that politi-
> cal purposes existed. MGM was the home of Andy Hardy, of
> Judy Garland and Esther Williams, and no Communist
> ideology could ever penetrate or take root in such a play-
> land. When Louis B. Mayer of Minsk decided to make a
> movie about Russia, he would inevitably make it the
> Russia of Andy Hardy, accompanied by Tchaikovsky.

Accurate as that assessment may be, its release didn't avoid
the opprobrium that befell its screenwriters Richard Collins,
branded as an "unfriendly witness," and Paul Jarrico, who
pleaded the 5th Amendment when called before the Committee. The lives of both writers quickly unraveled as a result of
the hearings.

As for Chekhov, who had seen the horrors of the Civil War
first hand and lived through the subsequent famine, depriva-
tion, and political liquidations of staunch Bolsheviks, one can
only surmise what he felt about the comic-opera depiction of
his homeland before the onslaught of the German armies. He
was learning rapidly that art in America, even populist art like
motion pictures, was subject to certain ideological standards.

● ● ● ● ●

In Vincent Sherman's 1944 film *In Our Time*, Chekhov,
playing the rhetorical old uncle of an aristocratic Polish family

just before the invasion by Germany, enters with the lines, "If you drink you die. If you don't drink, you die anyway, so it's better to drink." This is a thought that had probably occurred to Chekhov himself more than once during the period when he was a suffering alcoholic. By the time the film was made, and with the help of his wife, he had licked the problem although it is very possible his film commitments during the war years may have tempted him to fall off the wagon.

In Our Time is yet another maudlin mid-forties propaganda film whose underlying purpose is to strengthen America's resolve in a war that had already claimed hundreds of thousands of casualties. Written by Ellis St. John and Howard Koch, it has a strong cast that includes a young and winsome Ida Lupino, the comedienne Mary Boland, the sinister Victor Francen, the wooden but morally upright Paul Henreid (the patriot husband who reclaims Ingrid Bergman from the clutches of a politically reformed Bogie in *Casablanca*), and Alla Nazimova, an alumnus of the Moscow Art Theatre and one of Hollywood's most predatory lesbians.

The storyline is a wartime version of the class-incompatibility conflict that beset star-crossed lovers in innumerable films from the thirties. A rich count (Henreid) falls in love with the working-class companion of a wealthy American antique collector (Boland), is firmly rejected by her husband's aristocratic family but winds up freeing him from their stuffy domination and bestowing a newfound sense of independence. Ultimately, she loses him to the Polish resistance, but they reunite to perpetrate a "scorched earth" maneuver (yet again) against the Nazis, and amidst blazing fields, stroll hand in hand toward a fuliginous but uplifting final fade out.

Chekhov and Lupino enjoyed each other's company, which helped the film immensely, as the loquacious old uncle of the family is supposed to be sympathetic to the working-class outsider who appears to be infiltrating the aristocratic fold. London-born Lupino, the daughter of Stanley Lupino, a popular musical hall comedian, and Chekhov shared a love of the craft of acting. (It was Lupino who suggested to Mala Powers that she seek out Chekhov as a coach in Hollywood thus triggering one of the most enduring professional relationships of both their careers.) In an era where female directors regularly bumped their heads against the glass ceiling, Lupino went on to become a prolific director of films and TV series.

Alla Nazimova and Chekhov have very little screentime together, but what they do have considerably enhances the proceedings. Chekhov, as the grumbly old uncle of the family who is basically freeloading off his more successful brother (Francen), squeezes all the comedy and pathos there is to be had from the meager script, and Nazimova gives a grandstanding performance, which tends to suggest that both Russian artists realize that, compared to Gogol or Turgenev, they are simmering in the juices of a potboiler. Despite the mawkish predictability of the script, there is a certain worthy aura to the film that stems from the fact that, in the mid-forties, a propaganda movie to help the war effort was considered an honorable action by all concerned and, in the dark days of 1944, would never need to be justified or even rationalized.

The film's director, Vincent Sherman, was a Jewish Southerner from Vienna, Georgia, whose best work included the Bette Davis–Miriam Hopkins vehicle *Old Acquaintance*, *Mr Skeffington* (with Davis and Claude Raines), *The Hard Way* (again with Lupino), and *The Hasty Heart* (with Ronald Reagan). His film distinctions fade almost entirely beside his romantic conquests. As he openly confesses in his memoir *Studio Affairs*, he had lengthy romantic imbroglios with Bette Davis, Joan Crawford, and Rita Hayworth. When I spoke to him he had just passed his ninety-seventh birthday, but to have endured Davis, Crawford, and Hayworth, and lived to tell the tale, makes him a very special kind of survivor.

Concerning *In Our Time*, Sherman frankly admits:

> I got roped into it. I didn't particularly want to do it as I didn't think we had a good story, and we *didn't*. And the

more I read about Poland, the more I realized that it was
a lot like the South just before the Civil War—landed
gentry and large estates being run on the backs of a peasant workforce, so I did the best I could. I was hoping
toward the end, we could shoot some battle scenes in
Warsaw, but Warner didn't want to spend any money.
What I remember most about Chekhov is that before
each take, he would limber up, swing his arms and body
about in order to relax himself. And he also "made
friends" with the set. He would walk around and feel the
furniture and make it part of his character's life.

Unremarkable as the film is, the presence of two of Russia's
most charismatic performers gives it a certain significance in
the archive.

Alla Nazimova, born Mariam Edez Adelaida Leventon
(which quite justifies her shortening her name to simply
Nazimova) studied at the Moscow Art Theater and made her
name playing leading roles in St. Petersburg. She arrived in
America inauspiciously at the Herald Square Theatre at the
end of the nineties in an unremarkable drama entitled *The
Chosen People*. Nazimova, however, was unruffled, and when
her disheartened company returned to Russia, she opted to
remain in America. Six months later, having mastered the
English language, she triumphed in Ibsen's *Hedda Gabler*, fol-
lowed with Nora in *A Doll's House* and Hilda Wangle in *The
Master Builder*, and became one of the foremost exponents of
Ibsen in America. Her crowning performance was probably
the role of O-lan in the Theatre Guild's production of *The
Good Earth*.

Receiving a salary higher than even Mary Pickford's, she
made a string of successful silents starting in 1917, mostly melo-
dramas such as *Revelation, Toys of Fate* and *Eye For Eye*. In
1921, she co-starred with Valentino in *Camille*. Her luck ran
out when she started producing a number of her own arty
films. After plummeting from fourth place to twentieth in

Photoplay's annual popularity poll, she was relegated to playing small roles for Vitagraph. In the thirties, with the film flurry behind her, she devoted herself almost entirely to the stage, but did resurface in cameo roles in the forties. After dozens of torrid and tempestuous screen demises as vamps and tragic heroines, the actress from Yalta died herself of a coronary thrombosis in California in 1945, by which time all the ingredients of her future legend were firmly in place.

Nazimova's approach was strikingly similar to Chekhov's. "The actor should not play a part," she proclaimed. "Like the Aeolian harps that used to be hung in the trees to be played only by the breeze, the actor should be an instrument played upon by the character he depicts. The wind had but to ripple through the trees and the harp would play without conscious effort." Like Chekhov, she refused to siphon roles though the narrow bottleneck of her own limited personality. "I am nothing. I am nobody. I have to reconstruct my whole self into this woman I am to portray—to speak with her voice, laugh with her laughter, move with her motion—I never see myself at all. An actor must never see himself in character." And then, as if she had imbibed every page of *To the Actor*, which had not yet been conceived or written, she declared: "First, last, and always, a player must have imagination. Without imagination, he might as well be a bootblack as an actor. Imagination kindles the feelings, steers the actor through the character into emotion, enables him to reproduce feelings he himself has never experienced."

Given the extraordinary symbiosis that existed between Chekhov and Nazimova as performers, one can imagine what a Nora and Torvald, Nina and Trigorin, Ranevsky and Lophakin they might have made. Instead, Chekhov was consigned to cuddly old men and eccentric professors, and Nazimova to Slavic bit parts in films such as *Blood and Sand*, *Since You Went Away*, and *The Bridge of San Luis Rey*. Their brief encounter during *In Our Time* is more significant for what it portended than what it actually delivered.

● ● ● ● ●

In Alfred Hichcock's *Spellbound* (1945), the conjunction between actor and role fit like pieces of tongue-and-groove flooring. Dr. Alex Brulov, a Freudian analyst with a remarkable resemblance to the Viennese creator of psychoanalysis, is supposed to be wise, erudite, insightful, avuncular, and subtle — qualities that perfectly matched Chekhov's own makeup. His scenes with Ingrid Bergman glimmer with the kind of intimacy one expects a loveable disciple to show for a revered mentor. In his scenes with Gregory Peck, we can sense the sly doctor's tacit understanding of the troubled amnesiac and the dangers he may present. Throughout, Dr. Brulov spreads a kind of canny benevolence over his pupil's dilemma, namely having fallen in love with a man who has lost his identity and is now on the run from the police. It is a performance rooted in the Chekhovian (Anton, that is, not Michael) naturalism that any good actor can slot into when the need arises. An outsized actor like Orson Welles did it all the time in films like *The Big Clock* and *The Lady from Shanghai*. What made it work so well for Chekhov was the fact that behind the ordinariness of the cagey psychoanalyst there was a warm, almost throwaway performance that, like the best kind of acting, never draws attention to itself as acting per se. Things bubble under the surface and in so doing, give the surface a shimmery sheen from which we cannot turn away our eyes.

In 1943, David O. Selznick, who had become an independent producer but lost the prestige of running his own studio, was urged to see a psychiatrist by his departing wife, Irene Mayer. He reluctantly sought out Dr. May Romm, a highly respected Hollywood analyst. He found that he thoroughly enjoyed pouring out his innermost thoughts to this admiring and receptive lady, and in the process, quickly became a staunch advocate of psychoanalysis. Like many analysands, he came to believe that Dr. Romm was falling in love with him. As he became more and more unruly and unpredictable, the

analyst, who had seen more transferences than Selznick had
seen movies, gave him the boot after only one year. But
Selznick was unfazed. By then, he had convinced himself, he
"knew more than she did" and could just as easily analyze her.

When Hitchock presented Selznick with *The House of Dr.
Edwards* by Francis Beeding, a murder mystery that mingled
witchcraft and psychoanalysis played out in a Swiss mental
clinic, it was the right book at the right time for Selznick and he
enthusiastically gave it the greenlight. Ben Hecht, in close conjunction with Hitchcock, turned it into an intellectual thriller
of sorts, and Selznick brought in Salvador Dali to spice it up
with a captivating surrealist dream sequence. It came at just the
right time for American moviegoers as well. They were imbib-
ing Freudian psychology in one film after another, juggling
terms like "psychosis," "neuroses," "Oedipus complex," "ego,"
and "id" to their hearts' (and heads') content. Psychoanalysis
had become fodder for pictures like *Dreams that Money Can
Buy* and musicals like *Lady in the Dark*. No film seemed to be
complete without a Freudian interpretation that revealed the
unconscious flaws of its characters or the suppressed motiva-
tions behind their actions. Although both Peck and Bergman
were intelligent performers, probably no one knew more about
the subject than Chekhov, who had integrated many of the
tenets of psychoanalysis into his acting theory. One must also
remember that Chekhov had had several run-ins with shrinks
in Moscow—like those brought in at Stanislavsky's behest—
that almost ended in his being institutionalized.

Spellbound was immensely successful. Although Hitchcock was nominated for an Oscar for Best Director, he lost out
to Leo McCarey for *Going My Way*. Chekhov was nominated
for Best Supporting Actor but Barry Fitzgerald won that Oscar.
Nevertheless, the nomination and the commercial success of
the film greatly enhanced his reputation both as an actor and
a teacher—and in a community that responds more noticeably
to industry acclaim than it does to anything else.

Despite industry recognition and the fillip it gave his film career, Chekhov still felt he had lost his way in Hollywood; a sentiment curiously echoed by Harold Clurman in a piece reviewing *Spellbound* that he wrote for *Tomorrow* magazine in 1946:

> The two major performers—Ingrid Bergman and Gregory Peck—were called on to tell this picture's unlikely story so that it might be temporarily acceptable and interesting. But though this task was handsomely fulfilled, there was no moment in their acting that was anything more than good imitation. The picture's only vitality was that of Michael Chekhov. He was not a cog in the machine of the story but a living person.
>
> Chekhov is one of the few great actors of our time, but he has abdicated from creation. What he does in pictures hardly represents even the surface of his talents. (Playing a Russian repertory, he gave us a series of magnificent stage portrayals in a season that passed practically unnoticed on Broadway in 1935.) His film performances—including the one in *Spellbound*—are not true samples of his art. They are routine performances. But with him an entrance, an exit, walking across the room with a glass of milk, lying down, looking, listening, become dramatic. No matter what the scene, we feel ourselves in the presence of human experience. What he does takes on meaning almost apart from the concrete instance of the picture's plot. It is as if he needed no actual role; his acting is a kind of agent of life—focused, pointed, and expressive. He makes the juices of life circulate. Through him we learn once more that we have but to watch any moment of concentrated behavior to be fascinated. The smallest action thoroughly carried out seems to contain a kind of universal essence. This, in little, is the mystery of acting, one might almost say the mystery of life! It illustrates anew that just as in painting, an apple may equal a Madonna, so in acting that has liv-

ing texture there is more real drama than in the most
technical ingenuity.

Astute as Clurman always was in recognizing great acting
on those rare occasions when he found it, it is a little unfair to
claim that Chekhov had "abdicated from creation," as if Misha
preferred to pass his Hollywood days coaching starlets and
wannabes rather than playing Dostoyevsky, Turgenev, or
Gogol. The fact is, serious theater managements, like those
with which Clurman himself was often associated, were entirely oblivious to Chekhov's talents. Given the availability of
extraordinary European actors such as Albert Basserman,
Oscar Homolka, Conrad Veidt, Ludwig Donath, Vladimir
Sokoloff, and Alexander Granach, Hollywood preferred to
employ cuddlesome types such as Mischa Auer, Leonid
Kinsky, Felix Bressart, Sig Ruman, Fritz Feld, and S.Z
"Cuddles" Sakall, who embellished lackluster screenplays
with moments of sappy comedy relief. One must also remember that Chekhov was ensconced in Los Angeles, where in the
late forties and early fifties there was no serious theater to speak
of. Had enterprising impresarios such as Dwight Deere
Wiman, John Houseman, or the Theatre Guild had the inclination, a project could have been created that would have
enabled an actor of Chekhov's stamp to fulfill himself on
Broadway in works by Ibsen, Strindberg, or Anton Chekhov.
But in the late forties, as Clurman's own criticism testifies,
there was a dearth of serious theater in America, with a few
sterling exceptions such as O'Neill, Miller, Williams, Inge—all
committed exponents of psychological realism. In truth, what
Chekhov was doing was not so much abdicating his creativity
as instilling it in a new generation of American actors that
would go on to produce some of the most outstanding motion
picture performances of the next three decades.

Chapter Thirty-One

IN 1946, Ben Hecht and Charles MacArthur repaired to Long Island to make films independent of the studio system, and presumably more intellectual and serious than the usual crop of pictures mass-produced in Hollywood. One of these films was *Specter of the Rose*, written, directed, and produced by Hecht and featuring a cast that included Judith Anderson, Lionel Stander, and Michael Chekhov.

The film has a distinct home-movie feel of about it and bears little relation to Hecht's other work, which included polished movies such as *Scarface, Rope, Notorious, The Black Swan, Wuthering Heights*, and dozens of others. *Specter of the Rose* is loosely based on the character of Nijinsky and concerns a ballet dancer, played by Ivan Kirov, who is suspected of having murdered his ballerina wife while in the throes of some mental aberration. He subsequently falls in love and marries a younger version of his former spouse, played by Viola Essen, who in his febrile imagination, he confuses with his former wife and also tries to murder. The new bride is spared the fate of the former, and in a hallucinatory dance sequence that conjures up the spirit, if not the skill, of Nijinsky, he performs a breathtaking leap through his bedroom window and falls to his death in the street below.

Lionel Stander, as a murky poet with a pronounced Brooklyn accent (loosely modeled on the Greenwich Village bohemian Maxwell Bodenheim), dispenses some of Hecht's most leaden, florid writing, and Judith Anderson (long before she became a Dame) spends a lot of time knitting and being soulful and aesthetic as a fading ballet mistress. Ivan Kirov, a highly enigmatic actor, was not much of a dancer, his specialty being acrobatic leaps off of walls, and his cinematic wife, Viola Essen, although she was something of a dancer, was not very much of an actress. Neither Kirov nor Essen ever made another film. *Specter of the Rose* is one of those curious "private movies" that are so intellectual, esoteric, and murky, they only tend to reaffirm the virtues of the oft-disparaged commercialism of the studio system.

Chekhov plays the role of Max Polikoff, an agent-cum-impresario based loosely, and somewhat wickedly, on Sol Hurok in which the actor comes very close to playing the "accent clown" that he so dreaded becoming in films.

Although the film *qua* film has very little distinction, it is perhaps the very best record we have of Chekhov's work as a comic actor. His Polikoff is a camp, blatantly homosexual *macher* unwaveringly devoted to art for art's sake. His way of dealing with people is to douse them with syrupy lashings of fulsome affection; an extravert, self-confident chiseler, quite possibly also modeled on the expansive Ukranian trickster who tried to persuade him to create his own theater in Czechoslovakia. We can see in the interstices of Max's behavior, when he temporarily drops his guard, just how conniving and intolerable he really is, despite his effusive bonhomie. The performance is illuminated with telltale flickers that enable us to glimpse his frustration, aggression, and intolerance of the mundane antagonists who regularly foil his plans to produce great art in a society devoted strictly to mammon. But these are only flashes, like those one gets when a shooting star suddenly brightens a darkened sky, then expires before one can properly take it in. The broad sweep of the characterization is of a funny little man who has somehow stumbled into the wrong world and is desperately trying to reconcile his values with those diametrically opposed to them. As Max fakes, fawns, cajoles, and ingratiates himself, we get fleeting impressions of what Chekhov's Khlestakov might have been like at the Moscow Art, and the kind of comic finesse and exquisite attention to detail he would have brought to his uncle Anton's vaudeville sketches during the Hurok season.

Another fascinating aspect of this ultimately unsatisfying film is watching Chekhov interact with his old friend and associate George Shdanoff, who appears as a frustrated designer trying to get his salary back from his bankrupt producers. This is a relatively young Shdanoff, and clearly in the film at Chekhov's behest. The two play marvelously together, and it is the only instance that I am aware of in which they appear on screen together. The joy of seeing Chekhov doing first-rate work in a comic persona, which in many ways was his natural element, almost justifies the entire misguided enterprise.

If one were to try to equate Chekhov in comparison to his fellow players in *Specter of the Rose*, one would have to say everyone else was going about 30 miles per hour while Chekhov, souped up and nitrous-oxidized, was speeding along at 180. His personal velocity was unquestionably greater; his degree of inventiveness, attack, and sheer energy flow overwhelming those around him. Whether released or restrained, that degree of torque is what distinguishes the great from the mediocre actors.

Ultimately, all acting boils down to personality. The more distinctive the personality, the more watchable the actor, and the distinctions are not based on moral considerations or manners, breeding or upbringing, plainness or beauty, but on how succinctly the constituents of that particular personality convey those elements to the outside world. You can be distinctively snide or bitchy, distinctively repressed or demonstrative, distinctively introvert or extravert; the specific qualities have no bearing on the matter. All that really matters is how definitively the actor's personality delineates itself within the proffered fiction. Distinctive personalities automatically radiate, and wan or insubstantial personalities can practice "radiation exercises" from now till doomsday without leaving an impression. A radiator radiates hot air and no amount of increased voltage can enable it to radiate music or aroma, imagery or invention. It is the inherent qualities of the personality that provide the artist with the means to convey the emotional demands of a text or the psychology of a character. Technique is merely an adjunct, never an alternative. What Chekhov does in *Specter of the Rose* is to reveal the complexity of the actor's inner workings, and although the material makes it a waste of his talent, it is fascinating to watch that talent in full flow.

In the late forties and early fifties, Chekhov had been involved with a string of unmemorable movies that included *Cross My Heart* (with Betty Hutton), *Abie's Irish Rose* (allegedly Chekhov's favorite film), *Texas, Brooklyn and Heaven*, *Holiday for Sinners* and *Invitation*. In 1948, when Lewis Milestone was assembling *Arch of Triumph* with Ingrid Bergman and Charles Boyer, he cast Chekhov in the role of a Gestapo agent. No sooner had filming begun than Chekhov suffered a second heart attack and was obliged to recuperate for an entire year. He was replaced by Charles Laughton. His last film appearance was in *Rhapsody* with Elizabeth Taylor in 1954. Chekhov had been cast in nine films, but by and large, and when health permitted, Chekhov's energies in Hollywood were directed toward teaching. That is where his greatest legacy lies.

Chapter Thirty-Two

IN THE MID-FIFTIES, the Method furor was at its height. Marlon Brando, James Dean, Eli Wallach, Montgomery Clift, Julie Harris, Anne Jackson, Karl Malden, E.G. Marshall, Ben Gazara, Paul Newman, Kim Stanley, Maureen Stapleton, Geraldine Page, Uta Hagen, Martin Ritt, Daniel Mann, Sidney Lumet, Elia Kazan, and a host of others, had firmly established the cult of glorified ordinariness, and the work of Strasberg, the Actors' Studio, and its illustrious alumni dominated both the New York stage and Hollywood films. Acting had been reduced to natural behavior and screenwriters were purveying an intense neo-naturalism which, in its wake, was also creating a new breed of playwright: writers such as Paddy Chayevsky, William Inge, Michael V. Gazzo, Leonard Melfi, Terence McNally, etc.

The dramatic rebirth of Stanislavsky's aesthetic in America could not help but rankle Chekhov who had been waging a war against naturalism since the twenties. Chekhov is supposed to have said in a lecture:

> Obviously, the "method" label has been too indiscriminately slapped on to all innovators in the theater because of the posturings and failings of an anarchic few who, rather than evolving new and valid concepts or improving on the old ones, have gone way out into orbit, like so many mis-

guided missiles, by disregarding all good form and taste of
the past. But it is cruelly unjust to condemn a whole profession and its genuine ideals because of a handful of ostenta-
tious rebels without a cause who, in an effort to launch
themselves with pretentious and tasteless styles, have not
even succeeded in getting off their "pad." The same may be
said for some of those New Wave playwrights whose works
are awash with enigmatic themes, wobbly construction,
and uncharacterized people. So let us hear no more about
"method" actors, and let us not tar the theater as a whole
with that term's derisive insinuations.

Allowing for liberties that the transcriber of these sentiments may have taken in regard to Chekhov's diction (and I
suspect there were several), the fact remains that the resurgence of naturalistic acting would have appeared almost as an
affront to the kind of work Chekhov had been publicly espousing for thirty years. One has to remember, however, that there
is no such thing as a style that so dominates an era that alternative styles are utterly banished. When the naturalism of Andre
Antoine's Theatre Libre was triumphing in France, Jacques
Copeau, Charles Dullin, and Louis Jouvet were refining a styl-
ish alternative, employing the works of Claudel, Dostoyevsky,
and Shakespeare, and Alfred Jarry was subverting even those
trends with Absurdist comedies such as *Ubu Roi*. But clearly,
Chekhov was bucking a trend, and undoubtedly a certain
amount of class time had to be spent countering Strasbergian
dicta and defending revisonist thinking. As he had done in the
twenties, Chekhov found himself in opposition to the prevailing orthodoxy.

His group classes often had a smattering of Polish and
Russian students among their tyros; the private classes were for
more established performers such as Marilyn Monroe, Jack
Palance, and Mala Powers. At some classes, there would be a
mixture of talented younger performers and celebrity actors
such as Akim Tamiroff, Gary Cooper, Thomas Mitchell,

Robert Wagner, Arthur Kennedy, Patricia Neal, Anthony Quinn, Debbie Reynolds, etc. They comprised a certain amount of straightforward lecturing, followed by exercises and, occasionally, improvised scenes based on short stories or scenarios suggested by Chekhov. Jack Larson recalls an improv based on a short story by Anton Chekhov and a scene from Hamlet.

On one occasion, Gary Cooper, who usually just sat quietly and observed, was coaxed into an improvisation with Akim Tamiroff. The scene was loosely based on a poker game between three or four of the male actors. Cooper placed the action around a small table and, miming the playing cards, shuffled the deck and doled out cards to his fellow players. After a few hands, two of the men had folded and only Tamiroff and Cooper remained in the game. "My deal," said Cooper as he shuffled the cards and flicked out five cards to Tamiroff and himself. "How many do you want?" asked Cooper. "One," said Tamiroff. The two men eyed each other intensely as the cards flew out between them. "I pass," said Cooper. "I bet fifty dollars," said Tamiroff. "I'll see you," said Cooper, "and raise you fifty more!" Tamiroff's lips began to tremble and his eyes narrowed and began blinking uncontrollably. "I raise you a hundred," he said. "And I raise you another hundred," answered Cooper. Suddenly, Tamiroff lurched back in his chair and exclaimed, "You're cheating!" He was about to pull out his gun but Cooper beat him to the draw and, holding two fingers straight under Tamiroff's chin to simulate his double-barreled weapon, whispered, "You say that once more, and neither one of us is going to leave this game alive." The tension between the two men caused everyone in the room to stop breathing and the charged pause between them went on a good two minutes.

"It was the scariest improvisation I ever saw," said Anthony Quinn.

Most of the time, Chekhov would be elucidating some subtlety in the actor's arsenal, citing experiences from his own past or performances he had witnessed abroad. If scenes or improvs were not up to scratch, there would be no recriminations or harsh words. Actors would be coaxed to seek out alternative ways of achieving desired effects. But despite Chekhov's nonargumentative style, the sessions were not always placid.

On one occasion, Chekhov was explaining that while performing, an actor must simultaneously maintain an inner freedom and outer poise—like the trapeze artist who presents a free-flowing form while executing strenuous feats at great heights, rather than the boxer who is grounded and constantly exerting himself with volleys of violent movements. Burt Lancaster, who was sitting in on that class (and was himself something of a boxer), exploded in disagreement, insisting that it was the boxer exerting maximal physical power that should be the actor's model, and not the cool-headed trapeze artist, and that Chekhov was crazy. Many of the more practiced students who comprehended the paradox of expressing strong emotion while still retaining a "sense of ease," perfectly grasped Misha's point, but Lancaster was unyielding. These disputes were not frequent. Most of the time (according to Jack Colvin), a good deal of what the professor discussed went over the heads of many of the beginners who seemed to believe that mere physical exposure to Chekhov, as if to some kind of benevolent gamma ray, was sufficient to absorb his theories and improve their skill. John Abbot, the Hollywood character actor who was a senior member of the Stage Society in 1949 and founded the Drama Society in 1955, concurred with Colvin's view. "I don't think, of all the actors living," said Abbot, "there are more than two percent who could avail themselves of what he had to say."

Abbot was there on the night of Marlon Brando's visit and recalled that "Chekhov suggested some kind of improvisation to make some kind of point, and Marlon knelt on a chair, bent over it, stuck his behind out to all the company present, and stayed like that until the improvisation was over. When it was

done, Chekhov said dismissively, 'That was ridiculous!'"
Sometimes there was violent, antagonistic chemistry between
Method-trained actors and those buying into the Chekhov
technique—not unlike the antagonism that sparked between
Stanislavsky and Chekhov themselves in that last meeting in
1928, when each pitted his own acting theory against the other.

● ● ● ● ●

At the 1998 Golden Globe ceremony where he collected
the best actor award for his performance in *As Good as It Gets*,
Jack Nicholson, reminiscing about his early career, told the
audience: "While my mother and sister were hiding in the
dark and kind of watching me, y'know, hoping I was going to
be in the movie business, I turned around and imagined I saw
my director making fun of my newly acquired 'psychological
gesture' from Michael Chekhov." Chekhovians all over the
world perked up their ears. Actors such as Anthony Hopkins,
Clint Eastwood, and Anthony Perkins have acknowledged
Chekhov's influence. In many instances, these are performers
who have either brushed up against George Shdanoff or some
other Chekhovian coach, or simply read and were impressed
by Chekhov's published works, such as *To the Actor* and *On the
Technique of Acting*.

Just as there are many actors and teachers who loosely iden-
tify themselves with the Stanislavsky system, there are many
more who have acquired only the superficies of Chekhov's
techniques and vaunt them as artistic credentials. There is
more to Stanislavsky than "units," "emotional memory,"
"actions," and "objectives," and a great deal more to Chekhov
than "radiation," "atmosphere," and "psychological gestures."
These are the convenient handles of an acting theory that is
more like a series of Chinese boxes than it is a suitcase. To fully
come to grips with what Chekhov is espousing involves a protracted exposure to disciplines that underpin a metaphysical
view of what an actor does and how he achieves his most pro-

found results.

When Chekhov was teaching, he drew on insights that he personally experienced as an actor, and tried, by means of practical applications, to re-create sensations he had known first hand. Like any master teacher, he was drawing on a fund of personal acting events that had actually happened to him. It was the quality and frequency of those insights that made him a great actor and enabled him to engender similar experiences in his students. But there are many Chekhovian-styled teachers throughout the world who, being neither great actors nor great teachers, simply apply the technique as a consciously formulated modus operandi—which is a little like a fortune-teller without prescience reading tea leaves, or a psychic without extrasensory perception stroking a crystal ball. In the case of actor training, the touchstone is the teacher's inherent skill in identifying and reproducing the gifts that make acting remarkable and mesmerizing. Without those inherent skills, teachers are reduced to rehashing the tenets of a methodology that can produce results only when its formal precepts are transcended. A true believer, they say, has "seen the face of God," and something of that vision is retained in his nature that instinctively persuades others. A person who has never had an epiphany or throbbed with the sensation of spirituality is only going through the motions.

An acting technique, like any learned skill, depends not on the textbook but on the vouchsafed experience of the teacher applying it. In the case of Chekhov, there is an enormous gap between articulating the goal and getting to the goalposts. The goal is an enrichment of the imagination and a subsequent increase in natural resources, a result that produces the kind of "affective athleticism" that Antonin Artaud wrote about in *The Theatre and Its Double*. This is very different from simply honing one's technique or finding new ways to improve one's diction. If there is a curse to Chekhovian technique, it is that without actually mastering the steps required to achieve it, it can easily be dismissed as transcendental hogwash or soupy mysticism. Without qualified instruction by sensitive artist-teachers who have themselves experienced what they are trying to instill in others, it can simply dwindle into cosmic psycho-babble.

Chapter Thirty-Three

THERE WERE TWO SATELLITE TEACHERS that circulated around Chekhov in the last decade of his life. One was the aforementioned George Shdanoff, his close friend who became his leading disciple and, ultimately, a respected teacher in his own right. The other was Shdanoff's wife Elsa Schreiber, one of the most prestigious coaches in the Hollywood of the forties and fifties.

Schreiber was born in Vienna a few years before the turn of the twentieth century and at sixteen was an outstanding young actress in Germany and a piquant beauty. She played Juliet opposite the great German actor Alexander Moissi (often referred to as "the Barrymore of Berlin"), and subsequently, opposite Joseph Schildkraut. She made a number of silent films in the twenties, one of them with Joseph's eminent father Rudolph Schildkraut. After her early success, she was put under contract by the Berlin Staatsteater, where she was a memorable and much-lauded Lady Anne in *Richard III*. An early marriage diverted her from her stage career, but by the time she retired she had developed acting insights and literary perceptions that grew quietly—like underground bulbs—and gradually came to fruition.

In Berlin, she was frequently swept up into the company of theartical luminaries such as Fritz Kortner, Bruno and Leonard Frank, and Bertolt Brecht. She was highly touted by

Beate Moissi, the daughter of Alexander, and the word
"genius" came to be regularly attached to her persona. Elsa
started coaching actors a few years before she relocated to
London. She eschewed the title "coach" and always described
what she did as "privately directing prominent actors in their
parts." Within one year of arriving in London, she had mastered English and began working privately with actresses such
as Margaret Rawlings, Phyllis Calvert, Valerie Hobson, and
Lili Palmer, who proclaimed loudly and often that Schreiber
was "the only female genius that I ever met in my life."

Shdanoff was bewitched by Elsa the moment he first saw
her at a supper party thrown by Fritz Kortner in Berlin. She
swept him off his feet with her charm and intellectual agility.
They married in 1938, moved Los Angeles in 1939, and in 1943,
settled in Los Angeles.

In Hollywood, while Shdanoff was in his downstairs studio
coaching actors such as Cyd Charisse, Yvonne de Carlo,
Patricia Neal, Gary Cooper, Jack Palance, Robert Stack, Leslie
Caron, and Betsy Blair, Elsa, in the upstairs studio, serviced a
roster of private students that included Tyrone Power, Rex
Harrison, Sterling Hayden, Robert Walker, Jennifer Jones,
James Arness, Paul Newman and Gregory Peck, the latter pub-
licly acknowledging Schreiber's invaluable assistance when he
picked up a Golden Globe as best actor for *To Kill a Mocking
Bird* in 1962

Shdanoff was also a direct beneficiary of his wife's talents, as
he acknowledged in the nineties:

> Elsa was the most decisive influence, the most powerful
> stimulant, the greatest inspiration in my professional and
> daily life. While I am an impractical dreamer, a stranger
> in this universe, Elsa combined her spiritual talent, her
> metaphysical inclination, her artist's sensibility, with this
> surrounding life and all its problems. She knew better
> than I how to face and solve those problems. She had an
> incredible vitality, a childlike quality all her life; a mixture

of childish spontaneity and a mature woman's sharp outlook. She had the keenest observation—nothing escaped
her. As her great friend Beate Moissi said of her: "Elsa
hears the grass grow."

In the discreetly veiled world of Hollywood coaches, where
teachers do not publicize the help they give nor stars admit
that they often rely on such help, Schreiber's reputation has
grown exponentially with Chekhov's. Unlike Shdanoff, who
filtered and embellished precepts absorbed over a thirty-year
exposure to his mentor, Schreiber was very much her own
woman. She possessed an astute, steeltrap mind that could
parse the intricacies of film scripts and zone in on precisely
where the crucial problems lay. She would have made a fine
film director, and in fact, in 1946, when she was employed as a
script consultant at Universal Studios, she was asked to direct a
film test between Douglas Fairbanks Jr. and a new leading lady
being considered for a major role. Fairbanks was so enchanted
by the perception and flair of the Germanic lady who efficiently took control of him, he immediately sought out the head of
the studio and urged him to assign Schreiber as the director of
the film. "Wait, she has to learn the technical side of making
pictures," he was told. "We're grooming her. In time she will be
directing pictures." As often happens in the film business, studio chieftains and top honchos are systematically replaced by
others in Hollywood's nonstop game of musical chairs, and
this directorial opportunity never materialized. But Schreiber
could take solace from the fact that many of the performers
whom she molded in private sessions—like Gregory Peck and
Paul Newman—achieved outstanding national recognition
that could be directly traced back to her teachings.

It was during his period in Hollywood that Chekhov put his
mind to adapting his technique to the specific requirements of
motion-picture acting; a medium that required instantaneous
results rather than the ability to build, embellish, and sustain a
characterization over a long period of time. The underlying

principles of his technique might still pertain, but they had now to be deftly compressed if a practical end was to be achieved. In that sense, he *was*, as Shdanoff had complained, training actors to fulfill the needs of people like Louis B. Mayer.

Chapter Thirty-Four

MICHAEL CHEKHOV entered Mala Powers' life in the late forties. It was at the suggestion of her friend Ida Lupino that she sought him out at one of his Hollywood sessions.

> On a never-to-be-forgotten evening that changed my life forever, I nervously knocked on the door of that house. It was opened by a small, kind, meticulously dressed, unassuming man with a strong Russian accent—Michael Chekhov. He welcomed me with a warmth that enveloped me and that I experienced as flowing right from his heart. Soon he began to demonstrate means for creating a character—and this rather frail, slender man grew to be a giant in front of us. Enthusiasm, humor, artistry, and love of the theater radiated from him and penetrated each of us while we watched and listened, spellbound.

Powers recalls what so many experienced in Chekhov's presence—the incongruous expansion of personality that rose magically from a small, unprepossessing frame. As one of his students put it, "He was a giant in the slender body of a child."

At the age of sixteen, Mala Powers started taking private lessons, and the relationship between the young actress and the middle-aged teacher became one of the most important in both of their lives. Chekhov coached her in every film role she played, but more important, he shaped her intellect and influenced her belief system. "The astonishing quality about him as a teacher," she said, "was that nothing he ever taught related only to acting or to the theater. Chekhov's method and manner of teaching was so completely based on deep truths that whatever one learned from him about art could also be applied to life, to a richer understanding and interaction with one's fellow man. He was concerned with the whole human being." Powers learned, as the students at Dartington had, that each person in his care was considered a thoroughly unique individual with, as she put it, "an unknown, bottomless depth and capability slumbering within, which was constantly on the verge of awakening."

After six years, she had not only assimilated his system of acting, but absorbed his religious and philosophical ideas as well; so much so that she too became an anthroposophist. She was embraced by Xenia as well as Misha, and was treated almost as one of the family. She often officiated at the Chekhov classes and was a constant buffer for the Chekhovs in the often rough-and-tumble world of Hollywood.

After establishing herself as a film actress, Powers, whose parents were both journalists, began a successful writing career. Her books *Follow the Year* and *Follow the Star* have been translated into several languages. Her most outstanding film performance was undoubtedly Roxanne in the Jose Ferrer/Stanley Kramer film of Rostand's *Cyrano de Bergerac*, but even more significantly, she went on to become one of the most respected and accomplished teachers of the Chekhov technique in America, giving lectures, workshops, and demonstrations in schools, universities, and theaters throughout the world. At Chekhov's death, she was appointed the executrix of his estate.

Mala Powers is only one of the women who played a crucial role in Chekhov's career. Throughout his life, there were many, and without them it is quite possible his life might have read very differently.

It was Anton Chekhov's wife, Olga Knipper Chekhova, who finessed Michael's way into the Moscow Art Theatre; Xenia Karlovna Zeller who cured him of alcoholism and was a solid psychological support for the more than twenty-five years of their itinerant marriage; Georgette Boner who was his ardent producer and invaluable aide-de-camp during the period in Paris, Riga, New York, and England; Beatrice Straight who made it possible for him to begin the Chekhov Studio in Dartington; and her mother, Dorothy Whitney Elmhirst, who financed the venture and became the staunchest of all his allies. And then there was Deirdre Hurst du Prey, who, starting as his amanuensis at Dartington, went on to become something of his Boswell in America.

Du Prey grew up in the wilds of Vancouver in the early decades of the twentieth century. She was drawn strongly to dance, but her sensible mother made sure she developed more practical skills just in case her artistic ambitions were not fulfilled. One of these was shorthand, at which she became highly adept. Du Prey's life changed dramatically in 1932 when she was sent to Dartington Hall and was suddenly exposed to a multitude of unconventional influences. She wrote of that time:

> I fell in love with it immediately and experienced it fully. What they were really trying to do was establish a community in which everything necessary would be provided. There was a very modern school that was often much criticized. The students would go down into the River Dart, which was just at the foot of the school buildings, and go splashing in there, naked boys and girls! For the locals, that was really a little bit too much.

She and Beatrice Straight, who became a fast friend and remained one until her death, went to see the Hurok season of Chekhov plays in New York and were "thunderstruck." Together they began a campaign to lure Chekhov over to

Dartington. He arrived in 1935 and du Prey became a constant observer of the classwork. Chekhov noticed that she was constantly taking shorthand notes, and not having as yet mastered English, he relied more and more on du Prey's help. Because she constantly had a pencil wedged in her hair, she was nicknamed "the Pencil," and gradually took to assisting Chekhov in all his literary activities. As he became more fluent in the language, du Prey transcribed virtually every word that came out of his mouth. "Whenever we could get the time together, I took notes. He would write in a very peculiar way. He had very little use of English in a written form. His spoken English was good otherwise, but writing was very difficult. So I began from the very beginning working with him on everything that he wanted written."

By 1942, she had accumulated more than five hundred English language lessons derived from the Studio's inception at Dartington Hall, up to and including the lectures he gave in New York. Along with her colleague Paul Marshall Allen, she assembled all of this material into a manuscript entitled *The Actor Is Theatre*, which provided the raw material out of which *To the Actor* was eventually written in 1942. When Chekhov left for Hollywood, he took the du Prey–Marshall Allen version of the book with him, but it was impossible to find a publisher. Many of them balked at the preponderance of material about Steiner and anthroposophy, and could not see the connection between that and a primer on acting. Frustrated by his inability to find an American publisher and progressively more dissatisfied with the actual content of his manuscript, Chekhov decided to publish it himself in a Russian edition. In 1946, *O Texnike Aktera* appeared and Chekhov announced: "That was what I meant to say." (Thirty-eight years earlier, in 1928, Chekhov's autobiography *The Path of the Actor* had been an unexpected best-seller in Russia and despite the official proscription of his work, there were many Russians who still remembered him fondly.)

The Russian edition of *O Texnike Aktera* was distributed among émigrés in various parts of America, and several copies were smuggled into the Soviet Union by friends and subversive theatrical types. Chekhov then attempted to translate the book into English himself, but his lack of language skills defeated him. It was at this juncture that Charles Leonard, a playwright-producer-director, entered his life. Leonard agreed to edit the book and proceeded to convice Harper & Row to publish it. In 1953, *To the Actor—On the Technique of Acting* finally saw the light of day. But here, too, many of the Steiner references and more spiritually based material from the original were excised. (Eight years after Chekhov's death, Leonard produced a sequel to *To the Actor*, entitled *To the Director and Playwright*, composed of lectures given by Chekhov to the Drama Society in Hollywood culled from notes provided by John Dehner, John Abbott and Fanya Miroff. The book contains an interesting comparison of the styles of Stanislavsky, Meyerhold, Vakhtangov, and Tairov, and a few brief essays on standard Chekhovian subjects, but two-thirds of it is given over to Charles Appleton's rehearsal record of the 1946 Actors' Lab production of *The Inspector General*, a work that vividly demonstrates how the worst results can sometimes issue from the best of intentions. The problem with the Los Angeles revival of *Revisor* was not only that an ad hoc and uneven collection of American actors were unable to muster the style that a classic of such proportions required, but also that Chekhov's own attempt to resurrect a success, now a quarter of a century old, was motivated more by ego than zeal. Providing a detailed record of a director's approach to what was clearly a flop seems a wayward exercise in theatrical scholarship.)

It wasn't until 2002 when, under the aegis of Mala Powers, the reissued version of *To the Actor* appeared that Chekhov's work could be read in its entirety. But the du Prey transcriptions of the early classes (particularly the ones in New York between November 7 and December 29, 1941) are in many ways the best way to experience the full breadth of Chekhov's teachings. Perhaps one day they too will find their way into print.

But how providential that "the Pencil" should have been sharpened and waiting for Misha in Devon in 1935, at precisely the moment when officials in the Soviet Union were doing everything in their power to erase his memory.

Chapter Thirty-Five

ALTHOUGH CHEKHOV INTERACTED with many members of the Hollywood community, both stars and students, there is no clear-cut perception of the man or his character. To most of his students, the garrulous little Russian with the strong theoretical bent was simply thought of as "the professor." He exuded another time, another world, and there was something about his being ensconced in Hollywood that was simultaneously exotic and incongruous. However, many actors who knew him more intimately found him anything but "professorial."

Chekhov's great phobia was small talk. Having been weaned on rich intellectual stimuli by his father, he was incapable of discussing permutations in the weather or the box office takings regularly printed in *Variety*. He was rooted in writers like Schopenhauer, Steiner, and Nietzsche, and nothing pleased him more than philosophical speculation or discussing recent trends in psychoanalysis. He was eloquent discoursing on art, religion, literature, and aesthetics, but became mute when the conversation turned to show-biz gossip. Shdanoff remarked:

> Melancholic, complicated, a profound thinker he was also capable of laughing until the tears ran down his cheeks. His sense of humor was profound, but never evil. It was always loving and directed, most of the time,

against himself. He loved it when I imitated his self-conscious, shy, bizarre behavior. "Show me that again," he would cry through raucous, uncontrollable laughter. He was outgoing, loving, full of desire to help, yet introverted as well, withdrawn, seeking solitude, shielding himself from the surrounding world. Egotistical, selfish sometimes, yet at the same time altruistically concerned, ready to help. All these contradictions combined in one soul.

In a break during rehearsals of *The Inspector General* in Los Angeles, Morris Carnovsky asked him if he ever intended to return to acting himself. "No," he answered, "I've reached a point in my life where I've come to believe that it is too foolish a pastime for adults." When Carnovsky pressed him on the subject, "he persisted that acting was a useless waste of time and he had become disillusioned with the whole business. Later that afternoon," Carnovsky reports, "he was scheduled to give a lecture to a group of young students and I popped in at the back of the hall to catch some moments of it. The man addressing the group was so full of vigor, fire, and enthusiasm, so clearly inspiring the group of young actors around him, it was impossible to reconcile him with the depressed director I'd spoken to only an hour ago. Watching him illuminate and excite that group of young people about the art of acting, I somehow felt *that* was the real Michael Chekhov."

The unbridled improvisational skill that made his Khlestakov such a devastating comic creation and that permeates his performance in films such as *Specter of the Rose* was, to a great extent, the main components of Chekhov's personality. He was a Puck-like pixie that delighted in deflating the pomposities of the world, an absurdist long before the phrase became a cult label. But the legacy from Steiner and his own Christian principles also rooted him in a deeply entrenched humanism. None of his colleagues can remember an instance when he was sharp or wounding to an actor. Jack Colvin, in all the years he knew him, recalls only one hostile outburst when he was driving Chekhov home from an acting class at which a complacent, middle-aged, fairly well-established actor had said he had no need to study, as he already was "a master of my craft."

"This sent Chekhov through the ceiling," said Colvin, "He is *not* the master of his craft! He is a merchant who peddles shopworn clichés!" And of course, Misha felt that Hollywood's attitude toward him was also a welter of dispensed clichés, routinely casting him as little old professors, cuddly little foreign Russians, or German types."

When Marilyn Monroe confessed to Colvin that Chekhov was "the only man I ever really loved," it is clear that what she was testifying to was not some clandestine romantic amour, but the strong, benevolent, paternalistic affirmation of a teacher who shared the actress' view of her own uniqueness as an individual, and not the "shopworn cliché" the studios routinely recycled in one film after another.

Other students whom he befriended conjure up equally affectionate memories. Jack Larson, who had a ten-year stint on the *Superman* series with George Reeves, recalls that some of his most intense conversations with his mentor had to do with astrology and palmistry, two subjects that thoroughly fascinated Chekhov. "He would forever be taking my hand and following the lines in my palm with a slow, careful navigation of his finger through all its bends and turns. He often asked friends the exact hour of their birth in order to cast astrological charts for them." Both subjects are offshoots of Chekhov's deep-seated view that behind even the most commonplace externals, there is a mystery to be divined. After his death, Chekhov bequeathed to Larson several rare books on both astrology and palmistry. "He was a really loveable guy and I loved the long, private conversations we had together," Larson said. But many of Chekhov's younger students found him remote and unapproachable. Tuned into wavelengths beyond those reporting commercial triva, he *could* be remote, and when exposed to egotists who thought acting was easy, he could be surly. All teachers, in the presence of genuine talent, incline like flowers to sunlight and withdraw inwardly from mediocrities.

Although generally remembered as a cuddly, smiling, endlessly agreeable little man with a cultivated Russian accent, much of that persona was a façade for the angry, sometimes irascible man underneath. Shdanoff once challenged him precisely on that point. "Misha," he said to him one day, "you are wearing a mask in your daily life! Is it for defensive purposes?" Misha laughed good-naturedly at the criticism and told Shdanoff the following anecdote:

> When I was a young schoolboy, I was very aggressive, cocky, sure of my physical strength and would get into heated fights with other boys. One day, a boy much stronger and taller than myself whom I had provoked and challenged to a fist fight, beat me up so thoroughly that I found it difficult to even get back onto my feet. When I finally did get up, all black and blue from his blows, I began to smile. Since then, I go on smiling to all strangers—especially to policemen. It is what I call my "Russian sugar" and I pour it out regularly in my everyday life.

This explained much to Shdanoff, who recalled that whenever he accompanied Chekhov to a bank or to any official government agency, "he would perpetually smile and sweetly repeat 'Yeees, yeees, yeees, I see, I see....'" Afterward, Shdanoff would turn on him: "Misha, you didn't understand a word that person was saying!" Misha would immediately agree, mime sprinkling out a dose of his Russian sugar, and the two friends would laugh uproariously.

There were so many demons locked up behind the social façade of Michael Chekhov, it made perfect sense that when they found release in a role, they would literally swamp the stage.

Chapter Thirty-Six

IN TRYING TO BE SCRUPULOUSLY OBJECTIVE about Michael Chekhov and his achievements, I have to begin by acknowledging his debts both to Stanislavsky and Vakhtangov.

From Stanislavsky he appropriated the notions of "actions" and "objectives," "concentration" and "atmosphere"; he decidedly gave them his own twist, but the categories were initially carved out by his mentor. As for his "sense of the whole," that is as much Aristotle as it is Chekhov. His strictures on what one might call "bipolar characterization" (the assimilation of contradictory traits) are an extension of the Stanislavsky dictum to avoid one-dimensionalism, urging the actor to find complementary aspects of the role. Of course, that insight is not exclusive to Stanislavsky either; examples of it can be found in characterizations drawn from some of the greatest works of the Elizabethan and Jacobean canon. It is simply an acknowledgement of the fact that people are complex rather than single-celled. Morris Carnovsky, the accomplished Group Theatre actor, was a great admirer of Chekhov, but was also aware of his debt to his most influential teacher. "Where Stanislavsky spoke of 'relaxation of muscles,'" Carnovsky has written, "Chekhov did not hesitate to call it 'feeling of ease.' Where Stanislavsky broke off his brilliant observations on 'action' and 'objective,' Chekhov combined them with 'character' in his marvelous intuition of the 'psychological gesture.'"

From Vakhtangov, Chekhov inherited a sense of external theatricality, the conscious use of stage imagery to insinuate meaning and convey dramatic insights. Vakhtangov added innumerable colors to the actor's palette, and went further in demolishing the fourth wall than any Russian innovator, save Meyerhold. Chekhov's improvisational flair was influenced by the example of his earliest collaborator; the inventions, of course, were entirely his own.

Deirdre Hurst du Prey's book *Michael Chekhov: Lessons for Teachers of His Acting Technique*, a transcription taken in shorthand of Chekhov's lectures from Dartington Hall in 1936, is sprinkled with quotations such as: "You radiate very vividly in life. Try to find out how to capture that power for your art...always be conscious of radiating," and "Keep thinking constantly, 'I am a creative person.' I am *radiating* and doing everything in a creative way." Etc. etc, etc. "Radiation" is passionately exhorted and rigorously advocated, but the means by which this magical force can be engendered are never articulated. It remains an intriguing abstraction.

An actor who is powerfully playing his "action," expressing his "want," and pursuing his "objective" is going to be radiating energy more effectively than one who is uncertain of his "action," unclear about his "want" and half-heartedly pursuing his "objective." To the extent that an actor is *radiating* these energies, he will be more defined, more compelling, more watchable than one who isn't. But that quality is the result of nothing more than concentrated intent, technically fueled and imaginatively embellished. In that sense, every successful performance radiates from the stage to the audience. But to designate radiation as a quality distinct from the actor who is conveying it as an integral part of his performance is like saying every actor using his larynx and vocal cords is vocalizing. Of course he is. That's what acting is all about.

Certain actors, because of the force of their personality, because they innately possess "presence," cannot help but radiate a kind of personal magnetism because it is rooted in their metabolism. Others not so endowed always appear to be playing in poor light simply because, as personalities, they are less defined.

To be fervently induced to radiate when you lack this personal magnetism is like being urged to be beautiful when you are incontrovertibly plain. We have all had the experience of being mesmerized by a gifted performer with a dazzling personality (i.e., star quality) and left cold by a mediocre player who does not stir our interest or command our attention. Here, Chekhov's theory seems to be relying more on exhortation than elucidation.

Although "The Higher I" is an idea from Rudolph Steiner incorporated into the Chekhov technique, it is sufficiently removed from its source to qualify as an original concept. It points the actor away from the mundaneness of his own personal makeup toward a more elevated plateau where unexpected characteristics can be explored and appropriated. It is responsible for those startling transformations that are sometimes found in the work of actors such as John Barrymore, Paul Muni, Laurence Oliver, Orson Welles, Michael Gambon, and Anthony Hopkins where we feel possession has taken place and another being has taken residence in the psyche of the actor. The recorded performances of Chekhov himself are the personification of this idea; had these examples not existed, it might have remained an abstract concept.

Often, in the classes conducted both at Dartington and in Hollywood, Chekhov constantly warns the actor against being seduced only by the mind. This disparagement of the intellect is usually coupled with a strong advocacy of feeling. This begs the question: Can a theory of acting, which is essentially an intellectual construct, be embodied in anything but suggestive, theoretical language directed to the intellect? Can an injunction made to the consciousness to *feel* be acted upon by any process other than ratiocination and is there any route to sensibility that does not involve mental process? This does not deny the fact that some of the most effective acting comes from some area beyond human cognition.

When we are swept up by an actor's performance and attempt to describe it, we use words such as "extraordinary," "fabulous," "divine," "fantastic," and "out of this world" and none of these are empty hyperbole. When we are transported by great acting we *are* in the presence of something otherworldly, something that our language cannot easily define except by reference to preternatural causes. Chekhov's theories are the only ones that I know of that have actively gone in search of that transcendent quality; that have identified it and attempted to find a practical means of achieving it. The best of his technique stands in relation to acting theory as space probes do to our knowledge of the known universe. By going deeper they take us further and by taking us further, they add an extra dimension to an art that, from the very beginning, has probed the profoundest secrets of human experience. For this alone, there is a certain reverence due to Chekhov that cannot be paid to Stanislavsky, Meyerhold, Vakhtangov, or any other of the treasured pioneers that experimented in early-twentieth-century Russia.*

Chekhov's most significant contributions are in defining the psychological gesture and directing the actors' energy to forces beyond ostensible truth. The psychological gesture is in many ways the most ambiguous of his insights, and the words them-

---

* Chekhov's experiments into the paranormal are of concern, not only to teachers of acting but also to scientists who for years have been exploring the existence of some zone beyond the reach of conventional scientific knowledge. One of these, Freeman J. Dyson, Professor of Physics Emeritus at the Institute of Advanced Study in Princeton, has written as follows: "The hypothesis that paranormal phenomena are real but lie outside the limits of science is supported by a great mass of evidence. The evidence has been collected by the Society for Psychical Research in Britain and by similar organizations in other countries. The journal of the London society is full of stories of remarkable events in which ordinary people appear to possess paranormal abilities. The evidence is entirely anecdotal. It has nothing to do with science, since it cannot be reproduced under controlled conditions. But the evidence is there. The members of the society took great trouble to interview first-hand witnesses as soon as possible after the events, and to document the stories carefully. One fact that emerges clearly from the stories is that paranormal events occur, if they occur at all, only when people are under stress and experiencing strong

selves are rather misleading. It is not so much a psychologically crafted physical gesture per se, although it may take that form; it is more like a seedbed from which all physical characterization stems. Unlike the spine, which is an extension of Stanislavsky's idea of a "super objective," the psychological gesture is like the quintessential genetic code that determines the difference between one person and another. By discovering a character's most fundamental drives, it shapes the physical life of that character in ways that become consistent with that discovery.

Chekhov has written:

> The psychological gesture is your own secret. It is the basis on which you stand, but how you act is quite a different thing. If you act without the psychological gesture it may seem that your acting is pieced together. If you have the psychological gesture, you can act freely without paying attention to whether it is shown outwardly or not. In almost

emotions. This fact would immediately explain why paranormal phenomena are not observable under the conditions of a well-controlled scientific experiment. Strong emotion and stress are inherently incompatible with controlled scientific procedures." Although, of course, they are almost inescapably present in stage performances where "stress" and "strong emotions" are de rigueur. Dyson continues: "I am suggesting that paranormal mental abilities and scientific method may be complementary. The word 'complementary" is a technical term introduced into physics by Niels Bohr. It means that two descriptions of nature may both be valid but cannot be observed simultaneously. The classic example of complementarity is the dual nature of light. In one experiment light is seen to behave as a continuous wave, in another experiment it behaves as a swarm of particles, but we cannot see the wave and the particles in the same experiment. Complementarity in physics is an established fact. The extension of the idea of complementarity to mental phenomena is pure speculation. But I find it plausible that a world of mental phenomena should exist, too fluid and evanescent to be grasped with the cumbersome tools of science." (*New York Review of Books* Vol. LI, No. 5, March 25, 2004)

all cases, the psychological gesture must not be shown outwardly, because then it has more charm, more power.

But once that link between the character's psychology and
his body has been made, it automatically conditions all aspects
of the character's behavior; stance, posture, moral attitude,
social demeanor, as well as physical gestures.

Like Henri Bergson's *élan vital*, George Bernard Shaw's
"life force" or Wilhelm Reich's "Orgone energy," the psychological gesture is an all-encompassing concept in no way
restricted to human functionality. It can just as readily be found
in nature and the inanimate world. (A tree, a cloud, a building,
a neighborhood are all perpetually making their psychological
gestures in space.) From the actor's standpoint, it is imaginatively derived from various aspects of the play in question, and
as with many of Chekhov's theories, appears intellectually elusive until experienced—at which time it becomes crystal clear.

Chekhov's work, both as actor and theorist, opened up the
minefield that lay beneath subtext. He was bold enough to assert
what the ancients had earlier professed; namely that great acting
was allied to extra mundane causes that, though difficult to
define, were unquestionably present in the work of great performing artists. In doing that, he widened the horizon of acting
theory, and today we are all scanning the heavens to locate some
of the outerterrestrial bodies he intuited. He encouraged the
actor to practice yoga and meditation, and to look into clairvoyance and the supernatural, and all locked chambers of the imagination. He reaffirmed the supremacy of spirit over matter, and
like Artaud, added a philosophical dimension to an aesthetic
that tended to be fixated on the reconstruction of plausible
behavior. Chekhov, and Chekhov's ideas, will be sending out sig-
nals into the future for centuries to come. Because there was a
Chekhov, we will never again be satisfied with a simulacrum of
human nature. We will always be striving for a glimpse of that
otherness that we look for in religion, postulate in metaphysics,
and encounter in dreams.

Chapter Thirty-Seven

BY THE EARLY FIFTIES, when he was coaching actors in Hollywood and fluttering through, on the whole, unremarkable films, Chekhov had been separated from his homeland for a good quarter of a century. We know from the fate of artists such as Stravinsky, Solzhenitsen, and Nabokov that the tug of Mother Russia is a great one. Americans like Henry James, Ernest Hemingway, and Henry Miller could become expatriates and still retain their native culture, but the umbilical cord with Russia is not so easily severed.

Looking back, Chekhov could visualize the fond fraternity of the Maly Theatre, the inspiring days at the Moscow Art, the stimulating collaboration with Sulerzhitsky and Vakhtangov, playing Khlestakov, Eric XIV, and Hamlet to wildly enthusiastic houses, and an intimate association with the genius of writers such as Gogol, Strindberg, Shakespeare and Anton Chekhov—all stewing in a culture where almost every project represented some bold experimental gamble or innovative leap. Surveying his life at fifty, he would have had to recall a tangential episode in Germany, an abortive experience in France, a frustrating detour to Latvia and Lithuania, and a checkered career as a teacher, theorist, actor, and coach in a land where he was ineradicably an émigré. The deeply rooted lack of seriousness in his adopted land would have had to enforce a heavy depression as he rehearsed often ungifted actors in productions like *The Inspector General* (in which he had gloried under Stanislavsky's direction), or expostulated idealized theories to starstruck students who had no sense of ensemble and scant knowledge of the rich tradition of European classics on which Chekhov had been bred.

The City of Angels, where actors desperately sought to be included in mediocre projects that dashed their spirits and offended their intellect even as they spurred on their ambition, was as alien to Chekhov's Russia as the Nevsky Prospect was to Hollywood Boulevard. Many of his students acknowledge that, genial as he always was, Chekhov could not shake off the frustration that had become a staple of his life in America. The ebullience, the fastidious approach, the scrupulous delineation of character that sporadically illuminate his film appearances are like sparks from an engine that cannot quite manage to ignite. It is the classic case of the fish out of water, except that this fish is a beached great white whale.

Chekhov's power in America was always immanent rather than manifest. What he represented was more impressive than what he was allowed to deliver. The theories and the technique, except when related to his own past performances, remain abstract; an augury rather than hard evidence of a proven system. Even to the most gifted of his students, what their mentor was proselytizing seemed vague and elusive — something that might be possible to achieve in a different milieu and under very different circumstances than those that obtained in Hollywood. Perhaps that was their reason for being in those classes in the first place — to escape the confines of a certain tantalizing drudgery by becoming a different kind of actor and, ipso facto, more liberated human beings.

There is no shortage of performers who exemplify the Stanislavsky system or its Strasbergian counterpart. Starting with the pioneers of The Group Theatre, actors such as Garfield, Cobb, Carnovsky, Meisner, Lewis, Stella and Luther Adler, etc. extending outward to film stars such as Brando, Dean, Newman, Tandy, Clift, Stanley, Wallach, etc. But one would be hard-pressed to assemble a comparable list of Chekhovian artists; that is, actors and actresses who not only adhere to the principles of Chekhov's approach but clearly exemplify them in an aggregate of performances in either medium. This is mainly because Chekhov's ideas exist to underpin members of an ensemble; an acting style in which individual qualities, like so many hues on a palette, contribute to the overall texture of the entire canvas. Does that mean that Chekhovian technique cannot strengthen and enhance the skills of individual performers? Obviously not. We know from the work of actors such as Jack Nicholson, Clint Eastwood, Anthony Hopkins and Patricia Neal that a Chekhovian approach can produce exemplary results in performers who privately apply its precepts to particular roles in specific projects. But Chekhov himself, first at the Maly, then the First Studio, and then the Second Moscow Art, honed his talent within a collective framework, and the purpose of realizing, sharpening and extending his talent was to enrich the group of which he was an integral part.

There are some acting techniques that, like rules of grammar and syntax, enable artists to perfect their personal powers of expression in whatever work they undertake. Stanislavsky was a masterful actor who had the ability to research his own experience in order to codify a system of acting that could then be generally applicable. But he too was doing so within the context of ensemble work. The assumption in the cases of both Chekhov and Stanislavsky was that the actor was simultaneously donor and recipient of the training for the greater glory of the collective. If this was the basis on which Chekhovian technique first took shape, it raises an alarming question: Can it ever be fully realized by disparate actors wandering through plays and films where no shared aesthetic unites all the participants? I believe this was one of the doubts that gnawed away at Chekhov when coaching his diverse collection of Hollywood students. Could individual artists, no matter how skilled they became in Chekhovian Technique, ever truly realize those precepts in television sitcoms, unhomogenized movies or loosely assembled, one-off stage productions containing a variety of artists of very different acting backgrounds? And if not, what *was* a technique but a kind of aesthetic oddity that served as a beacon to ships beyond the sight of its signal?

Chapter Thirty-Eight

IN THE MID-FIFTIES, Chekhov became increasingly nostalgic about Russia, and increasingly aware of the incongruity of a seasoned Russian actor trying to hew out a life for himself in America, particularly at a time when harsh gusts from the Cold War would blow through the papers day after day. The strain of teaching others to do what he could no longer undertake himself became a growing burden. (He had already survived two heart attacks.) He did his best to insure that his despondency would not affect his students or his standing as a teacher, but Xenia got the full blast of it, and when he consorted with the Russian émigré community, many of who shared his frustrations, it poured out of him like sewage.

Future projects were always in the air: a revival of *The Cherry Orchard*, the perennial dramatization of *Don Quixote*, a new production of *Hamlet*. But secretly he knew he was merely planting seeds in fallow soil. These were either triumphs from the past or unrealistic ambitions that had petered out many years before. One must be forward-looking, he told himself. This was America. He lived in the film capitol of the world. He must, like those around him, hustle, bargain, and strive to keep up with the times. The Russia of his boyhood and early manhood was now a dungeon in which feckless laborers struggled to stay alive and elude the clutches of a malevolent regime in what had become a shameless, godless country.

Of course, he had tried to say all of that with *The Possessed* in 1939 and no one wanted to know. But, he had to admit, he was no political activist, no champion of the downtrodden. His heroes were Shakespeare, Molière, Dickens, Gogol, and Steiner. His forte was comedy; his refuge, art. His doctors had strongly advised him to give up smoking. That was a practical goal. That was achievable. He would attend to that.

A certain frailty was now visible in Chekhov. Unable to teach classes in person, he had taken to taping his lectures and then having them played to an assembly of his students. His health had always been fragile since the first heart attack in Latvia, and try as he might, he could not entirely give up cigarettes. But this was not so much an addiction as it was the dry tendrils of an uprooted plant that rejected the soil into which it had been transplanted. His oldest friend noticed it when he visited him to say goodbye.

Shdanoff had received an invitation to go to Europe, and recognizing that Misha had become progressively more frail and he might never see him again, he went to Beverly Hills consciously to make his farewells. Misha sensed the tacit import of the visit but remained bubbly and lighthearted. "Here's Herr 'Doctor,'" he said to Xenia, gently mocking Shdanoff, whose erudition he always admired. "He's off to Europe to become famous. He's come to say goodbye. When we see him again, he'll be too rich to even know us anymore." Shdanoff embraced Chekhov, each man trying to maintain a conviviality that neither really felt. The embrace turned into a song and then a dance to the folk tune from *The Dybbuk*. The two men danced clumsily into the living room laughing and gasping for breath as they clung to each other, and joyfully collapsed on the couch. That was Shdanoff's last memory of Chekhov.

On September 30, 1955, a few hours after James Dean was killed in a car crash, Michael Chekhov, who had ignored his doctor's instructions to give up smoking, reached over to light up a cigarette and slumped backward, dead from a heart seizure.

● ● ● ● ●

All the obituaries duly mentioned that he was the nephew of Anton Chekhov, had worked with Stanislavsky, and was the director of the Second Moscow Art Theatre. Apart from a small and loyal cadre in Hollywood, it is unlikely that too many Americans took note of his passing. Dean, who had become a towering figure in films and was widely associated with Lee Strasberg's Actor's Studio, was by far the more charismatic figure and the one whose death at twenty-four would cause the greater stir. Xenia may have wondered to whom in Russia the news of Misha's passing should be conveyed; Olga, his first wife, had virtually disappeared; Michael and Olga's daughter Anya had died in an air crash over Dresden shortly after the war. In Paris, Shdanoff received a cable from a friend that simply said: "Michael Chekhov died yesterday." On reading the news, he went out into the pouring rain and walked the streets without an overcoat. When he finally returned hours later, he was wringing wet and shaking with fever. He spent the next three days in bed with pneumonia. Beatrice Straight would have profoundly felt the immensity of the loss, as would Yul Brynner, Hurd Hatfield, and the alumni of Dartington Hall. To Mala Powers, the quasi-adopted daughter, it would have seemed as if her own father had passed away. Marilyn, then in thrall to Strasberg and on the brink of announcing her marriage to Arthur Miller, and being deeply sentimental, would have cried copiously and sent flowers and solicitations to Xenia. A few aged Russians in Los Angeles would have huddled together to recall spectacular performances they had seen as young men in Moscow or St. Petersburg.

At the funeral, the atmosphere was leaden and somber. Had Chekhov been there in more than spirit, he would have drawn the mourners' attention to the ceremony as a perfect example of a dramatic atmosphere, something that might be usefully re-created in an improvisation. Mala Powers recalls:

I was rescued from the utter despair in which I was imprisoned when a dear little old man acting as an usher tried to set up a folding chair. Each time that he opened it, the chair immediately closed up again and yet the old man, with the deepest seriousness, continued unfolding the chair and watching it close up again. Suddenly, in my mind, I saw Misha standing there with me, laughing until the tears came into his eyes at this wonderful, unconscious "clown routine." It saved me. In that moment I knew that throughout my entire life, Michael Chekhov would never be very far away from me.

The memorial service was held in a living room in a nearby home that had been converted into a chapel. It was one of those insufferably hot California days, the temperature veering around 102 degrees. The mourners included Fyodor Chaliapin's son, a large sampling of Russian émigrés, a gathering of older Hollywood actors, and Marilyn Monroe, dabbing away both tears and sweat with a wet silk handkerchief. In the living room, a Rasputin-like Russian Orthodox priest was waving a sensor and chanting. In the adjoining room, the mourners, each holding a lighted candle, were packed tight, almost faint with the heat.

"Death on the stage," Misha had said, "should be a slowing down and the gradual disappearance of the sense of time." The clock had stopped clicking for Misha rather suddenly. Had it happened on stage, he would have criticized the abruptness. It would probably never have occurred to him that some essential part of his being, his "higher I," perhaps, was about to be reborn in theaters and academies throughout the world; that it was possible to segue from being an ordinary person, to a celebrated person, to a "non-person," to a legend.

Chapter Thirty-Nine

AFTER CHEKHOV'S DEATH, George Shdanoff continued to teach Chekhovian technique in Los Angeles, but alluded less and less to the sources from which it sprang. A certain tension developed between the Shdanoffites and Chekhovians, the latter believing that Shdanoff was withholding proper credit from the primal source of his teaching. Shdanoff, who spoke five languages and was a charismatic and erudite teacher, had a healthy ego and coached some of Hollywood's best known stars, but as often happens with disciples who, having tried their wings discover they can fly on their own, he tended to play down his origins. Chekhov's 1939 production of Dostoyevsky's *The Possessed*, which failed on Broadway, had been adapted by Shdanoff but there was very little stage authorship after that. His film career was sixty years behind him. Efficient as he was, without Chekhov's example before him, it is unlikely Shdanoff would have developed into the teacher he eventually became. Nikolai Guzov, a talented Chekhovian instructor in Los Angeles, knew Shdanoff in his last years. He contends that, during the obscure period when Chekhov had become a non-person in the USSR, it was Shdanoff's staunch advocacy of the Chekhov technique that kept his reputation alive on the West Coast. Certainly, Chekhov fell off the radar screens in the sixties and seventies, and was officially neglected in the Soviet Union. The resurgence of interest in him seems to date from the Gorbachov period.

Toward the end, a rather treacherous Russian ingénue inveigled herself into Shdanoff's life. (He, like Chekhov, was particularly susceptible to feminine allure.) When Shdanoff passed away in 1998, the ambitious ingénue became the legatee of many of his last effects. A manuscript detailing his close relationship with Chekhov, and not assigned in his will, disappeared, allegedly spirited away by the overzealous actress who had contractually undertaken to prepare a biography of Shdanoff. None ever appeared.

Marilyn was dead by 1962, by which time she had been entirely colonized by Lee and Paula Strasberg. Xenia, subsisting on a meager subsistence provided by Monroe's will and still pining for her homeland, died in 1970. Brynner, after an extended illness, was dead from cancer in 1985; Hurd Hatfield, in 1998. Beatrice Straight died of pneumonia in 2001. Waves of young students who had been inspired by Chekhov's writings continued to immerse themselves in his technique and Chekhov studios continued to spring up throughout America and all over Europe. Chekhovian teachers such as Marjolein Baars, Lisa Dalton, Nikolai Guzov, Sarah Kane, Joanna Merlin, Ted Pugh, and David Zinder emerged as keepers of the flame and today, Chekhovian alternatives to the "method" continue to mushroom wherever actors assemble and the Stanislavsky-Strasberg aesthetic is found wanting. Mala Powers remains a zealous Chekhovian apostle, conducting Chekhovian workshops and organizing international conferences. William Elmhirst, son of Dorothy and half-brother of Beatrice, still lives a stone's throw from Dartington Hall, still treasures his memory of the estate when Chekhov's personality pervaded the place and is endowed with a certain fervid spirituality that he associates with both his mother's influence and his brief exposure to Chekhov when he was merely a boy. Survivors of the Chekhov Theatre Studio and Ridgefield, many of them in their eighties or nineties, either cherish their memories at Devon and Connecticut, or don't want to be reminded. Eager young actors train, argue about new acting theories, form companies, pursue agents, hustle for work, become stars, sell out, give up, and fade away.

When I visited Dartington Hall to research this biography and began wandering the grounds late one afternoon, I came across a grassy knoll that I recognized from photos as the site where Chekhov and his students performed their exercises. It was probably just a trick of the light, but I heard a rustling, and through a haze felt the presence of Misha in the air. It was probably nothing more than the Devon wind blowing through the coastal fog, but it would be nice to believe that someone who had been so convinced of an afterlife was still milling around his old haunts.

Bibliography

Barron, Stephanie, and Maurice Tuchman. *The Avant Garde in Russia 1910–1930*. MIT Press, 1980.

Beevor, Antony. *The Mystery of Olga Chekhova.* Viking/Penguin, 2004.

Braun, Edward. *Meyerhold on Theatre*. Methuen & Co. Ltd., 1969.

Chekhov, Michael. *Life and Remembrances*. Unpublished manuscript, 1944.

_____. *On the Technique of Acting*. Harper Collins, 1991.

_____. *To the Actor*. Harpers & Brothers, 1953.

Clurman, Harold. *The Collected Works of Harold Clurman*. Applause Books, 1994.

_____. *The Fervent Years*. Hill & Wang, 1945.

Corrigan, Robert W. *Theatre in the 20th Century*. Grove Press, 1963.

Danchenko, Nemerovitch. *My Life in the Russian Theatre*. Little Brown & Co. 1936.

du Prey, Deirdre H. *Lessons for Teachers of His Acting Technique*. Dovehouse Editions, 2000.

Friedrich, Otto. *The City of Nets*. Harper & Row, 1986.

Gorchakov, Nikolai M. *Stanislavsky Directs*. Funk & Wagnalls, 1954.

Houghton, Norris. *Moscow Rehearsals*. Harcourt, Brace & Co. 1936.

Kirby, Michael, ed. *The Drama Review*. MIT Press, Fall 1983.

Leonard, Charles. *Michael Chekhov's to the Director and the Playwright*. Limelight Editions, 1984.

Lewis, Robert. *Slings and Arrows*. Stein & Day, 1984.

Margashack, David. *Stanislavsky on the Art of the Stage*. Faber & Faber, 1950.

Markov, P.A. *The Soviet Theatre*. G.P. Putnam's Sons, 1935.

Marowitz, Charles, ed. *Alarums and Excursions*. L.A. Theatre Center Vol. 2, 1988.

Monroe, Marilyn. *My Story*. Stein & Day, 1974.

Munk, Erica. *Stanislavsky and America*. Fawcett Publications, 1967.

Rudnitsky, Konstantin. *Russian and Soviet Theatre, 1905–1932*. Harry N. Abrams, Inc., New York 1988.

Schmidt, Paul. *Meyerhold at Work*. University of Texas Press, 1980.

Slonim, Marc. *Russian Theatre*. Collier Books, 1962.

Stanislavsky, Konstantin. *My Life in Art*. Foreign Languages Publishing House, USSR 1925.

Van Gyseghem, Andre. *Theatre in Soviet Russia*. Faber & Faber, 1938.

Vineberg, Steven. *Method Actors*. Schirmer Books (Macmillan), 1991.

Williams, Jay. *Stage Left*. Charles Scribner's & Sons, 1974.

Young, Stark. *Immortal Shadows*. Hill & Wang, 1948.

TAPED, WRITTEN OR TELEPHONE INTERVIEWS WITH:

Phoebe Brand	Jack Larson
Phil Brown	Robert Lewis
Jack Colvin	Joanne Merlin
Lisa Dalton	Daphne Moore
William Elmhirst	Gregory Peck
Mel Gordon	Mala Powers
Nikolai Guzov	Anthony Quinn
Mary Haynsworth	Ford Rainey
Frederick Keeve	Beatrice Straight

Charles Marowitz is the founding artistic director of the Malibu Stage Company and has been co-director, with Peter Brook, of the Royal Shakespeare Company Experimental Group. He is the author of the following Applause titles: *Directing the Action: Acting and Directing in Contemporary Theatre*; *The Other Way: An Alternative Approach to Acting & Directing*; *Recycling Shakespeare*; *Alarums & Excursions: Our Theatres in the '90s*; and *Roar of the Canon: Kott and Marowitz on Shakespeare*. In 2004, he directed Vaclav Havel's play *Temptation* in Prague for the National Theatre of the Czech Republic, the first American director to be so honored. He is a faculty member at the American Academy of Dramatic Arts in Los Angeles and is on the Artistic Directorate of the Shakespeare Globe Theatre of London. He lives in Malibu, California.

Index